TEACHING SEEING & WRITING 2

TEACH

SEEIN

WR

Donald McQuade
Christine McQuade

NG
G &
TING2

PREPARED BY
Anne Kress and Suellyn Winkle
Santa Fe Community College

Dan Keller
Southern Illinois University, Edwardsville

Bedford / St. Martin's
Boston ◆ New York

7   6   5   4   3   2
f   e   d   c   b   a

For information, write: Bedford/St. Martin's,
75 Arlington Street, Boston, MA 02116   (617-399-4000)

ISBN: 0-312-40006-3

Preface

We have designed every aspect of *Seeing & Writing 2*, including what you will find in this helpful guide to teaching the book, with one overarching goal in mind: to improve the ability of each student to read and think more critically, and to write more effectively. In this second edition, we continue to focus our efforts on strengthening the analytic and compositional skills of student users by encouraging them to think and write more insightfully about the visual and verbal dimensions of contemporary American culture. Because most students today have grown up in a culture dominated by visual texts, and because many are acquainted with the basic workings of highly sophisticated visual processes, we believe that such materials can serve as excellent resources for teaching critical thinking and effective writing.

The first edition of *Teaching Seeing & Writing* was thoughtfully and imaginatively prepared by Suellyn Winkle and Anne Kress from Santa Fe Community College in Florida. Dan Keller, our colleague at Southern Illinois University, Edwardsville, has skillfully enriched and extended the pedagogical strengths of this guide to teaching *Seeing & Writing 2*. This new edition of *Teaching Seeing & Writing* is an even more useful compendium of engaging and productive instructional resources. It provides a wealth of strategies and exercises that will enable you to extend your specific instructional purposes well beyond the time limitations of any one class period. We hope that you will respond to the instructional suggestions as they were intended: as conversational — and compositional — promptings to initiate productive dialogue and writing among your students and faculty colleagues.

To that end, Dan Keller has gathered for each selection and special feature in *Seeing & Writing 2* a wide range of imaginative "field-tested" instructional resources under four general rubrics: Generating Class Discussion and In-Class Writing; Additional Writing Topics; Connections to Other Texts; and Suggestions for Further Reading, Thinking, and Writing. Each contains clusters of questions and further instructions and provides an opportunity to thicken and widen the instructional impact of the visual and verbal materials you might chose to work with in your classes. Suggestions for Further Reading, Thinking, and Writing for each selection can prompt additional instructional activities in which students work with other materials drawn from print, web-based, and audio/visual media.

Each of the four general rubrics contains multiple suggestions for broadening and strengthening the classroom activities and writing exercises prompted by an individual verbal or visual selection. In addition to these resources, *Teaching Seeing & Writing 2* provides suggestions on how to use more theoretical selections in the text's appendix; this will help students understand more about the intellectual and cultural contexts within which questions about the interrelations of the visual and the verbal are discussed.

This instructional supplement also includes detailed strategies for helping students to respond effectively to the range of genres represented in *Seeing & Writing 2*. Some genres will be more familiar than others to first- and second-year undergraduates: the image, the advertisement, the painting, the photograph, the essay, the poem, the short story, and the various forms of mixed media that appear with increasing frequency in contemporary American culture.

We trust that you will find in this compilation of *Teaching Seeing & Writing* not only a wide range of teaching possibilities but also a great deal of flexibility about how best to adapt these materials to the particular instructional circumstances and challenges your students bring to each class. We invite you to visit the companion web site to the book, Seeing & Writing Online, at www.bedfordstmartins.com/seeingandwriting. You'll find there the web links printed in this manual as well as additional research links and visual exercises. We would be most grateful to hear from you about which exercises worked most effectively for you in the classes you teach.

We hope that *Teaching Seeing & Writing 2* will serve as a useful teaching tool for you. We are confident that your students will enjoy — and learn a great deal from — working with challenging visual and verbal texts, and that they will benefit from responding to the instructional exercises contained in this volume. Ultimately, we hope students will discover that the achievements of all the writers and visual artists whose work is presented in *Seeing & Writing 2* are within their analytic and compositional reach.

Donald McQuade and *Christine McQuade*

Contents

Appendix   272

Chapter 1

Observing the Ordinary

Introduction

GENERATING CLASS DISCUSSION AND IN-CLASS WRITING

The introductory material for Observing the Ordinary asks students to acknowledge the acts of visual perception they perform every day and to become more aware of this very powerful and highly developed skill that they often take for granted. In connection with the discussion of passive and active seeing, you might ask students to take a few moments to jot down an impromptu list of what they see in their classroom. Then, ask them to read their lists aloud. Use what they've written as a springboard to a discussion of how and why people notice the things that they do. For example, you could talk about how we may *actively* view surroundings or people that are new to us, whereas we often *passively* view those places and people after we become familiar with them. The key is to clarify what "observing the ordinary" means.

This exercise will also demonstrate that "even if we all had the same object [or in this case, the same space filled with a finite number of objects] before us, each of our descriptions of it would likely be different, depending on who we are" (p. 40, para. 1). Some students will undoubtedly see different things in the room and/or name them in a different way. Try to get students to move from their concrete lists of objects to what those lists imply about how they understand their classroom space. You may also want to point out that what they see probably depends on where they've chosen to sit. How does perspective from one position differ from another? How can they distinguish the space of the teacher from the space of the students? What do they notice about the things in the room in addition to color? For example, how are the people in the room dressed? Fashion—clothing style, cut, and color—is a major industry in Western culture. We are expert at "reading" clothing. But we are expert at reading other visual cues as well, such as body language. In what different ways have people entered the classroom and chosen to sit? What do students bring with them? What does the instructor bring? What visual clues tell students they are in a classroom? How do they know which person in the room is the instructor? Ask them to "read" the classroom, using *only* visual cues as their data.

All these questions tie directly to the idea that we use observations to draw informed inferences. By accumulating visual data, concrete and specific observations about what we *see*, we can begin to make informed inferences about possible meanings. To better understand the readings and images that follow in this chapter—and in the rest of the book—students need to understand the kinds of observations they can make about what is visible to them and how these observations come together to create meaning.

To return to the text, ask students to consider the two-page photograph that precedes the introduction—the predominantly white objects on a white background. As students identify these commonplace objects, ask them to consider what ties this group of images together (color, size, function, composition). The objects are immediately identifiable—so much so that some students may ask, "So what?" Have them articulate the elements of the photographic composition—the use of white, the equal spaces between the objects, the similarity of the size of the objects, and so on. Explain that composition—the way something is put together—can bear its own meaning. In this case, the composition might suggest that we are so accustomed to seeing these everyday objects that they are becoming less and less visible to us: They are literally fading into the background. The similarity of the foreground and background, and the colors of the objects themselves, suggest that a viewer must look very closely in order to see the ordinary. To become careful observers and better writers, students need to be able to make the important distinction between what they are seeing (objects on a page) and what they are thinking or what inferences they are drawing (everyday objects are becoming invisible).

 For additional resources for the selections in this chapter (including exercises and annotated links), go to www.seeingandwriting.com.

Roe Ethridge, *Refrigerator*

GENERATING CLASS DISCUSSION AND IN-CLASS WRITING

Students might have a hard time understanding why they are studying a picture of a refrigerator. You might ask each student to write a description of the refrigerator in his or her home, making sure to describe any magnets, pictures, and photos on it. You could then ask students to read the descriptions to the class. Between readings, ask students to make inferences about each person's kitchen, family, and lifestyle based on the description of the refrigerator. The descriptions and the inferences are bound to vary.

After this exercise, students might have an easier time making inferences from Ethridge's photograph. Ask students—either individually or in groups—to spend a few minutes writing a description of the refrigerator in the photograph; then have students read their descriptions to the class. Which details stand out the most? Do students report the same details or different ones? If the same details are consistently listed, ask students why they think these details are so prevalent. Have students pick a few words that describe the refrigerator, the kitchen, and the family.

Make sure students understand that Ethridge intended to have the dog in the picture. Ask students how the dog's presence affects the image. Does it give the picture a sense of life? If the dog were fully visible, would students wonder what was beyond the picture's edges?

ADDITIONAL WRITING TOPICS

1. Have students write a description of something that belongs to them. It could be a refrigerator, a car, a closet, a dresser—something that could be described inside and out. Tell students to avoid describing a pair of shoes, an outfit, a hat, or a piece of jewelry. The thing described should reveal the personality of the writer. After students pass in their descriptions to you, briefly read each one to the class. Have the students guess who wrote each description.

2. Ethridge's photograph has been used for commercial and artistic purposes. Ask students to find other photographs that could also be used in multiple ways. They should then write a short essay that explains how the photographs fit the different purposes. In their essay, they should describe the pictures as clearly as possible.

3. Ask students to freewrite about the family based on the photograph of its refrigerator.

1. Ask students to examine the son's bedroom in Pepón Osorio's *Badge of Honor*. This room is also devoid of people. Ask students to draw inferences about the teenage boy based on the appearance of his bedroom.

2. In his essay "Three Minutes or Less," Norman Mailer states that "a sense of place" could be a thought in a room. Using this photograph and the thoughts it inspired in your students, have students write a short expository essay about how a photograph can create a sense of place through the thoughts it brings out in its viewer.

SUGGESTIONS FOR FURTHER READING, THINKING, AND WRITING

print

Barrett, Terry. *Criticizing Photographs: An Introduction to Understanding Images.* Mountain View, CA: Mayfield, 1990. This book and the next offer helpful insights into the subject of this chapter.

Roberts, John. *Art of Interruption: Realism, Photography, and the Everyday.* New York: St. Martin's Press, 1998.

 web

For links for the selections in this chapter, go to www.seeingandwriting.com.

Fruit Labels

The ancillary picture provides students an opportunity to see a wide variety of fruit labels. Students will probably be unfamiliar with most of these labels. You might ask which labels stand out to them and why. Most students will recognize the "Chiquita" and "Sunkist" labels but will then probably notice only the labels with large print. Most of these labels are simple and do not bear slogans. Ask students to think of labels on soda or water bottles; they will most likely recall intricate designs and catchy slogans. You could then discuss the possible reasons for these differences.

Billy Collins, *Horizon*
Michael Collins, *Seascape*

GENERATING CLASS DISCUSSION AND IN-CLASS WRITING

Even though these pieces were made independently of each other, they serve as useful comparisons for how differently they represent the same scene. You might direct students to read Billy Collins's poem and look at Michael Collins's photograph before discussing each in detail. With this brief background, some students might begin to compare/contrast the pieces as you discuss them separately.

Michael Collins's photograph *Seascape* features a few feet of shore before the incoming tide, which dissolves into a gentle blue that mirrors the sky above. Neither ships nor clouds are visible—only a few feet of earth, then endless sea and sky. Given a casual viewing, one can barely tell where the sea ends and the sky begins. In this photograph, the horizon does clearly separate the sea from the sky as it does in Billy Collins's poem.

Ask students to relate the details they noticed when they first looked at this picture. Most probably noticed the blending of the sea and sky. Ask students to consider how their reading of the photo would change if Collins had not included the tiny section of shore. What if he had not included the incoming tide?

In "Horizon," Billy Collins focuses on the power of imagination and of simple artistic representation. The poem promises than any drawing tool can be used to create a horizon—"the brush of a Japanese monk / or a pencil stub from a race track." Ask students why Collins chose to mention such different drawing instruments in the first two lines. What do the first two lines suggest about the instrument and the person holding it?

Collins uses the sharp contrast between these items to stress that the instrument does not matter since "the effect is the same: the world suddenly / divided into its elemental realms." Note the line break between "suddenly" and "divided" to emphasize how quickly the drawn line causes the division in the world. Collins makes the horizontal line on the page sound magical, transporting the reader from "a small room" to "a vast desert" or "a winter beach." Ask students how Collins expects so much to be seen from a simple line drawn across a specific point on the page. After all, he does not give directions to draw the earth, sea, and sky. Ask students to explain whether he is relying upon the drawer's imagination, the power of the horizon, or both?

Then ask students to discuss which piece better represents the scene. Have them point out concrete details that influence their judgments. Do some students favor "Horizon" because it asks them to rely upon their imagination? Do others favor *Seascape* because it gives them visuals they can examine? Do any students find that imagination is required to see the horizon in *Seascape?* If so, how?

ADDITIONAL WRITING TOPICS

1. Ask students to follow Billy Collins's directions for creating a horizon on paper. Then ask them to freewrite about whether or how the horizontal line transforms the page. Do they see the significance of the horizontal line that Collins does?

2. Using *Seascape* and "Horizon" as examples, students could write an essay in which they consider whether poetry or photography is more effective at capturing a scene.

3. Ask students to write a descriptive essay about a natural scene. They should tie the scene together through paragraphs that detail different parts of the scene (e.g., if Collins's *Seascape* were an essay, the paragraphs would involve the shore, the sea, and the sky). The thesis could explain why the scene has a special meaning for the author or why people in general are struck by it.

CONNECTIONS WITH OTHER TEXTS

1. Ask students to read Carl Sagan's speech and view the *Pale Blue Dot* photograph it was based upon (pp. 108–109). Does Collins's *Seascape* inspire awe and humility in students as *Pale Blue Dot* does in Sagan? Ask students to freewrite about what they know and feel regarding the ocean. If they struggle, ask them to write about the differences between *Pale Blue Dot* and *Seascape.*

2. Ask students to read the pair in Chapter 2, Edward Hopper's painting *House by the Railroad* and Edward Hirsch's poem "Edward Hopper and the House by the Railroad". Even though Hirsch's poem is based upon Hopper's painting, ask students to ignore the connection for this exercise. Have students compare the strategies used by the four artists to create a scene. You might direct students to compare the verbal artists and the visual artists separately at first, but they should consider all the works together by the end of the discussion.

SUGGESTIONS FOR FURTHER READING, THINKING, AND WRITING

print

Collins, Billy. *The Art of Drowning*. Pittsburgh: University of Pittsburgh Press, 1995.

———. *Sailing Alone around the Room: New and Selected Poems*. New York: Random House, 2001.

www.bigsnap.com/billy.html Web site devoted to Billy Collins. Provides links to interviews, articles, and all of Collins's poems.

www.loc.gov/poetry/laureate.html Information about Billy Collins as the new Poet Laureate at The Poetry and Literature Center of the Library of Congress. Includes a cybercast of Collins's reading and lecture.

Links for the selections in this chapter can be found at www.seeingandwriting.com.

audio

The Best Cigarette. Audio CD. 34 tracks. 1997. Cielo Publishing. Billy Collins reads his poetry.

Larry Woiwode, *Ode to an Orange*

GENERATING CLASS DISCUSSION AND IN-CLASS WRITING

Larry Woiwode's "Ode to an Orange" is a personal narrative essay devoted to a childhood memory of a specific season, place, and object. The place is North Dakota, the season is winter, and the object is an orange. As the use of the word *ode* in the title suggests, Woiwode's essay is a lyrical meditation on the subject of a fruit—the orange. You might want to begin discussion by explaining that something called an ode usually refers to a formal, rhymed poem and not to an informal, personal, anecdotal essay; the word *ode* is itself not ordinary. It supposes a certain literary expertise on the part of the reader; it alludes to the tradition of poetic longing. Invoking this serious literary tradition for such a mundane citrus gives the title an almost quaint connotation as well; and the notion that a family seriously regards an orange as an extraordinary treat will certainly seem outlandish to some of your students. Remind them that Woiwode grew up in a different time and place and that the family's appreciation of and the brothers' passionate hunger for the oranges is sincere. You might direct your students to note the tone of lines like "there was no depth of degradation that [they] wouldn't descend to in order to get one" (para. 10).

Once you've established that the words *ode* and *orange* in the title hint at the mix of elements to come, ask students how the serious and mundane are balanced by the end of the essay. Have the students developed a new or different appreciation for the fruit? What kind of image of an orange did they have in mind before and after reading the essay? What has the orange come to represent?

In terms of content, Woiwode's essay is not only about, for example, the poverty suggested by the modesty of the two brothers' desire for a Christmas orange. It is also about what constitutes our personal visions of luxury. These are visions that each reader brings to the essay, an example of how "we also invest ordinary objects with private and public meanings" (p. 41). You might ask students to discuss what everyday objects in their personal histories embody their nostalgia for the desires of childhood (e.g., Cabbage Patch dolls, Tonka trucks, or Happy Meals), how parents establish power by giving and withholding desired objects, or even what magical properties a vivid childhood image can summon.

A discussion of how images can be created through words could lead to a consideration of the elements of composition in a written or visual text. For example, both kinds of texts have a distinct shape and form. When we read or write an essay, we make certain assumptions about the shape the writing will take. A personal narrative offers detailed description and presents one author's perspective, but the reader still assumes that the essay will have a point or a thesis and that it will be organized into paragraphs. You might ask students what their assumptions are about the essay form. What do they expect to see when they open their textbooks? Would it seem odd *not* to have columns of print, with the title in a large bold font and the author's name underneath? How do readers expect an essay to be organized? What does the image of the essay itself on the page communicate to them?

ADDITIONAL WRITING TOPICS

1. Woiwode invites readers directly into the world of a bleak Great Plains winter in the 1940s, and then he introduces a world of color summoned by the arrival of the oranges into his town. In what ways does the essay itself have a visual orientation? It is not only titled after a color, but it also creates a little color movie as we read. Have students identify the various scenes that Woiwode depicts: begging for the oranges, peeling an orange, eating an orange. Invite students to imagine this theoretical movie shot by shot, to cast it, to provide the set design, and to plan the camera angles.

2. Woiwode is able to evoke an entire time and place through his memory of a simple orange. His essay evokes nostalgia for (1) an idyllic, wholesome farm life that is disappearing from our culture and (2) the idealized American nuclear family of our recent past. Using Woiwode's essay as a model, ask students to write a description of an important object that represents for them something larger and more personal about family, home, or community.

3. Part of the strength of Woiwode's essay arises from its ability to play the harsh chill of winter against the warmth of the orange, as expressed in its color, its smell, its taste, and so on. Ask students to write an analytical essay in which they explain how Woiwode contrasts these two elements: winter and orange.

CONNECTIONS WITH OTHER TEXTS

1. After they read Woiwode's essay about the oranges and the boys' longing and desire for them, have students look at the Sequoia Citrus Association's orange crate label (p. 52). Ask them to consider the following questions: What is suggested by the relationship of the hand to the orange? by the shape of the orange? by the fact that the flesh of the orange is partially revealed and lusciously presented? How is this visual presentation of an orange similar to or different from Woiwode's verbal presentation? Which one do the students find more inviting, and why?

2. Woiwode's descriptions are powerful because they appeal to the five senses. Ask students to read the Coca-Cola advertisement in Chapter 2. The ad makes a brief appeal to the sense of taste: "And, yes, when you're thirsty, it's the taste of ice-cold Coca-Cola." Instead of referencing the five senses, the ad links Coca-Cola with America and appeals to the readers' patriotism. Ask students to consider why the advertisers chose this tactic. You could even ask students to rewrite the ad, appealing to the readers' five senses.

SUGGESTIONS FOR FURTHER READING, THINKING, AND WRITING

print

Ackerman, Diane. *A Natural History of the Senses.* New York: Random House, 1990. A beautifully written book about the senses.

Woiwode, Larry. *Beyond the Bedroom Wall: A Family Portrait.* New York: Avon, 1976.

———. *The Neumiller Stories.* New York: Farrar, Straus and Giroux, 1989.

———. *Silent Passengers.* New York: Atheneum, 1993.

[www] *web*

www.fruitcratelabels.com   This site offers an online gallery of fruit crate labels from the same era as the book's reproductions, as well as an array of other product labels from that period.

www.ultimatecitrus.com   A web site created by the Florida Citrus Growers that offers a wonderful counterpoint to the memoir by Larry Woiwode and the assorted older citrus ads shown on page 52 of Chapter 1.

Links for the selections in this chapter can be found at www.seeingandwriting.com.

audio/visual

King of the Hill. 103 min. NTSC, 1993. Videocassette, color, rated PG-13. Distributed by MCA/Universal and Gramercy Pictures. Director Steven Soderbergh's film captures the extraordinary in the ordinary and makes a wonderful and moving parallel to Larry Woiwode's memoir; it could also be tied to Annie Dillard's essay. The protagonist is a young boy, Aaron Kurlander, growing up alone during the Depression and struggling to survive. The film is based on A.E. Hotchner's memoir, *King of the Hill*.

Larry Woiwode Interview with Kay Bonetti. 60 min. 1984. Recording. Distributed by American Audio Prose Library.

Larry Woiwode Reads "The Street" from Beyond the Bedroom Wall. 42 min. 1993. Recording. Distributed by American Audio Prose Library. "A paradigm of fiction that strongly evokes a sense of time and place."

Mystery of the Senses. 5 cassettes (60 min. for each sense), or as a set. Videocassette. Distributed by NOVA. Inspired by Diane Ackerman's book *A Natural History of the Senses*.

Sequoia Citrus Association, *Have One*

GENERATING CLASS DISCUSSION AND IN-CLASS WRITING

The ad for the *Have One* brand can be seen as reflecting "the accelerated pace and more sophisticated look of urban life: bolder typography, darker colors" (p. 52). You might direct students to discuss how the ad is "more sophisticated," to look at details like the bangle bracelet on the woman's arm and her shiny and polished nails. Is this the hand of a rustic farmwife? You might also point out that the orange is removed from the grove (as compared to the labels below on p. 52), and that this image seems more photographic, more like contemporary ads for food products.

You might also ask students to consider the graphic design of this ad. Direct them to the repeated figure of the circle: the orange, the "o" in *one*, the bangle bracelet, the curve of the hand. Students might also note the similarity between the woman's fingers and the sections of the orange. All these elements constitute an ad that is forceful and sensual (and that ties in perfectly with the essay that precedes it).

ADDITIONAL WRITING TOPICS

1. Ask students to search their own kitchens for examples of food packaging that has evocative power. Each student should bring in one such package. Have them write a brief reflection on what meanings this package holds for them and how the meanings are conveyed through graphic design, attaching the package itself that they've annotated to explain important details.

2. Ask students to contrast the different connotative meanings (what design elements *suggest*) in *Have One* and in smaller California Orange Growers' ads. How are the advertising styles different? Have students answer that question in a three-page essay, using specific details from the ads to back up their points.

3. Ask students to write an essay that compares the *Have One* ad to a current ad for oranges or for orange juice. In their essays, they should consider how corporate interests are reflected in contemporary advertisement. Students might also consider if the message delivered by their current ad is as direct as the injunction to "Have One."

CONNECTIONS WITH OTHER TEXTS

1. Ask students to compare and contrast the text and imagery of the *Have One* ad and the Coca-Cola advertisement from Chapter 2.

2. Ask students to look at the Mercedes-Benz ad at the beginning of Chapter 6 (p. 464). Today many businesses rely on an icon or a logo to build product recognition and to tie their company to a given product, whereas the orange crate labels were an example of beautiful graphic art used to sell products and distinguish one brand from another. Have students freewrite on which approach they think would be more effective, and why.

VISUALIZING COMPOSITION: **Close Reading**
Richard Estes, *Central Savings*

GENERATING CLASS DISCUSSION AND IN-CLASS WRITING

Richard Estes's painting was crafted with such realistic detail that it seems photographic. The details seen through the diner's window and in its reflection call for careful examination, making this an especially useful selection if students seem to have difficulty analyzing images. If students have not examined this selection before class, you might ask them to state their first impressions of the picture, ignoring the text on the page. Most students would guess it to be a photograph. When they realize or are told that it is a painting, ask which details, if any, suggest this.

Then you might direct students to read the paragraphs and to complete the exercise under the "Visualizing Composition" heading on the same page.

If students have difficulty with the exercise in the book, you might ask them to form groups to analyze the painting and the student's annotations. As they analyze the painting, they should make notes about the details they notice. Point out the careful observations made by the student in the text, which might seem simplistic to your students at first. Ask them what they think of the annotations, particularly #3 and #5. Do they agree, as the student states in #3, that the counters "seem to reflect images that seem to repeat themselves over and over"? Do they think Estes intended this effect? Can they tell whether the clock is a reflection in the window (as the student wonders in #5)?

By analyzing both the painting and the annotations, students should gain some useful skills for analyzing other images in the text. Before you move on to another selection, be sure to suggest that students write similar annotations for the essays and the images they encounter in Seeing & Writing.

ADDITIONAL WRITING TOPICS

1. If students have difficulty analyzing images, ask them to freewrite about the nature of their problem.

2. Ask students to write an exploratory essay about what they think Estes's purpose was in this painting. In this essay, they should describe the specific techniques used by Estes and explain their effects.

CONNECTIONS WITH OTHER TEXTS

1. Ask students to examine the photorealistic paintings by Tim Gardner. Have students apply this selection's exercise to his work.

2. Ask students to read Larry Woiwode's "Ode to an Orange" and analyze the techniques he uses to draw a larger picture from his memories of an orange.

SUGGESTIONS FOR FURTHER READING, THINKING, AND WRITING

print

Arthur, John. *Richard Estes: Paintings and Prints.*
Rohnert Park, CA: Pomegranate Communications, 1993.

Meisel, Louis K., and John Perreault. *Richard Estes:
The Complete Paintings, 1966–1985.* New York:
Harry N. Abrams, 1986.

web

www.artcyclopedia.com/artists/estes_richard
.html   Artcyclopedia's page on Estes
contains numerous links to his work on the
Internet. You could ask students to practice
their close reading skills on other works by
Estes.

Links for the selections in this chapter can be
found at www.seeingandwriting.com.

---

www. Re: Searching the Web

If students are unfamiliar with the web, you might tell them to start with a standard search engine, such as yahoo.com or goto.com, and enter the product they want to find. They may not be able to locate the information requested in the assignment on the web for all products, so they may need to augment their online research with some library research.

As an additional assignment, you might ask students to consider how the Internet has transformed ordinary activities: corresponding, shopping, researching, working, and so on. They might brainstorm as a group, then work as individuals to write a comparative process essay that depicts the way in which one of these acitivities is conducted today as opposed to just a few years ago.

Students can complete the Re: Searching the Web exercises online at www.seeingandwriting.com. Additional tips and links for each exercise are also available.

Anne Fadiman, *Mail*

GENERATING CLASS DISCUSSION AND IN-CLASS WRITING

Fadiman's essay begins with her father's fascination with reading mail (paras. 1–3); then Fadiman leads readers through a brief history of the British postal system (paras. 4–10). Eventually, her essay becomes a critique of e-mail (paras. 18–22). Students will probably be most interested in the section that deals with e-mail, so you might choose to start your discussion with that subject; however, Fadiman's critique depends upon the previous sections, so those should be reviewed as well. You might begin the discussion by asking students about their familiarity with e-mail. Most students probably have the opposite experience of Fadiman: They have more experience writing e-mails than letters. If students have written letters, ask them to discuss the similarities and differences in writing letters and e-mails. During this discussion, you might direct them to Fadiman's critique of e-mail.

Students might think that Fadiman dislikes e-mail, but she both praises and criticizes it. She appreciates its speed: "pretty soon I was batting out fifteen or twenty e-mails a day in the time it had once taken me to avoid answering a single letter" (para. 16). However, she also criticizes e-mails because they are brief and because they are "frequently devoid of capitalization, minimally punctuated, and creatively spelled" (para. 18). To what extent does her description of e-mail fit the experiences of your students? Do they find punctuation and spelling problems distracting in their e-mail?

Next you might direct students to Fadiman's comments on e-acronyms and "emoticons" (para. 21). What is her tone regarding these e-mail shortcuts? What do students think of these? Can anything similar be found in letters?

Students might be confused by the essay's organization; they might not see the connections between Fadiman's father, postal history, and e-mail. Here you might point out how Fadiman unifies her essay by making allusions to earlier statements. In paragraphs 5 to 8 she explains how, until 1839, the postage of out-of-town letters was paid by the recipient; this outraged Rowland Hill, who came up with the national Penny Post, which put the postage burden on the sender. The Penny Post is alluded to later when Fadiman praises e-mail for its removal of distance at a low price: "E-mail is a modern Penny Post: the world is a single city with a single postal rate" (para. 17).

In another allusion she expresses her concern over the poor writing caused by the ability to send e-mail quickly: "In effect, it's always December 26; you are not expected to write *Middlemarch*, and therefore you don't" (para. 18). This comment makes sense only when it is connected with an earlier comment regarding how long Fadiman would let letters sit before replying: "The longer they languish, the more I despair of my ability to live up to the escalating challenge of their response. It is a truism of epistolary psychology that, for example, a Christmas thank-you note written on December 26 can say any old thing, but if you wait until February, you are convinced that nothing less than *Middlemarch* will do" (para. 13). These comments also complicate Fadiman's view of e-mail. Since she praises and criticizes both mail and e-mail, she cannot be written off as a Luddite. She enjoys the convenience of e-mail but acknowledges the price that accompanies convenience.

The ancillary image "Man Turning into a Barcode" depicts the features of a human face dissolving and then re-forming into a barcode. Students might notice the relationship between e-mail and the barcode—both are electronic means of quickly and conveniently transmitting information. Whereas Fadiman presents e-mail with a somewhat balanced view, this image suggests a stark view of humanity's reliance upon technology.

ADDITIONAL WRITING TOPICS

1. Fadiman's essay seems inspired partially by her father's love of mail. In fact, she has acquired her father's passion for mail (para. 12). Ask students to freewrite for ten minutes about the commonplace events or objects that their parents love; then have students write for another ten minutes about the commonplace events or objects that they love. Do they share their parents' passions? They could then write a comparison/contrast essay based on their freewriting.

2. Ask students to write an essay in which they respond to Fadiman's critique of e-mail as an effective means of communication. They should use quotations from Fadiman to strengthen their argument.

3. Have students research the history of another form of communication, such as the telephone or e-mail. You might ask them to write an essay similar to Fadiman's—especially in the way she moves from the personal to the historical, explaining not only how the form of communication has changed but also how it affected the past. Students could also imagine its role in the future.

CONNECTIONS WITH OTHER TEXTS

1. Larry Woiwode's "Ode to an Orange" also uses a mundane object as a springboard for other subjects (pp. 48–51). Just as Fadiman uses mail to discuss her father, postal history, and e-mail, Woiwode uses an orange to transport readers to the 1940s and to discuss poverty and luxury. Ask students to compare the strategies used by Fadiman and Woiwode in order to accomplish these effects.

2. Fadiman seems to regard the letter as an art form and sees e-mail as a convenient means of communication. Have students read Dorothy Allison's "This Is Our World" (pp. 259–64), in which Allison states that art holds "a bit of magic" (para. 27). Ask students to consider Allison's definition of art and write an argumentative essay demonstrating how e-mail could fit into that definition.

print

Fadiman, Anne. *Ex Libris: Confessions of a Common Reader.* New York: Farrar, Straus and Giroux, 1998.

———. *The Spirit Catches You and You Fall Down: A Hmong Child, Her American Doctors, and the Collision of Two Cultures.* New York: Farrar, Straus and Giroux, 1997.

 web

www.theatlantic.com/unbound/bookauth/ba981 028.htm   An *Atlantic Monthly* interview with Anne Fadiman.

www.bathpostalmuseum.org/   Features the history of the British Postal System.

Links for the selections in this chapter can be found at www.seeingandwriting.com.

audio/visual

You've Got Mail. 119 min. 1998. VHS videocassette, rated PG. Distributed by Warner Bros. Directed by Nora Ephron. A romantic comedy about two rival bookstore owners who fall in love through e-mail. Performers include Meg Ryan and Tom Hanks.

William Eggleston, *Untitled*

GENERATING CLASS DISCUSSION AND IN-CLASS WRITING

Eggleston's photograph invites viewers to sharpen their vision, to truly observe the ordinary, and to consider the value of framing and focusing on a particular visual fragment of their lives or experience. This photo of the space under a bed reveals what is usually private, suggesting at the same time the material conditions of the more public part of the room that we *can't* see. The viewer may draw some inferences, as the photo "[suggests] stories or meanings seemingly visible only to those who know the subject" (p. 63).

Ask students to examine the photo and discuss what the details suggest about the person or people who live there. What inferences can they make about the condition of the bed and the shoes beneath it? about colors in the photo—the repeated orange and tan motif? You might ask students to consider why Eggleston focused on the bedroom for this photo. It is usually the most private area of one's home, which fits perfectly with his photographic motive (to capture the images of everyday life). His presence is felt in the photo by the glare of the flash on the illuminated carpet—he is making himself known.

As with earlier images in this chapter, Eggleston's photo asks students to acknowledge *how they see*. The shot is brightly lit and acutely focused. Unlike the photo on the chapter divider page of objects on a clean, white background, which focused on the *often seen*, this image focuses on the *usually unseen*. You might ask students to consider how often they actually "see" their home or notice the everyday mess of their lives. That which people habitually see may tend to disappear before their eyes; that which is unfamiliar to them may appear more vividly.

ADDITIONAL WRITING TOPICS

1. Ask students to write a paragraph describing exactly what Eggleston would see if he were to photograph the space beneath *their* beds. How would they feel about having this private space made public? Do photographers have the right to take their cameras anywhere?

2. Our culture has historically been fascinated with making the private public. Divide your students into three or four panels to investigate and analyze examples of this emphasis in the media today. Assign each panel a different medium: One panel might choose examples in the evening news; another, television talk shows such as *The Jerry Springer Show*; another, radio call-in shows like Howard Stern's; and so on. Have each panel member act as an "expert" on one particular show and write a brief overview of privacy issues in the show—each panel can then teach the rest of the class. At the end of your panel presentation, open up the floor to a discussion of how the different media compare.

3. Eggleston's "Untitled" is taken from a book entitled *The Pleasures and Terrors of Domestic Comfort*. Ask students to consider another phrase that might replace "of domestic comfort" in this title. For example, they might choose "of college life" or "of getting a job" or "of going on vacation." Then, have them write an essay in which they describe at least three photos that they would include in this newly titled book. Their essay should also explain why the photos fit within the collection.

CONNECTIONS WITH OTHER TEXTS

1. Eggleston's photo illuminates the hidden space beneath a bed, magnifying its importance so that the viewer can see the private in a public way. Ask students to consider this photo in relation to K. C. Cole's essay, "A Matter of Scale" (p. 111). You might direct them to Cole's observation: "As you zoom in, or out, the world looks simple, then complex, then simple again" (p. 115, para. 28). How does the newly seen world beneath the bed seem both complex and simple?

2. In his essay "Three Minutes or Less" (p. 165), Mailer states that a sense of place can be as large "as one's birthplace" and as small "as a thought that takes place in a room." As a writer, he observes that "there's nothing more difficult than to come up with a good description of place." You might ask students to consider how photographers create a sense of place. How does the portrayal of the ordinary in Eggleston's photograph create a sense of place?

SUGGESTIONS FOR FURTHER READING, THINKING, AND WRITING

print

Eggleston, William. *Ancient and Modern / Photographs by William Eggleston.* New York: Random House, 1992.

 web

www.blindspot.com   This online photography magazine includes a gallery with photographs by, among others, William Eggleston, Chuck Close, Richard Misrach, and Wolfgang Tillmans.

www.masters-of-photography.com   This site offers excellent reproductions of some of Eggleston's photographs, along with links and articles.

Links for the selections in this chapter can be found at www.seeingandwriting.com.

RETROSPECT: *Changing Gears*

GENERATING CLASS DISCUSSION AND IN-CLASS WRITING

You might first ask students to look at each bicycle ad individually, then read them as a timeline. As students discuss the first ad for Columbia Bicycles (1886), you might direct them to consider the extensive use of text along the sidebars. Each segment makes a terrific claim about distance traveled. Students might infer that this ad is selling the bicycle as a means of rapid transportation, a claim that might draw laughter today. The graphic design of the ad plays on the novelty of this new form of transportation, its great height, with the ad frame and the arches within the ad repeating the round, tall wheel.

In the ad for Cycle Trades (1920), the speed of the bicycle as a form of rapid transportation is still being emphasized. Now it is even faster than a streetcar. The audience for the ad seems to be businessmen (note the man's suit, tie, and hat!). And, as might be fitting for a business audience, the text highlights the ways in which the bike will actually make money for its rider. Visually, the ad stresses forward momentum: Those on bikes are moving toward the reader, whereas those waiting for the streetcar are facing backward. Students might note that the slogan, "Ride a Bicycle," is quite similar to the orange crate slogan, "Have One," in its imperative simplicity.

The Roadmaster ad (1953) marks a significant change. Now a bicycle is a child's toy. In both images within the ad the bike is static, like any other toy. The selling point and the excitement are conveyed by color. A vibrant red runs through the ad and connects the boy to the logo to the bike to Christmas. If students are able to read the small text, they will notice that there may be a reason why this bike is not moving. The ad is aimed at "Mom and Dad," who are being sold on the safety features of this bicycle.

The 1998 ad does not portray the bicycle as a toy or a means of transportation. Instead, the ad appeals to the appreciation of freedom with the slogan "The place is not important. It's the freedom that counts." The conceit is that the all-terrain bikes provide the couple with the "freedom" to arrive at this coastal vista. Ask students how they interpret the slogan. Students will probably note that this ad features the least amount of text and that none of the text mentions the bike's specific features. Does the reliance upon the notion of freedom help or hinder the ad's effectiveness? Ask students if any other vehicles could easily replace the bikes in this ad.

Have students examine these ads closely and discuss the changing image of the bicycle in the four ads. In what ways does each one place the bicycle within the frame—in both the text and the image? Ask students to consider how the purpose of the bike shifted over the time span represented—over a century—from a standard form of transportation to a form of recreation, and why this shift may have occurred. Why don't people ride bicycles to work anymore? Students might also consider how American culture may be reflected in these ads.

ADDITIONAL WRITING TOPICS

1. Ask students to write a short essay that compares the ad from 1920 with the ad from 1998. Their essays might focus on the inferences they draw about the changes in American ideas of work and play that are suggested by the two ads. For their conclusion, have students speculate about what a bike ad might reflect in the year 2040.

2. Have students write an essay in which they analyze the gender roles featured in these bicycle ads. Or they might focus on how the ads reflect social changes. In addition, students could analyze current television commercials, many of which focus on women being in the driver's seat.

CONNECTIONS WITH OTHER TEXTS

1. You probably discussed the social changes reflected in these ads. Ask students to turn back to *Have One* and *Orange Crate Labels* earlier in Chapter 1. What can students infer about American society from each ad?

2. Refer students to the Phat Farm ad in Chapter 5, which features a picture of two men and brief Classic American Flava text. Readers are expected to make connections between the limited text and the figures presented in the picture. In contrast, the bicycle ads, for the most part, feature more text. Which method do your students find more effective? What are the risks involved with the Phat Farm ad's minimal text? with the abundance of text in the bicycle ads?

SUGGESTIONS FOR FURTHER READING, THINKING, AND WRITING

print

Catalog of the Cycle Collection of the Division of Engineering, United States National Museum. Bulletin 204. Washington: U.S. Government, 1903.

Palmer, Arthur Judson. *Riding High: The Story of the Bicycle*. New York: Dutton, 1956.

web

Links for the selections in this chapter can be found at www.seeingandwriting.com.

Tracey Baran, *Untitled 2*

GENERATING CLASS DISCUSSION AND IN-CLASS WRITING

Baran's photograph focuses on an older woman ironing a few feet away from a younger woman in a small, cluttered room. Ask students to examine the photograph and to point out the details that first strike them. Do they focus on the brighter section of the photo on the left featuring the older woman, or the section on the right with the younger woman? Ask students why Baran focused on such an ordinary activity. Does the photograph seem staged, or does it reflect a subtle attempt to capture a slice of "real" life?

Ask students to discuss what the details in the photo imply about the people who live there. What do the overflowing table and bookcase suggest? What about the clothes hanging above the window? The details seem to indicate that this family does not have a large living area and may be of low socioeconomic status. What do the positions of the women suggest about their relationship? It seems to be comfortable, but not close. With her head down, the older woman seems to be focused on ironing; the younger woman is looking away and appears to be biting her fingernails, not at all interested in the older woman's activity.

ADDITIONAL WRITING TOPICS

1. Ask students to write a detailed paragraph about what a photograph taken by Baran would reveal about an ordinary activity that occurs in their homes. Suggest an activity other than ironing: washing dishes, vacuuming, dusting, cooking. Have students imagine the scene as a snapshot before they write about it.

2. During discussion students might have debated whether this photograph should be considered artistic. Students could write an argument essay in which they support or oppose defining Baran's photograph as a work of art. They should provide their own definition of art and include examples of what they consider to be art. Tell students to write for an audience unfamiliar with Baran's picture, so they have to provide a detailed description of the photograph.

3. Ask students to create a title for this photograph and then write a short essay that explains and defends the title.

CONNECTIONS WITH OTHER TEXTS

1. Roe Ethridge's photograph is primarily of an inanimate object, a refrigerator. Although no family can be seen in the picture, the details lead to inferences that can be made about it. Ask students to examine both photos and to imagine Baran's as empty of its two figures. How much does the photograph change? What kind of people would your students imagine in Ethridge's picture?

2. Baran's photograph and Shizuka Yokomizo's photographs of people (pp. 288–90) are both staged, but in different ways. Both Yokomizo and Baran had permission from their subjects, but Yokomizo never met hers; they agreed to stand at their window at a certain time to be photographed. Ask students to compare the body language of the figures presented in the photographs of Yokomizo and Baran. Discuss the influence of the photographer on the photographed. If Yokomizo's subjects had invited her in, how might they be posed differently?

SUGGESTIONS FOR FURTHER READING, THINKING, AND WRITING

print

Bernhardt, Debra E., Rachel Bernstein, and Robert F. Wagner. *Ordinary People, Extraordinary Lives: A Pictorial History of Working People in New York City.* New York: New York UP, 2000.

[www] *web*

Links for the selections in this chapter can be found at www.seeingandwriting.com.

Tillie Olsen, *I Stand Here Ironing*

GENERATING CLASS DISCUSSION AND IN-CLASS WRITING

Olsen's story is a first-person narrative in which the main character reflects on her experience of raising Emily, her oldest daughter. The mother's memories are triggered by a concerned statement from an unnamed person: "'She's a youngster who needs help and whom I'm deeply interested in helping'" (para. 2). As the mother states, the concern will cause her to "become engulfed with all I did or did not do, with what should have been and what cannot be helped" (para. 4). Students might be concerned about the identity of this person, the "you" to which the mother speaks in her interior monologue. This person is probably a teacher or a school counselor; beyond that, the person is a device used by the author to spur the mother's monologue. You might ask students to imagine being in the role of this concerned educator. How would he or she react to the narrator's statements? Because students often trust a story's narrator, this role-playing exercise might prompt them to reconsider carefully the mother's claims.

Students might also criticize the mother. If this is the case, you might ask them to imagine their own lives from their parents' perspective. How would their parents describe the childhood or teenage years? Do your students think their parents have ever felt as helpless as the mother in this essay does? Direct your students to the third paragraph in which the mother states: "She has lived for nineteen years. There is all that life that has happened outside of me, beyond me."

The mother is complicated—and, therefore, realistic—because she cannot be characterized simply as either a good or a bad mother. She encountered circumstances beyond her control, yet she feels remorse for the possible ramifications. Emily's father left when she was eight months old because he "'could no longer endure' (he wrote in his good-bye note) 'sharing the want with us'" (para. 8). She states that Emily "was a miracle to me," but the father's absence meant that she had to work, leaving Emily with a "woman downstairs to whom she was no miracle at all" (para. 8). She also put her in day care when she was two years old, unaware of "the lacerations of group life in the kinds of nurseries that are only parking places for children" (para. 12). Although the mother feels remorse, she also states that it could not have been any other way: "It was the only way we could be together, the only way I could hold a job" (para. 13).

At this point, it seems difficult to blame the mother, and she has not blamed herself. However, she does recall a man once telling her to smile more at Emily. She wonders: "What *was* in my face when I looked at her? I loved her. There were all the acts of love" (para. 17). You might ask your students about the possible meaning of the word *acts* in that statement—could it mean that she acted out of love, or perhaps that she performed the necessary actions? It's not an easy question to answer since the possibility is only subliminally suggested by Olsen, yet it might cause students to read more carefully for what the mother briefly mentions or does not explain. For instance, in paragraphs 10 and 19, the mother mentions that she had to send Emily away but does not explain why. You might ask students to find similar sections that need more explanation.

Of course, the point is not to find evidence to indict the mother but to understand the complexity of her situation. As she states in the first paragraph, she is "tormented" by the concerned educator's request. Such torment is especially apparent in paragraph 24 when she recalls how she did not comfort Emily when she had nightmares. In the last sentence of the paragraph, the mother admits that she put forth more effort for another daughter, but she tries to excuse the unequal treatment by stating that it only happened twice: "Twice, only twice, when I had to get up for Susan anyhow, I went in to sit with her".

In the end, the mother seems both hopeful and pessimistic. She believes that her daughter will not reach her full potential: "So all that is in her will not bloom—but in how many does it?" She has hope, though, that Emily will learn that her life has not been determined by her mother's actions: "Only help her to know—help make it so there is cause for her to know—that she is more than this dress on the ironing board, helpless before the iron" (para. 56). Students might notice that the iron is prominent at both the beginning and end of the story. Ask them why Olsen might have placed the mother at the ironing board for the duration of the story. Why isn't she reading or cooking? How is the iron symbolic? How does Emily's life suggest that she has been and still is "helpless before the iron"?

ADDITIONAL WRITING TOPICS

1. Ask students to write a narrative from Emily's point of view. Students should consider what her life has been like. How does she view herself and her mother?

2. Invite students to write an essay that explains how "I Stand Here Ironing" is a feminist text. They should cite specific details from the story and explain the feminist viewpoint to an audience unfamiliar with feminist literary theory.

3. In discussion, students might have debated how much the mother is to blame for her daughter's situation. Students could write an argument essay about the level to which parents should be held responsible for their children's actions and happiness. Students should use personal examples to buttress their claims. They might also consult sociological research.

CONNECTIONS WITH OTHER TEXTS

1. Ask students to examine Tracey Baran's photograph, which depicts a scene reminiscent of Olsen's story. An older woman stands ironing several feet away from a younger woman (possibly her daughter); despite their physical proximity, they seem incredibly distant. Discuss the similarities and differences between the two texts, asking students to consider how each uses different techniques to create a scene and establish a tone.

2. Students could read Eudora Welty's "The Little Store" (p. 134) and write an essay that compares how Welty and Olsen use characters of different ages and backgrounds to create different views of the world.

SUGGESTIONS FOR FURTHER READING, THINKING, AND WRITING

print

Faulkner, Mara. *Protest and Possibility in the Writing of Tillie Olsen.* Charlottesville: University Press of Virginia, 1993.

Nelson, Kay Hoyle, and Nancy Huse, eds. *The Critical Response to Tillie Olsen.* Westport, CT: Greenwood Press, 1994.

Olsen, Tillie. *Tell Me a Riddle.* New Brunswick, NJ: Rutgers University Press, 1995.

 web

www.mockingbird.creighton.edu/NCW/olsen .htm   The Nebraska Center for Writers web site includes a short biography, quotes, an interview, and critical reviews.

Links for the selections in this chapter can be found at www.seeingandwriting.com.

audio/visual

Olsen, Tillie. *Tillie Olsen Interview with Kay Bonetti.* 1 cassette (77 min.). 1987. Distributed by American Audio Prose Library.

PORTFOLIO: Tim Gardner, *Untitled (Sto and Mitch, Daytona 2001); Untitled (S. Rod and Nick Eating Wings); Untitled (Bhoadie in Hot Tub II); The Summit, 1999*

GENERATING CLASS DISCUSSION AND IN-CLASS WRITING

Gardner's paintings mimic photographic realism so effectively that most students will mistake them as photographs. Gardner's attention to detail seems to suggest that he wants viewers to reexamine their notions of painting and photography. You might ask students to list qualities often associated with painting and photography before examining Gardner's work. During the discussion, students will probably note that photographs capture real life whereas paintings imitate or alter it. Of course, technology allows for the alteration of photography. For example, photographs in glamour magazines are often airbrushed to the point of seeming fake.

After this discussion, you might direct students to Gardner's paintings and the Seeing questions in the text. The first three paintings feature young men in rather ordinary situations: eating chicken wings and drinking beer, posing for a picture in front of a hotel, relaxing in a hot tub. As students discuss these pictures, revisit the qualities they listed in the previous discussion. Ask them to locate photographic details in these watercolors. A detail students might miss is the re-creation of the camera flash: in *S. Rod and Nick Eating Wings*, it can be observed on the arm and face of the man gnawing on a chicken wing on the left side of the image; in *Bhoadie in Hot Tub*, it can be seen on the face and shoulder of the man as well as on the lining of the hot tub.

Students could compare and contrast the fourth painting—*The Summit*—to the others because it seems the least photographic and involves older men in a different activity. Although the two men seem realistic, the sky and mountains behind them bear obvious brushstrokes. The background resembles a traditional watercolor, whereas the foreground calls to mind the photographic realism in Gardner's other watercolors. Ask students which details seem photographic to them. To what extent does the rock formation in the foreground look realistic? Ask students how they view the way in which Gardner challenges their expectations and perceptions.

ADDITIONAL WRITING TOPICS

1. Ask students to write an essay comparing and contrasting the details in Gardner's paintings.
2. *The Summit* is different from the other watercolors in several respects—for example, the age and activity of the people presented. Have students write an essay that explains what Gardner's watercolors suggest about the people and the activities presented in them. Students should use details from each watercolor to support their thesis statement.
3. Invite students to choose which watercolor they find most appealing. They should then write an essay that analyzes the elements of the watercolor and explains its appeal.

CONNECTIONS WITH OTHER TEXTS

1. Tracey Baran's photograph *Untitled 2* is far different from Gardner's watercolors of college youth in pursuit of leisure. Gardner's paintings are striking reproductions of photographs that catch people in candid moments. Ask students to examine both Baran's photograph and Gardner's photographic watercolors for details that reveal the candid or staged nature of each. How does the artist create or intrude upon a scene? Discuss the difficulties of capturing reality through art.
2. Ask students to examine Nikki S. Lee's photographs (pp. 374–75), which present the photographer immersed in different subcultures. Ask students to discuss the lifestyles presented in her photographs. Then have them apply a similar strategy for an essay on Gardner's watercolors: Describe the lifestyles and personalities of the figures presented. Throughout their descriptions, students could ruminate on how easy it is to make generalizations based upon appearances and isolated moments. To what extent can a person's essence be captured in a photograph or painting?

SUGGESTIONS FOR FURTHER READING, THINKING, AND WRITING

print

Meisel, Louis K., and Linda Chase. *Photorealism at the Millennium.* New York: Harry N. Abrams, 2002.

 web

www.columbia.edu/cu/pr/00/04/timGardner .html   Columbia University News article about Tim Gardner's rise to success. In-

cludes a watercolor and some insight from Gardner into his work.
www.offoffoff.com/art/2001/gardner.php3
OFFOFFOFF.com's review of Gardner's work. Includes six images.

Links for the selections in this chapter can be found at www.seeingandwriting.com.

Zoe Ingalls, *Teaching Architecture Students "The Discipline of the Hand"*

GENERATING CLASS DISCUSSION AND IN-CLASS WRITING

In this article from the *Chronicle of Higher Education,* Ingalls writes about Sue Ferguson Gussow's freehand-drawing course for architecture students. In the course, Gussow attempts to make students more aware of detail by having them draw peas, green peppers, and the human figure. She also teaches freehand drawing as a way of generating ideas.

You could start the class discussion by asking your students to draw or write a description of something familiar in the room or on the campus—the chalkboard, a building, a stature, a painting. Inevitably they will miss some details, which will illustrate the idea behind Gussow's pea pod lesson.

When she asks students to draw a pea pod from memory and then hands out real pods, the students become aware of the details they missed (paras. 1–3). Gussow wants her students to become more aware of the world around them, so they can, as Ingalls states, "breathe the illusion of life into two-dimensional surfaces" (para. 4).

Gussow has her students draw freehand to help them generate ideas. She states: "'The drawing and the brain work are feeding each other back and forth. You're making marks; they're giving you more ideas'" (para. 8). You might bring up the subject of freewriting, a technique used by writers to get their thoughts on paper. Ask students to compare freedrawing and freewriting. If there are any students who write or draw outside of class, ask them to share their techniques. Do the writers sometimes sketch as they write or prepare to write? Do the visual artists write about their drawing or painting before they begin?

Have students comment on how the following statement could apply to other art forms: "'In order to get the gross idea of a form down, you have to generalize. Yet in order to make the drawing come alive, to become individuated and fascinating, you have to notice what is unique about this situation, what catches the eye'" (para. 10). This statement could also apply to writing: Writing that is engaging often has details that are commonly missed, that make the piece "individuated and fascinating." Challenge students to think about writers whose prose fits this description.

Gussow asks her students to study and draw the human figure because she wants them to "'understand the human condition and how you can make something for it'" (para. 13). Students even learn that drawing the human figure is similar to drawing a building. Gussow notes the similarity: "'We talk about the skeleton of a building, the spine of a structure'" (para. 25). Have your students consider how important an understanding of the human condition is for not only architecture, but all art.

ADDITIONAL WRITING TOPICS

1. Ask students to freewrite about Gussow's teaching philosophy.

2. Have students write an analysis of an essay or work of fiction that uses details that fit the description in paragraph 10.

3. Ask students to write an expository essay of their writing process. Because the writing process is different for everyone and changes according to type of writing, students should describe and assess their process for different types of writing. Students could even describe the process they use for this assignment.

CONNECTIONS WITH OTHER TEXTS

1. Gussow wants her students to understand the human condition so they will design buildings with consideration for the occupants. Ask students to view the *Pale Blue Dot* photograph and read Carl Sagan's speech based upon it. Discuss the importance of accommodating humanity in architecture as well as the importance of gleaning aspects of humanity from a photograph.

The text here asks us to consider the nature of the television sitcom in our everyday lives and recommends watching a rerun of *Seinfeld* as an example of how the routines of daily life can be brought to our attention in an entertaining way.

Television is, of course, one of the most common places we look for information about the world in this decade. Thus, it is more important than ever to bring your students a sense of critical awareness to this medium.

You might also invite students to examine and write about other predominant television genres—the nighttime soap opera, such as *ER*, or the teen angst shows such as *Dawson's Creek*, or the tongue-in-cheek heroic sagas of *Buffy the Vampire Slayer* or *Xena: Warrior Princess*. Students might write comparison/contrast essays or use other rhetorical forms, such as definition (how *Buffy* treats everyday life with a demonic spin) or classification (such as the kinds of activities and objects that make up *Xena*'s world).

Alfred Leslie, *Television Moon*

GENERATING CLASS DISCUSSION AND IN-CLASS WRITING

Leslie invites our eyes to focus on his abstract painting of a television set. Is a painting of a television really art? (Is a painting of a soup can really art?) Further, is television art? *Television Moon* seems to suggest that we view the television set itself as an aesthetic object. Leslie's television stands in a room with a chair beside it and reflects the moon from a world outside. Using a "serious" painting style reminiscent of a still life, Leslie offers a contemporary version of the tradition of painting mundane objects in the home. The portrayal of the inside of private homes and ordinary people was a shift from the more traditional portraiture of ancestors in formal poses or religious or historical events. This modern domestic still life, however, is not a bowl of fruit or a vase of flowers—the traditional subjects of an older style. The domestic environment has changed. Leslie has said that he wants his art to "influence the conduct of people"; ask students how they think he intends his painting to influence our conduct. What statement do the objects in *Television Moon* make as a group? What does the reflection of the natural world suggest on a surface that usually serves as a gateway to man-made entertainment?

 For an interactive visual exercise for this selection, go to www.seeingandwriting.com.

ADDITIONAL WRITING TOPICS

1. Ask students how television—or any other technology—functions in their lives. How important is it? What part of their time do they spend watching or using it? Have them write a short essay describing how this technology might shape the way in which they observe life (i.e., through TV news, through surfing the web, through listening to music).

2. Have students write an essay in which they compare and contrast looking at nature with looking at television. Do they use the same kind of skills for each? Is it the same kind of looking? Why or why not?

3. In addition to the one-page verbal still life of *Television Moon* suggested by the first Writing question on page 89 of the book, you might set up a still life of objects in your classroom—the textbook, a Diet Coke can, a baseball cap—and instruct students to write a detailed description of it. Ask them to draw conclusions about how the objects, as the second Seeing question suggests, "serve as a commentary on contemporary American" educational practices and assumptions.

CONNECTIONS WITH OTHER TEXTS

1. Another everyday object is captured in Roe Ethridge's *Refrigerator*. How would students examine these works if the medium were reversed in each? That is, how would they approach *Refrigerator* as a painting, or *Television Moon* as a photograph? What expectations do students have regarding photography and painting? How do these expectations influence their reading?

2. Have students look at the still of *The Simpsons* in Chapter 5 (p. 387). Leslie's painting can be categorized as "serious" art as opposed to Matt Groening's "comic" art, but both are critiques about the central role that TV plays in our culture. Which medium is a more effective vehicle for delivering a message about our culture? Have students break into groups and brainstorm an ad campaign with a social message (don't smoke, don't drink and drive, read more books, etc.) that would use three different media: comic art, "serious" art, and print ads. Which medium do the students think would work best to deliver their message?

Pepón Osorio, *Badge of Honor (Detail of Son's Bedroom)*

GENERATING CLASS DISCUSSION AND IN-CLASS WRITING

In this work, Osorio has fabricated a teenager's bedroom. You might begin discussion by asking students to examine the boy's room in comparison to their own. What is different about this room? Students will instantly note the obvious difference: The owner of this room has an image of himself projected onto a wall. Ask students to ignore the image for a moment and to examine the room for other details. Which objects stand out the most? What do they suggest about the boy's interests? Students might notice the bicycle, the basketballs, or the basketball posters. They might also notice a room full of masculine images—Bruce Lee and various sports figures.

You might have students consider the reality of the boy's room. Does it seem exaggerated to them? Students will undoubtedly point to the video screen as evidence of the room's fabrication. Apart from the video screen, what else makes the room seem fabricated? Consider its sheer excess: Golden light gleams on the reflective floor, hundreds of baseball cards cover the back wall, and a dozen basketball posters crowd the other wall, which is lined with at least nine pairs of shoes.

Finally, you might ask students to consider why Osorio would fabricate an exaggeration of a teenager's room. Does this image say something about teens' preoccupation with material items? Is it attempting to counter popular media portrayals of Latinos?

This image is only a section of Osorio's work; the other section shows a wall that attaches the boy's room to his father's prison cell. You should keep that information out of the discussion and focus on the son's room. When students come to the next reading that includes the complete picture, they should note how their observations change when the first picture is put into its original and complete context.

ADDITIONAL WRITING TOPICS

1. Ask students to use their observations of the room to write a brief profile of its owner. How would they describe his personality? What are his interests? What is his socioeconomic background?

2. Put students into groups and ask them to brainstorm ideas as to why Osorio included the video projection in the room.

3. Ask students to do some research on Osorio and to write a formal essay on how his art addresses Latino culture. They should use examples from *Badge of Honor* as well as his other works. They should also consult interviews and articles written about Osorio.

CONNECTIONS WITH OTHER TEXTS

1. William Eggleston's photo of the space beneath a bed is also useful for making observations and inferences. What do the objects under the bed suggest about the bed's owner? Does this view provide any details as to how the rest of the room might appear?

2. Ask students to examine Moyra Davey's photograph *The City* (p. 363), which invites viewers to make inferences based upon the objects on top of a desk. As they examine the desk, have students comment on the owner's interests and personality. Your students will not be able to see the top of the boy's desk in Osorio's picture, but based on the rest of the room, how do they imagine it would compare to Davey's?

SUGGESTIONS FOR FURTHER READING, THINKING, AND WRITING

print

Osorio, Pepón. *Badge of Honor.* The Newark Museum, 1996. Exhibition catalogue with essays.

——. *Con To' Los Hierros: A Retrospective of the Work of Pepón Osorio.* New York: El Museo del Barrio, 1991.

Rodriguez, Clara, ed. *Latin Looks: Images of Latinas and Latinos in the U.S. Media.* Boulder: Westview Press, 1998.

[www.] *web*

www.feldmangallery.com/pages/artistsrffa/artoso01.html   This page of the Feldman Gallery features some of Osorio's work.

www.giarts.org/conf_01/Keynote_Pepon.htm   An address by Osorio.

Links for the selections in this chapter can be found at www.seeingandwriting.com.

VISUALIZING CONTEXT: **The Complete Picture**

GENERATING CLASS DISCUSSION AND IN-CLASS WRITING

In the previous reading, students encountered one-half of Osorio's mixed-media installation *Badge of Honor.* This selection gives them an opportunity to see the boy's room in its original context, that is, attached to his father's prison cell. Each room has a video screen that features its inhabitant conversing with the other. Osorio invites viewers to think about imprisonment and the separation of family. The boy's lavishly decorated room is contrasted with the father's stark cell, which emphasizes their separation.

You might begin discussion by directing students to the image of the complete installation (p. 93). Ask them to comment on how they view the boy's room differently now that they see it connected to the prison cell. Does it confuse or enlighten their previous reading? Since they now see a video screen in the cell, can they intuit a reason for the screen in the boy's room? After discussing how the different context changes their reading of the boy's room, direct students to the pages preceding the image (pp. 90–92) for background information on the installation and a definition of *context*.

Ask them to compare the boy's room to the father's cell. Because they cannot see much of the cell, have your students imagine its appearance: its walls, its contents, its floor. In what ways are the two rooms different? How do these details shape your students' perception of the boy's relationship with his father? How do they suggest more than a physical distance, despite the two rooms being joined?

In their examination of the boy's room, students might have noticed the wealth of objects: basketballs, posters, baseball cards. When they view the father's cell, they will notice its dearth of objects. Students might have also noticed the posters depicting masculine figures—Bruce Lee, basketball and baseball players. Now these figures seem especially meaningful since they can be connected with the absence of the boy's father.

As students consider the different contexts in which this installation has appeared—an empty storefront, a museum, and a gallery—ask them to discuss how seeing the installation in a textbook creates a different context.

ADDITIONAL WRITING TOPICS

1. Direct students to write dialogue for a conversation between the father and son. If students have difficulty in doing this on their own, you might put them in pairs and have each person take a role. What is the father's crime? How does the son view his father? How does honor affect their relationship? Discuss the written dialogues. How does the context of the full installation change the students' views of the son?

2. Ask students to imagine the father's cell, and then have them write down details about the cell that engage each of the five senses. Direct students to write a comparison/contrast essay about the jail cell and the boy's room. The purpose of the paper, though, is to assess how differently they view the boy's room now that they see it joined to the father's cell. You might direct students to refer to their notes and writings from their previous reading of the son's bedroom.

1. Ask students to look at Roe Ethridge's photograph of a refrigerator. The photograph was shown in a gallery and was also used as an advertisement. Have students consider how much control artists truly have over the meaning of their work when different contexts can change it so easily.

2. Direct students to Andrew Savulich's photographs of violent and accidental events (pp. 268–71). A description of the event is provided at the bottom of each picture. Ask students to look at each photograph and note their first impressions before they read the provided description. After they read each description, discuss how the text changes the context of each picture. What other descriptions could apply to these pictures?

Annie Dillard, *Seeing*

GENERATING CLASS DISCUSSION AND IN-CLASS WRITING

In this excerpt from her Pulitzer prize–winning book, *Pilgrim at Tinker Creek*, Annie Dillard takes us on her daily walk to the creek as she draws figurative arrows on the sidewalk and pursues her passion to see things closely—her focus is often on minutiae. Her tone is childlike, personal, enthusiastic; her arrows lead the willing reader to discover the "SURPRISE AHEAD" (para. 1) and the "unwrapped gifts and free surprises" (para. 2) that are like the pennies she hid for lucky passersby as a child. Rather than writing about dramatic vistas like the Rocky Mountains or the Grand Canyon, Dillard encourages her readers to appreciate the small, often undervalued visual spectacle that nature offers—blackbirds flying out of a tree, the green ray at sunset, what she calls "the bright coppers at the roots of trees" (para. 4).

As darkness falls, however, her initial enthusiasm and acute observations give way to an increasing sense of threat. She says, "Night was knitting over my face an eyeless mask" (para. 12), and as her ability to see diminishes, her fright increases ("A distant airplane, a delta wing out of nightmare, made a gliding shadow on the creek's bottom that looked like a stingray cruising upstream"; para. 12). By the end of the essay, though, Dillard has begun to appreciate the vision that is given to her by the darkness ("I close my eyes and I see stars, deep stars giving way to deeper stars, deeper stars bowing to deepest stars at the crown of an infinite cone"; para. 14).

It may be interesting to ask students what kind of image they have of the writer by the end of the essay. Is this a scientific description of the natural world? an essay about a woman who becomes frightened because she "stayed at the creek too late" (para. 10)? a larger commentary about the relation all of humankind has to both light and darkness? We are, Dillard writes, "fearful aliens in an enemy camp with our arms crossed over our chests" (para. 12). Ask students what they make of that statement. Do they agree? Dillard's desire to share the insights she gleans from Marius von Senden's book, *Space and Light* (para. 22), further demonstrates her method of careful observation followed by careful thinking. The very concrete world she perceives leads her to the abstract world of inference. Her passion to see and her ability to share her vision through her writing are examples of the highly productive role that being a careful observer can play in our writing lives.

ADDITIONAL WRITING TOPICS

1. Ask your students to write a short piece in class on a natural space that they value. They should include as many details as possible, using Dillard as a model.

2. Have your students isolate one portion of Dillard's excerpt and write a short essay based on the imagery she offers. The passage, for example, in paragraph 11 that begins with "Where Tinker Creek flows under the sycamore log bridge to the tear-shaped island" and ends in paragraph 14 with "I close my eyes and I see stars, deep stars giving way to deeper stars, deeper stars bowing to deepest stars at the crown of an infinite cone" offers escalating images of fright as the darkness falls.

3. Seeing question 2 suggests asking students to consider Dillard's use of the phrases "the artificial obvious" and "the naturally obvious." Have stu-dents write detailed explications of a single example of each type of seeing. (You might want to make sure that they understand the distinction: The naturally obvious is what we laypeople expect to see, whereas the artificial obvious is evident only to experts.) As examples of the artificial obvious, students may want to choose something they consider themselves experts in—running shoes for the runners, computers for the cyberexperts, clothing for the fashion bugs, and so on. Ask students to conclude by agreeing or disagreeing that the "experts" come back with "three bags full," as Dillard suggests (para. 8), even though to the uneducated all running shoes may look alike, all computers may seem alike, all clothing may seem ordinary.

CONNECTIONS WITH OTHER TEXTS

1. Discuss with your students the question of scale in Annie Dillard's piece and K. C. Cole's piece (p. 111). Both authors are interested in the natural world, and both focus on the significance of being able to see from more than one perspective. Dillard wants to take her pet amoeba outside, show it the Andromeda galaxy, and "blow its little endoplasm" (para. 20). On the other hand, Cole impresses on us how scale can be a critical factor in the physical survival of a species. Discuss with your students the significance of scale in their own lives, and ask them to write a classification essay that demonstrates categories of importance in their own lives and the criteria they used to select and order them.

2. Ask students to read Dorothy Allison's "This Is Our World" (p. 259) in Chapter 3. Both Allison and Dillard are interested in describing our world—Allison is interested in the man-made part of it, whereas Dillard is more invested in describing the natural. Which perspective do students find more compelling, and why? Have them write a personal narrative that starts with their responses to both essays and then moves to an analysis of why one subject interests them more than the other—or why both are equally compelling.

SUGGESTIONS FOR FURTHER READING, THINKING, AND WRITING

print

Dillard, Annie. *An American Childhood*. New York: Harper and Row, 1987.

———. *The Living*. New York: Harper Collins, 1992.

———. *Living by Fiction*. New York: Harper Colophon Books, 1983.

———. *Pilgrim at Tinker Creek*. New York: Harper Colophon Books, 1982. Dillard's full book on "seeing" and experiencing nature.

———. *Teaching a Stone to Talk: Expeditions and Encounters*. New York: Harper Colophon Books, 1982.

———. *Tickets for a Prayer Wheel: Poems*. Toronto: Bantam Books, 1975.

———. *The Writing Life*. New York: Harper and Row, 1989.

Sacks, Oliver. *An Anthropologist on Mars*. New York: Knopf, 1995. Dr. Oliver Sacks, the well-known neurologist, includes an essay in this book entitled "The Case of the Colorblind Painter," about an artist whose vision becomes black and white after he sustains a head injury.

[www] *web*

www.artandculture.com/cgi-bin/WebObjects/ ACLive.woa/wa/artist?id=529   This site includes biographies and information on Annie Dillard and her work, and links to related sites.

Links for the selections in this chapter can be found at www.seeingandwriting.com.

audio/visual

Annie Dillard Interview with Kay Bonetti. 47 min.
1989. Recording. Distributed by American
Audio Prose Library.

King of the Hill. 103 min. NTSC, 1993. Videocassette, color, rated PG-13. Distributed by
MCA/Universal and Gramercy Pictures. Director Steven Soderbergh's film captures the
extraordinary in the ordinary and makes a
moving parallel to Larry Woiwode's memoir;
it could also be tied to Annie Dillard's essay.

The protagonist is a young boy, Aaron Kurlander, growing up alone in the Depression,
struggling to survive. The film is based on
A. E. Hotchner's memoir, *King of the Hill.*

The Living. 4 cassettes (6 hrs). 1992. Recording.
Performed by Laurence Luckinbill. Distributed by Harper Audio.

Pilgrim at Tinker Creek. 7 cassettes (1.5 hrs. each).
1993. Recording. Read by Grace Cassidy. Distributed by Blackstone Audio Books.

Looking Closer:
Seeing Is Believing

GENERATING CLASS DISCUSSION AND IN-CLASS WRITING

With the possible exception of Close's *Self Portrait,* most of these selections involve the
subject of the Millhauser excerpt—the fascination of the miniature. Indeed, even
Close's work could said to be involved with the miniature; although his canvas is
large, his attention to minute detail is clear. You might read the Millhauser together
first because it is relatively short and works as a good introduction to the other pieces
in the section. You could then separate the students into groups and divide the selections among the groups. As they read each selection, ask them to note the specific details that present the ordinary in a different way. When they are done, they should
report their findings to the rest of the class for discussion.

Steven Millhauser, *The Fascination of the Miniature*

You could start discussion by asking students to name any miniature objects that interest them. Some students might name Mini-Me, the miniature version of Dr. Evil in
the second Austin Powers film; others might point out children's clothes that are
miniature replicas of adult's clothes. Ask if they agree with Millhauser's assertion that

the miniature fascinates because it "shock[s] us into attention: the inattentive and jaded eye, passing though a world without interest, helplessly perceives that something in the bland panorama is not as it should be. The eye is irritated into attention" (para. 2). The excerpt ends with the observation that the fascination of the miniature could be better understood by examining the discrepancy of the gigantic. Which do your students find to be more interesting: gigantic objects or miniature ones?

Tom Friedman, *Aspirin Self-Portrait*

Friedman displays a fascination with the miniature in this self-portrait carved into an aspirin tablet. Students could compare Friedman's miniature self-portrait to Close's gigantic one. Which image do they find more interesting? Students will probably be divided on the issue, but their reasons for choosing Friedman or Close could give them some insight into the Millhauser excerpt.

Carl Sagan, *Reflections on a Mote of Dust*, May 11, 1996
Voyager 1, *Pale Blue Dot*

The picture taken from *Voyager* 1 at a distance of 4 billion miles presents the earth as a tiny white speck in a sea of darkness. The sight humbles Sagan and fills him with a sense of responsibility: "To my mind, there is perhaps no better demonstration of the folly of human conceits than this distant image of our tiny world. To me, it underscores our responsibility to deal more kindly and compassionately with one another and to preserve and cherish that pale blue dot, the only home we've ever known" (paras. 5–6). You might ask students to write a few paragraphs about what this view of the earth means to them before they read Sagan's speech.

David Scharf, *Kitchen Scouring Pad*

Ask students to guess what this image of intertwined blue and yellow fibers might be. After discussing the possibilities, you could pass an actual scouring pad around the room, letting students realize that much of this object is hidden from their view. Does this close-up view of an everyday object fascinate your students? Does it unsettle them?

K. C. Cole, *A Matter of Scale*

K. C. Cole addresses the notion of scale in this verbal text. She discusses the biological and physical laws that apply to living creatures, and she emphasizes how size defines our capabilities in a universe ruled by gravity. Cole also suggests that our size acts as an editor to our perception. She quotes Berkeley microbiologist Norman Pace: "We're so hung up on our own scale of life that we miss most of life's diversity. . . . 'Who's in the ocean? People think of whales and seals, but 90 percent of organisms in the ocean are less than two micrometers'" (para. 26).

Harold Edgerton, *Milk Drop Coronet*

The image of Edgerton's photograph of a milk drop illustrates the point of scale well. Not many of us perceive the visual events of our daily lives—or the beauty of them—on the scale of the milk drop presented in this microscopic and mesmerizing image.

Felice Frankel and George M. Whitesides, *Compact Disc*

You might pass a compact disc around the class for students to examine as you discuss the picture and essay. In this essay, Whitesides explains how a CD player reads information from a disc. He compares the CD player to the human brain and eye: "Faces, moods, coming changes in the weather: a glimpse recognizes all. By comparison, a CD player is a one-eyed robot working in the dark with a head lamp" (para. 3).

Whitesides also notes another important difference between the machine and the human: "A beam illuminates the disc, and a photoreceptor registers the information faster than any human eye can appreciate, but there is no appreciation of style: just 1001011011001" (para. 4).

Chuck Close, *Self-Portrait*

Close duplicates photographic detail in this self-portrait. Students should know that the painting's true scale is not represented in the text. Most of Close's portraits are over 8 feet long, and this piece is no exception. Ask students why they think Close would create portraits so large and so distorted. How does the size of the portrait make a statement about vanity? Students might be able to analyze Close's work more effectively if they were asked to list the qualities of traditional portraits and the effects of those qualities. If traditional portraits seem to gloss over physical imperfections, are Close's portraits an attempt to capture the imperfections?

ADDITIONAL WRITING TOPICS

1. Ask students to research miniature and gigantic objects online. In a sense, they could finish Millhauser's essay, explaining the fascination with gigantic and miniature objects, possibly taking a position as to which is more fascinating.

2. Students could research how tapes and vinyl records are made and how they function. On the basis of this research, they could compare and contrast tapes, vinyl records, and compact discs.

CONNECTIONS WITH OTHER TEXTS

1. The images and texts here are concerned with scale. Edgerton's photograph of a milk drop would be less impressive without its microscopic detail. Friedman's self-portrait would not be as striking if it were captured on a larger scale (in a pancake, for example). Ask students to look back on the images from this chapter and consider the importance of scale in each. You might put students into small discussion groups, giving each group an image to consider in terms of scale.

SUGGESTIONS FOR FURTHER READING, THINKING, AND WRITING

print

Bodanis, David. *The Secret House: 24 Hours in the Strange and Unexpected World in Which We Spend Our Days and Nights.* New York: Simon & Schuster, 1986. A 24-hour account of the microscopic life of a house and its two inhabitants.

Sagan, Carl. *Broca's Brain.* New York: Random House, 1979.

———. *The Demon-Haunted World—Science as a Candle in the Dark.* New York: Random House, 1995.

———, and Ann Godoff (editor). *Pale Blue Dot: A Vision of the Human Future in Space.* New York: Random House, 1995.

www web

www.carlsagan.com   Official Carl Sagan web site.

www.culturevulture.net/ArtandArch/TomFriedman.htm   Includes a brief article about and a few photos of Friedman's work.

www.genegillminiatures.com/   Provides a gallery of miniature historical buildings and landmarks created by artist Gene Gill.

www.howstuffworks.com   Fun and informative, this fascinating site gives information on how everyday things work. This might be a useful resource for students wanting to research other forms of audio recording in connection with the Frankel and Whitesides reading.

www.imaginationmall.com/   Provides numerous links to web sites that sell or provide information on miniatures.

www.skeptic.com/mag44.html   A tribute to Carl Sagan on *Skeptic Magazine's* web site. Includes three essays by *Skeptic* writers and quotes from Sagan's books.

Links for the selections in this chapter can be found at www.seeingandwriting.com.

audio/visual

Biography—Carl Sagan. 60 min. NTSC, 1996. Videocassette. Distributed by A&E.

Chapter 2

Coming to Terms with Place

Introduction

GENERATING CLASS DISCUSSION AND IN-CLASS WRITING

This chapter asks students to think about place. You might want to start discussion by asking students to list terms they use for place (*home, school, work, town, city, chatroom, library,* to name a few). Have the class sort terms according to their positive and negative connotations and then by whether they are *real* places or concepts. This should spur discussion on how we talk about place. Given Jerry Brown's comments that "People don't live in place, they live in space", you may also want to introduce the notion of virtual space and community. Students could look at sites such as iVillage.com or concepts such as Microsoft's Network Neighborhood that use language associated with community and communal space.

Direct your class to the image of a bird's nest on the chapter divider. What does the nest suggest? Does it clearly connote place? You could begin discussion by introducing the metaphor of "leaving the nest" or the "empty nest"—home as a nurturing space/place. You may want to point out that this particular image reinforces that notion, with the nest resembling a natural cushion, both dense and delicate. It offers comfort. The nest also links a sense of place to the familiar, to communities and relationships. Do students agree with this sense of place, or do they construct it in a different way (the unfamiliar, unknown)? Is place a literal point on the map or is it something more ineffable—an emotion or a memory?

For additional resources for the selections in this chapter (including exercises and annotated links), go to www.seeingandwriting.com.

Coca-Cola Company, *Advertisement*

GENERATING CLASS DISCUSSION AND IN-CLASS WRITING

Because the image in the chapter introduction is an advertisement for Coca-Cola, you'll probably want to start discussion by asking students to think about its visual rhetoric—how it gets our attention. The bottle is open, inviting one to drink; the word *America* is centered over the Coke bottle, linking the two visually. The fill-line of the bottle falls just below the Coca-Cola Company logo on the right so that it points to the logo. A tight visual connection also exists among the header *America,* the company logo, and the name *Coca-Cola* on the bottle: They are all in the same font. This further ties the company to the country and suggests that America is Coke.

The students should also look at the text of this ad carefully, because it makes huge leaps in logic. Ask your students what Coke has in common with the Grand Canyon, or autumn in New Hampshire, or the memories described in the text of the ad. Is Coke "the real thing" just like "all of the good things in this country are real"? Finally, what is being sold in the advertisement? How does it tap into our national sense of place? Do students find the ad effective?

ADDITIONAL WRITING TOPICS

1. Ask students to write a short description of a product they identify with a certain place. For example, they might write about a food available only in their hometown, or the interior of a car their parents once drove. Make sure students direct the details of their description to underscore exactly how the product is tied to the place.

2. Have students write a short response to a specific claim of authenticity—whether for Coke,

Levis, Lender's New York bagels, or any other product that is marketed as the "real" thing. After analyzing the rhetorical strategies that companies use to create a sense of place and make consumers feel at home, ask students to what degree they "buy" such claims.

3. Students might research a more recent Coca-Cola advertising campaign to see how the company has changed its advertising strategy over time. Does each student's ad connect Coke to traditional American values? Have students write a brief essay that answers this question and includes a close reading of one print or television advertisement for Coca-Cola.

CONNECTIONS WITH OTHER TEXTS

1. Ask students to examine the Ericsson ad in the Looking Closer section (p. 204). How is it similar to and different from the Coke ad? How does each create a sense of place? Both suggest movement yet offer a product that grants stability: No matter where you are, Coke and Ericsson will be with you.

2. Nature is used to sell products in the Coke ad and in the last bicycle ad in the Chapter 1 Retrospect (p. 69). Students might consider the language and images used in the ads. What is the relationship among product, concept, and consumer?

SUGGESTIONS FOR FURTHER READING, THINKING, AND WRITING

print

Allen, Frederick. *Secret Formula: How Brilliant Marketing and Relentless Salesmanship Made Coca-Cola the Best Known Product in the World.* New York: HarperBusiness, 1995.

Munsey, Cecil. *The Illustrated Guide to the Collectibles of Coca-Cola.* New York: Hawthorn Books, 1972.

Petretti, Allan. *Petretti's Coca-Cola Collectible Price Guide.* Dubuque: Antique Trader Books, 1997.

www *web*

www.cocacola.com/   The official Coca-Cola Company web site has links to international brand sites that offer students an interesting look into how a corporation creates a sense of place.

Links for the selections in this chapter can be found at www.seeingandwriting.com.

PAIR: Edward Hopper, *House by the Railroad*
Edward Hirsch, *Edward Hopper and the House by the Railroad (1925)*

GENERATING CLASS DISCUSSION AND IN-CLASS WRITING

This pair of verbal and visual texts are organically related; Hirsch wrote his poem about Hopper's painting. You might start by giving students this information and then asking them what reflections of the other they see in each. Hopper centers the house in the frame of the painting, the "exact middle." As Hirsch's poem comments, it is a solitary object, not surrounded by any sign of life—no trees, no people, not even a train on the tracks. The windows are either curtained, shaded, or black. The house is cast in various shades of gray, making it look old, almost discolored. The house could be seen as growing out of the similarly gray sky or as a stark silhouette superimposed on its environment. This is the message given by Hirsch's poem; ask students whether it is possible to see a welcoming presence, a "home" in the positive sense given the context of reading the painting next to the poem.

Ask students to consider how Hirsch personifies the house in the poem. It is "gawky," "ashamed," "desperately empty." How does the poem suggest that the house is a manifestation of the painter (Hopper)? The first two stanzas refer to the house as if it were a man; the third introduces the painter as a personality. You might want to work through the poem line by line with the class and track the way in which Hirsch shifts between the house and the painter. You could direct students to stanza 6: "the house begins to suspect / That the man, too, is desolate, desolate." The poem eventually becomes, in part, a meditation on how an artist's inner self, an emotional space, becomes the source of his or her art. Can students identify the story of this poem? Is it about a man creating a place or the place "writing" the man?

This pair also questions how one creates, defines, and delimits one space from another. Hirsch mentions the architectural elements of Hopper's paintings (the rooftop, the porch, the windows, the storefronts) as a method of building space from "white canvas." Ask students to study the picture. Has Hopper succeeded in building three-dimensional space out of flat canvas?

After you've read the poem closely, you may want to read the painting for what it reveals that the words do not. For example, Hirsch's poem contains the lines, "the house / Must have done something against the earth." However, the house as we are able to see it is, in fact, not literally "against the earth." Instead, it is visually foundationless and unsecured. You might want to discuss this concept in relation to the poem's final lines, "someone American and gawky, / Someone who is about to be left alone / Again, and can no longer stand it." Is there something singularly American about being "alone," both in the sense of being an individual and in the sense of being unsecured to place?

ADDITIONAL WRITING TOPICS

1. Ask students to write their own short description of Hopper's painting (if possible, *before* they read Hirsch's poem). Then ask them to compare their own descriptive language to the language Hirsch uses and to explain the points at which both converge or diverge.

2. Hirsch writes, "the man behind the easel is relentless; / He is as brutal as sunlight." Ask students to consider how sunlight is used within Hopper's painting, how the shadows it creates give the painting an "unnerved" tone. They should write a short essay that explains how Hopper uses light and dark in the painting to create meaning.

3. Hirsch writes, "The house must have done something horrible / To the people who once lived here." Popular culture is rife with the icon of the haunted house or place, including recent incarnations such as *The Amityville Horror, Poltergeist,* and *The Blair Witch Project*; students may even note a resemblance between Hopper's house and the hilltop home of Norman Bates in *Psycho*. Ask students to write an essay on how a place may be haunted by memories or ghosts, or on why this cultural icon holds such sway over people.

CONNECTIONS WITH OTHER TEXTS

1. Ask students to consider the graphic image of Hopper's solitary "American" house in relationship to the Coca-Cola advertisement (p. 127). In a comparative essay, students should explicate these two takes on America and explain which one they find more accurate.

2. Refer students to Jeff Mermelstein's photograph *Here is New York* (p. 221), which presents a desolate image of New York on September 11, 2001. Ask students to list five adjectives that describe Mermelstein's photograph and Hopper's painting. If students find that each work evokes similar feelings, ask them to consider how each artist achieves this.

SUGGESTIONS FOR FURTHER READING, THINKING, AND WRITING

print

Berkow, Ita. *Edward Hopper: An American Master.* New York: Smithsonian, 1996.

Hirsch, Edward. *Earthly Measures: Poems.* New York: Knopf, 1994.

———. *For the Sleepwalkers: Poems.* New York: Knopf, 1981.

———. *How to Read a Poem and Fall in Love with Poetry.* New York: Harcourt Brace, 1999.

———. *Transforming Vision: Writers on Art.* Selected and introduced by Edward Hirsch. Boston: Little, Brown, 1994.

Levin, Gail. *Edward Hopper: The Art and the Artist.* New York: Norton, Whitney Museum of Art, 1980.

Strand, Mark. *Hopper.* Hopewell: Ecco Press, 1993.

web

www.artcyclopedia.com/artists/hopper _edward.html   The Artcyclopedia guide to online sites on Edward Hopper.

Links for the selections in this chapter can be found at www.seeingandwriting.com.

audio/visual

Edward Hopper: The Silent Witness. 43 min. 1995. VHS videocassette. Distributed by Kultur. A docudrama tour of Cape Cod in conjunction with paintings by Hopper. "Chiefly criticism of his work."

Eudora Welty, *The Little Store*

GENERATING CLASS DISCUSSION AND IN-CLASS WRITING

"The Little Store" is a poignant remembrance of what a child sees (and misses) as she grows up, as well as a study of the way in which place can be at once incredibly expansive and narrow when viewed through the eyes of a child. Welty centers her memoir on a specific place; you might want to direct students to consider how she uses it to organize the structure of the narrative, walking together through the progression of the narrative. First comes her trip to the store, related through the sights, sounds, and smells that she encounters (paras. 1–10), a trip that helps her recall people as well as places. You might ask students to consider whether the insular world of a small town encourages these sorts of associations. Do all familiar places carry associations? To what degree do such associations determine our identities and memories? Welty writes, "Setting out in this world, a child feels so indelible. He only comes to find out later that it's all the others along his way who are making themselves indelible to him" (para. 10). Make sure students understand the word *indelible*; do they agree with Welty's observations?

Once Welty reaches her destination, her experience moves through the senses. The description begins with a catalogue of the store's items, description that situates the reader at a child's level: The cheese is "as big as a doll's house" (para. 15) and "a child's hand" reaches in for the candy (para. 16). As with the beginning of the narrative, however, this is not just the child's voice but also the adult's, as toys and candies are balanced against influenza and violent death. Students might miss what seems like a throw-away line in Welty's piece, "Is there always a hard way to go home?" (para. 20). Is this a comment on what happens when we remember our past? Ask students to compare the beginning and end of the essay: Welty begins with a pastoral description of her mother and ends with the disappearance of another family who she never really knew.

Talking about "The Little Store" is a good springboard for a more general discussion about how an author effectively creates a sense of place. Welty does this by appealing to all the senses, not just sight. She also evokes a realm beyond sense, what we cannot really see about places and people. When she writes of seeing things "at a child's eye level" (para. 16), she emphasizes not just what she could see but also what she could not. Welty tells us almost as much about what she can't see as about what she can: She had never seen the Monkey Man sitting down; she "seldom saw [the Sessions] close together"; they lived behind "shaded windows"; she had "never seen them sitting down together around their own table" (para. 27). The image—a photo taken by Welty—that follows the essay allows the viewer to see only half of the storekeeper clearly: half of his face, a little more than half of his body. How does what we cannot see of a place help to define our sense of it?

ADDITIONAL WRITING TOPICS

1. Ask students to list ways in which they experience their favorite place with all five senses and then use their lists to build a short paper, focusing on one sense in each paragraph. This will help students get a sense of structuring devices for essays and paragraphs.

2. Welty's last paragraph begins with the dramatic statement, "We weren't being sent to the neighborhood grocery for facts of life, or death. But of course those are what we were on the track of, anyway" (para. 30). Ask students to write an essay that analyzes "The Little Store," using this statement as a point of departure. How does the trip to the neighborhood store offer the young Eudora "facts of life, or death"?

3. Welty writes of the Sessions' grocery, "But I didn't know there'd ever been a story at the Little Store, one that was going on while I was there" (para. 27). It is only in retrospect that she comes to understand the importance of this place and story. Ask students to write a short memoir of a place, specifying that their goal is to reveal the "story" they hadn't realized was there.

CONNECTIONS WITH OTHER TEXTS

1. Ask students to compare the descriptive language used by Welty with that used by David Guterson in "No Place Like Home" (p. 157). What kind of language does each use to draw the reader into a specific place?

2. Have students compare the narrative points of view in Welty's memoir and Larry Woiwode's "Ode to an Orange" (p. 48). How does each use a child's point of view to convey a sense of wonder in relating the everyday experience?

SUGGESTIONS FOR FURTHER READING, THINKING, AND WRITING

print

Welty, Eudora. *Collected Stories.* New York: Harcourt Brace Jovanovich, 1980.

———. *Eudora Welty: Photographs.* Jackson: University of Mississippi Press, 1989. Foreword by Reynolds Price.

———. *The Eye of the Story: Selected Essays and Reviews.* New York: Random House, 1978.

———. *One Time, One Place: Mississippi in the Depression.* New York: Random House, 1971. Introduction and black and white photographs by Welty, including *Shopkeeper.*

[www] *web*

www.olemiss.edu/depts/english/ms-writers/dir/welty_eudora/   A directory of Eudora Welty photographs and a long article placing her works in the context of the South; the site is maintained by the University of Mississippi.

Links for the selections in this chapter can be found at www.seeingandwriting.com.

audio/visual

Eudora Welty Reads. 2 cassettes (1 hr., 38 min.). 1992. Recording. Distributed by Harper Collins, Caedmon. Includes "Why I Live at the P.O.," "A Memory," "A Worn Path," "Powerhouse," "Petrified Man."

Albert Bierstadt, *Among the Sierra Nevada Mountains, California, 1868*

GENERATING CLASS DISCUSSION AND IN-CLASS WRITING

This lush landscape by Albert Bierstadt uses light and natural majesty to romantic effect. A familiar motif can also be found: The mountains and the trees suggest the shape of a nest like that on the chapter's divider spread. It's a pristine scene: The light beams down on the valley with its crystal lake and abundant nature. You might ask students to consider how Bierstadt has used form, color, and light to reinforce the sense of nature's unity and interconnectedness. For example, the clouds repeat the shape of the mountains, as do many of the trees. Why has Bierstadt left human beings out of this painting? How might a human figure have changed the sense of nature the painting instills in the viewer? The implied human figure is the viewer; the purity of the experience might be sullied if the viewer were not alone.

Like Bierstadt, John Pfahl uses light and form to comment on nature. What is the effect of the subject—cooling towers rather than the Sierra Nevada Mountains? Is Pfahl's photograph (p. 142) romantic? What are the implications inherent in the different mediums—an oil painting and a photograph? Bierstadt's paintings brought early developers to the West; how is that ironic?

ADDITIONAL WRITING TOPICS

1. Ask students to freewrite about the emotions that Bierstadt's painting evokes. Then, have them consider what formal elements within the work raise these emotions.

2. The headnote accompanying Bierstadt's painting explains that "throughout his long career he celebrated the sublime beauty and power of romanticized landscapes" (p. 142). Ask students to write a short essay in which they explain how this painting is romanticized. They might discuss scale, color, light, and so on.

3. Bierstadt is credited with creating the quintessential image of the American West. Ask students to write a short essay on an artist or author (of any genre) who has created what they feel is the classic image of a specific place; have them explain how this artist's works have captured the sense of this place. For example, you might suggest Woody Allen or Martin Scorsese for New York, Paul Gaugin for Tahiti, Barbara Kingsolver for the Southwest, John Berendt for Savannah, or Aaron Spelling for Beverly Hills.

1. Ask students to compare and contrast this painting with Edward Hopper's *House by the Railroad* (p. 130). What is the tone of each work? How does each artist convey tone through color? How might Bierstadt's painting change if Hopper's house were present in it? What if Bierstadt had surrounded Hopper's house with trees?

2. Bierstadt's painting captures the abundance and beauty of nature. In Chapter 7, Sebastião Salgado's photograph *State of Roraima, Brazil* depicts a different scene—a wasted landscape caused by deforestation. Ask students to consider these works as images of potential and exploitation. Have students consider the methods used by each artist to fulfill his purpose.

SUGGESTIONS FOR FURTHER READING, THINKING, AND WRITING

print

Gussow, Alan. *A Sense of Place: The Artist and the American Land.* San Francisco: Friends of the Earth, 1972. Paintings of American landscapes by American artists. Introduction by Richard Wilbur.

Hendricks, Gordon. *Albert Bierstadt: Painter of the American West.* New York: H. N. Abrams, 1974.

Pfahl, John. *Altered Landscapes: The Photographs of John Pfahl.* Carmel: Friends of Photography, Robert Friedus Gallery, 1981.

————. *A Distanced Land: The Photographs of John Pfahl.* Albuquerque: University of New Mexico Press, 1990.

————. *Picture Windows: The Photographs of John Pfahl.* Boston: Little, Brown, 1987.

Robotham, Tom. *Albert Bierstadt.* New York: Crescent Books, 1993.

 web

Links for the selections in this chapter can be found at www.seeingandwriting.com.

Scott Russell Sanders, *Homeplace*

GENERATING CLASS DISCUSSION AND IN-CLASS WRITING

Sanders's essay initially seems to be a celebration of commitment to place, but it evolves into something more: a celebration of our connection to the land as a tangible, physical tie. Students might be directed to chart how Sanders moves from the general geographical idea of "staying put" (para. 4) to a tightly focused and ethical lens on each individual's responsibility for the fate of the planet. The structure of the essay mirrors his increasingly interior contemplation and singular conception of self and space, symbolized by the "words of Zen master Thich Nhat Hanh" (para. 15). Sanders asserts, "If you stay put, your place may become a holy center" (para. 15). He then asks us to consider what it means "to be alive in an era when the earth is being devoured, and in a country that has set the pattern for that devouring" (para. 20). In fact, by the end of the essay, Sanders expresses his confirmed belief that "there is only one world, and we participate in it here and now, in our flesh and our place" (para. 22).

The accompanying Larson cartoon mocks the effects of moving from one place to another. How does the cartoon assert the quote Sanders uses by Thoreau—"The man who is often thinking that it is better to be somewhere else than where he is excommunicates himself."

ADDITIONAL WRITING TOPICS

1. Ask students to write an essay that argues the exact opposite of Sanders's point: that movement is good and stasis is bad. They should collect their examples from the same types of sources that Sanders uses, modeling his structure.

2. Students might be asked to bring in two advertising images: one that represents staying put, and one that represents moving. Their task is to write a short essay analyzing how the elements of the ads combine to convey these messages and explaining which seems more convincing and why.

3. In large part, Sanders attributes our need to keep moving to the cultural belief that something better is always out there—he highlights the restlessness of the American character. Assign your students a narrative essay in which they tell the tale of their move to college.

CONNECTIONS WITH OTHER TEXTS

1. Tony Hiss's "The Experience of Place" (p. 182) also deals with our connection to the places around us. You might ask students to read Hiss's essay and compare it to Sanders's. Then have students write an essay that compares and contrasts the two, describing and analyzing how each presents mankind's relationship and responsibility to the world. Which essay seems more developed and convincing?

2. Direct students to investigate some of the texts that Sanders mentions in his essay: works by Salman Rushdie, Gary Snyder, or Thich Nhat Hanh, for example. Ask them to analyze Sanders's essay in light of their findings.

SUGGESTIONS FOR FURTHER READING, THINKING, AND WRITING

print

Larson, Gary. *The Far Side.* Kansas City: Andrews and McMeel, 1982. Cartoons from Larson's syndicated cartoon strip.

———. *The Prehistory of the Far Side: A Tenth Anniversary Exhibit.* Kansas City: Andrews and McMeel, 1989.

Sanders, Scott Russell. *Secrets of the Universe: Scenes from the Journey Home.* Boston: Beacon Press, 1991.

———. *Staying Put: Making a Home in a Restless World.* Boston: Beacon Press, 1993.

——— *Wilderness Plots: Tales about the Settlement of the American Land.* New York: Morrow, 1983.

web

www.aao.gov.au/images.html   A web site run by the Anglo-Australian Observatory that contains about thirty pictures of galaxies and nebulas. These could be used in relation to Scott Russell Sanders's "Homeplace" or K. C. Cole's "A Matter of Scale."

Links for the selections in this chapter can be found at www.seeingandwriting.com.

RETROSPECT: *Camilo José Vergara's Photographs of 65 East 125th St., Harlem*

GENERATING CLASS DISCUSSION AND IN-CLASS WRITING

This Retrospect offers twelve photos by Camilo José Vergara of the same address in Harlem over a 25-year span, from 1977 to 2002. The initial image shows a funky yet clean establishment, painted in bright colors. In January 1980 the building is painted black but is still clean, with decorated tiles leading to the front of the store. By October of that year the store has been split in two. Within three years the storefront is no longer safe at night—as we can infer from the security door and the deteriorating decorative tile. The second half of the store has again changed owners. In November 1988 the stores have new owners again, and one of the tenants will remain the same from this point forward. It is a small, dark "Grocery/Candy/Smoke Shop." You might want to ask students to consider why and how this store is able to stay open for eight years. What is it offering to the area residents? By November 1988 the decorative elements of both stores have completely disappeared, and from this point forward the shop on the left has trouble maintaining a tenant. You might ask students to identify the various tenants of this half of the building.

In September 1992 the first graffiti appear in the photo, on the now-closed store-front on the left. The street as a whole is cleaner in 2001 than in 1996, but it has lost all the charm and character it had in 1977. The decorative tile is gone, the paint is dull, and the empty store is battered.

In discussion, you may want to introduce the question of the address for this Retrospect. Why feature a street in Harlem? In part, the rationale would be the obvious decline over the years in the neighborhood. This decline reveals social, cultural, and economic changes that affected urban inner cities far more harshly than suburbs, and northern urban areas (that had often relied on industry) the hardest.

ADDITIONAL WRITING TOPICS

1. You might ask students to list the details that they immediately notice about these photos. What stands out, and why? Which photo draws their attention first? Ask them to write a short in-class piece on how one particular photo captures the viewer's eye.

2. Ask students whether these pictures reveal the transience of our society—our sense of space rather than place—or whether they are about the essentially unchanging urban landscape. In a brief analytical essay, the students should support one or the other thesis using the photos as evidence.

3. As this street decays, there is one striking consistency from 1988 on: the Grocery/Candy/Smoke Shop. You might direct students to investigate the issue of smoking and African Americans, a controversial topic within both the African American medical and social activist communities.

CONNECTIONS WITH OTHER TEXTS

1. Ask students to compare the later photos in this series to Mark Peterson's photo *Image of Homelessness* (p. 155). What similarities do they notice in the framing and the objects included within both compositions? Their essays should examine the ways in which photographers guide their viewers to form opinions about the subject matter.

2. Ask students to look at the pictures of Cindy Jackson in Chapter 4 (p. 370), before and after the many operations to change her appearance into that of a living doll. Whereas in the Retrospect the photographer shows a place changing gradually, the two photos in Chapter 4 show before and after with none of the steps in between. Have students write an essay in which they first "translate" each set of photographs into a verbal description and then compare the benefits and drawbacks of showing change dramatically and step-by-step.

print

Vergara, Camilo J. *The New American Ghetto.* New Brunswick: Rutgers University Press, 1995.

[www.] *web*

www.harlemlive.org/main.html   An online publication about Harlem by Harlem youth that includes valuable links and offers a solid counterpoint to this chapter's Retrospect.

Links to the selections in this chapter can be found at www.seeingandwriting.com.

David Ignatow, *My Place*

GENERATING CLASS DISCUSSION AND IN-CLASS WRITING

In their first reading of "My Place," students might think of Ignatow's place as being physical—possibly a house or an apartment. They might note that he comes to it "morning, noon and night" (line 3). Ask students how they would define Ignatow's place in this first stanza. What do they think of Ignatow's statement that his "place" gives him his bearings: "where I am going and what / I am going from, making me / firm in my direction" (stanza 1, 9–11). Of course, students could read this in the literal sense—Ignatow knows, for example, where the store is because it's two blocks south of his house. If students do sense that Ignatow is not being literal, ask them which phrases suggest this.

In the second stanza, the place to which Ignatow refers becomes less physical. Ask students to examine the lines "I am good to talk to, / you feel in my speech / a location, an expectation" (2: 12–14). Do they read this "location" as a dialect or an accent—or something else? How does this make him "good to talk to"? What do they make of "location" being referred to as "an expectation"? Discuss how locations can create expectations. Some students might reply that people create expectations of others from accents or dialects.

Ignatow's notion of "place" becomes even more complicated in the last few lines, in which another person "too grows his [place] / from which he speaks to mine / having located himself / through my place" (2: 19–22). How do we create a sense of place through others? If students are focused on speech—accents, dialects, and so on—you might direct them to think about the mental spaces created by roles. You could ask them to imagine explaining their thoughts on this class to a friend. How would their wording and tone change when explaining the same thoughts to their parents, or even their instructor?

ADDITIONAL WRITING TOPICS

1. Ask students to write an essay explaining and defending their interpretation of this poem.

2. Ask students to write three letters about this class; each letter should be written to a different audience: a friend, a parent, and the instructor. They don't have to turn these in, so urge them to be honest. After they're done, ask how their personalities seemed to change in each letter.

3. Have students write a brief list of all the roles they fill. If students become stumped after a few entries, you could encourage them to broaden their thinking by pointing out such obvious examples as "human" and "male" or "female."

CONNECTIONS WITH OTHER TEXTS

1. Ask students to read Lucille Clifton's poem "When I Go Home" (p. 213), which presents her home through specific details. Discuss the strategies used by both Clifton and Ignatow to describe a sense of place. How does Ignatow create an internal sense of place? How does Clifton—despite her specific external details—suggest an internal one as well?

2. Ignatow notes in his poem how another person has "located himself / through my place." Discuss with students how they identified with Ignatow's poem, how they located themselves through it.

SUGGESTIONS FOR FURTHER READING, THINKING, AND WRITING

print

Ignatow, David. *Against the Evidence*. Middletown, CT: Wesleyan University Press, 1994.

————. *I Have a Name*. Middletown, CT: Wesleyan University Press, 1996.

————. *Shadowing the Ground*. Middletown, CT: Wesleyan University Press, 1991.

(www) web

www.webdelsol.com/ignatow/ Features biographical information on the poet and selected poems from *Against the Evidence*.

www.poets.org/poets/index.cfm The web site for the Academy of American Poets includes a short biography and links to Ignatow's poetry on the Internet.

www.poetrysociety.org/journal/articles/ tributes/ignatow.html   Poetry Society's tribute to Ignatow. Includes a poem by Ignatow and a poem written in his honor.

Links for the selections in this chapter can be found at www.seeingandwriting.com.

Talking Pictures

Invite your students to venture further into our national mythology: Have them write a critical research essay on the portrayal of American restlessness in the Hollywood western. Wagon train movies, cattle-driving movies, frontier movies, or homesteading movies, for example, all offer opportunities for analysis of both the written and/or visual aspects of a given film.

Mark Peterson, *Image of Homelessness*

GENERATING CLASS DISCUSSION AND IN-CLASS WRITING

Peterson's photograph may be jarring to students, especially after they have read Scott Sanders's glowing description of home, community, and place. If homelessness has not come up already in class discussion as you've moved through the chapter, this would be a good time to talk about the growing population of people who don't have a home—whether by choice or otherwise—as a prelude to the Looking Closer section at the end of the chapter. Many of the selections in this chapter focus on rural or small-town space, and many of the selections in the book have been produced by people who have been educationally and economically privileged. *Image of Homelessness* reminds us that some people don't have freedom of choice about which kinds of places to inhabit. You may want to ask your students how this image—a cardboard box with the pillow and blanket visible within—says something different about homelessness than a photograph of a person sleeping on a park bench would. How has this homeless person created a sense of place? What details in the photograph suggest a larger space? Do students think Peterson is trying to make a specific social statement?

ADDITIONAL WRITING TOPICS

1. Ask students to write a personal response to Mark Peterson's photograph: How does it make them feel to look at this image? What aspect of it causes a particular response? Would they respond in the same way to other images of homelessness?

2. Ask students whether they think the homeless have the same sense of home, place, and community as those who pay rent for an apartment or a mortgage on a house. Have students write an essay that considers the effects of a person's economic circumstances on his or her attitude toward issues such as place.

3. Have students spend some time researching homelessness in their community. How extensive a problem is it? What community efforts are being made to address it? Students should also obtain statistics about the number of homeless in their state and in this country as a whole so that they have a context within which to evaluate their own community. Ask them to write a paper that sums up their findings and draws conclusions about homelessness as a local, state, and national problem.

CONNECTIONS WITH OTHER TEXTS

1. Both Mark Peterson's *Image of Homelessness* and Camilo José Vergara's collection of images of a Harlem streetcorner (pp. 150–151) document urban settings. Have students write informally about the statement they think this group of photographs makes about urban environments.

2. Have students watch *My Own Private Idaho*, a movie that seems to glorify the lives of homeless youth. Assign a paper in which students define homelessness as the movie presents it and then compare it with the definition suggested by *Image of Homelessness*.

SUGGESTIONS FOR FURTHER READING, THINKING, AND WRITING

print

Kozol, Jonathan. "Are the Homeless Crazy?"
    Harper's Magazine, 277 (September 1988):
    17–19.

 web

Links for the selections in this chapter can be
    found at www.seeingandwriting.com.

David Guterson, *No Place Like Home*

GENERATING CLASS DISCUSSION AND IN-CLASS WRITING

Guterson's essay describes his trip to and encounters with residents of Green Valley, Nevada. He uses several rhetorical strategies to indicate that this place is really "no place like home." Guterson uses comparison to play the sterility of the community against the wildness of the desert. He encourages the reader to identify with the rebellious children, especially with Jim Collins, and to pity the frightened adults, like the Andersons. He even compares the failures of Green Valley with the failures of Eden: "even Eden—planned by God—had serpents, and so, apparently, does Green Valley" (para. 27). The reader is led to believe that those who have come to this place have found not utopia but an empty promise.

Green Valley is a planned community that "is as much a verb as a noun, a place in the process of becoming what it purports to be" (para. 2). You might ask students to consider how the city is a verb—how it is an action as well as a place. Guterson argues that residents of the town become part of the place, that it shapes them by "Green Valley-ing" them. The process involves increasing standardization so that one house looks like the next and the community becomes a "seamless façade of interminable, well-manicured developments" (para. 2). The city is one of a growing number of planned communities in the United States, and the proliferation of these developments is clearly troublesome to Guterson.

You may want to discuss Guterson's bias. What is his agenda? Did he go to Green Valley on a fact-finding mission, or did he start out with a predetermined conclusion and then gather facts? Authors often deploy information to make their own points, with varying degrees of subterfuge about that purpose. Guterson presents himself "as a journalist" (para. 25), which would lead a reader to think of his presentation as neutral and objective. However, although Guterson never comes out and says, "Green Valley is insidiously evil," this is essentially his message. If students don't see this, you might alert them to his use of connotation. When he writes, "I'd come to Green Valley because I was curious to meet the citizens of a community in which everything is designed, orchestrated, and executed by a corporation" (para. 3), he starts with an innocent term, *curious*, but ends with *executed*—a wonderful turn of phrase. Guterson also paints the citizens of Green Valley in rather unflattering terms. Do we need to know that Phil Anderson, the accountant, is "overweight" (para. 14)? Should we take at face value Guterson's characterization of the residents' responses to his queries as "almost never entirely forthcoming" (para. 25)? In the end Guterson's judgment of the citizens of Green Valley is harsh: They are fools who have traded very real "personal freedoms" for "false security" (para. 38).

Joel Sternfeld's photo, *Lake Oswego, Oregon,* accompanies the essay as an ancillary image. Ask students whether they think this image portrays the uniformity that Guterson addresses.

ADDITIONAL WRITING TOPICS

1. Ask students to consider how closely their neighborhoods resemble Green Valley. You might direct them to write a short comparison/contrast essay in which they argue for or against planned communities on the basis of their own past experience.

2. Guterson presents his research into Green Valley not just to inform his readers but also to persuade them to agree with his point of view about planned communities. Ask students to write an analysis of Guterson's persuasive language, paying special attention to how he characterizes both the community and the people he interviews. If you feel comfortable with the terms, you might explain the basic argumentative appeals

ethos, pathos, and *logos* to students and have them identify the ways in which Guterson appeals to authority, emotion, and logic.

3. Guterson notes that no one seems to use the Green Valley civic center plaza, describing it as "deserted, useless, and irrelevant" (para. 4). Ask students to identify a broad open area on their campus or in their town. They should do a brief field study of this area, sketching its layout, charting its use at different times of day, interviewing visitors, and so on. From this information, they should construct a persuasive essay that identifies two or three key reasons for the success or failure of this public space.

CONNECTIONS WITH OTHER TEXTS

1. In the Looking Closer: Going Home section of this chapter, Erica Jong writes, "Home is the place where you feel safe . . . despite disquieting news that arrives by cable or optical fibre" (p. 214, para. 1). Ask students to write a short essay that considers how the creation of a community like Green Valley is responding to a desire for safety and protection from the outside world.

2. At the end of *The Wizard of Oz,* Dorothy returns from Oz by clicking her ruby slippers together and repeating that "there's no place like home." Guterson borrows part of his title from Dorothy's repeated invocation. Have students draft an essay in which they consider the implications of Guterson's title and compare the description of the master-planned community with the wonderful world of Oz.

SUGGESTIONS FOR FURTHER READING, THINKING, AND WRITING

print

Frantz, Douglas, and Catherine Collins. *Celebration U.S.A.: Living in Disney's Brave New Town.* New York: Henry Holt, 1999. The authors and their children lived in Disney's planned community for two years.

Guterson, David. *The Country Ahead of Us, the Country Behind.* New York: Harper and Row, 1989.

———. *East of the Mountains.* New York: Harcourt Brace, 1999.

———. *Snow Falling on Cedars.* San Diego: Harcourt Brace, 1994.

Sternfeld, Joel. *American Prospects: Photographs.* New York: Times Books, 1987.

[www.] web

Links for the selections in this chapter can be found at www.seeingandwriting.com.

audio/visual

East of the Mountains. 4 cassettes (6 hr.). 1999. Recording. Read by David Guterson. Distributed by BDD Audio.

Interview with Douglas Frantz and Catherine Collins. 50 min. 1999. Recording. Distributed by National Public Radio. Terry Gross, host of NPR's *Fresh Air,* interviews journalists Douglas Frantz and Catherine Collins about their book *Celebration U.S.A.: Living in Disney's Brave New Town,* which describes their life in a planned community.

Snow Falling on Cedars. 2 cassettes (3 hr.), abridged. 1995. Recording. Read by B. D. Wong. Distributed by Random House Audiobooks.

Snow Falling on Cedars. 11 cassettes (15.75 hr.), unabridged. 1996. Recording. Read by George Guidall. Distributed by Recorded Books, Prince Frederick, MD.

The Wizard of Oz. 110 min. Directed by Victor Fleming, 1939. Videocassette. Distributed by MGM-UA. The film is alluded to in the title of David Guterson's essay and ties in perfectly with the Looking Closer section of this chapter. It is also an excellent primer in how an artist uses color and tone to establish place.

Norman Mailer, from *Three Minutes or Less*

GENERATING CLASS DISCUSSION AND IN-CLASS WRITING

In this excerpt from *Three Minutes or Less,* Norman Mailer briefly explains what a sense of place means to him and then observes how difficult it is for writers to create a sense of place. Ask students what the concept means to them. In his thinking about a sense of place, Mailer says that "it is as large as one's birthplace or the country one adopts. And it can be as small as a mood that has a ground, or as small as a thought that takes place in a room." As a writer, he observes that "there's nothing more difficult than to come up with a good description of place." You might discuss what constitutes a good description of place. You could even bring in a few examples for the class to read or direct them to examples in the text. (Ron Hansen's "Nebraska" [p. 171] is a good choice.)

Mailer also states that writers often credit hard work for successful writing but sometimes feel that they "get a gift from the various powers either up there or coming up from below." See how the students react to this statement. Are they surprised that an experienced writer would refer to mysterious "powers" in an essay about his craft? To what do your students credit their own successful writing?

ADDITIONAL WRITING TOPICS

1. Ask students to write a description of a place familiar to them. Have the students exchange and analyze the descriptions according to the criteria you developed in your discussion.

2. If the discussion went well regarding the meaning of a sense of place, you might ask students to write a definition essay on the subject.
3. You could ask students to expand on the definition essay by researching the views of various writers on the subject of a sense of place.

CONNECTIONS WITH OTHER TEXTS

1. Mailer states that a sense of place can be as large "as one's birthplace" and as small "as a thought that takes place in a room." Ron Hansen creates a vivid sense of place in "Nebraska" (p. 171) in both the small and large sense to which Mailer refers. Ask students to write an essay that explains how Hansen's story fits Mailer's definition of a sense of place.
2. Have students examine Tracey Baran's *Untitled 2* (pp. 70–71). Discuss how she creates a sense of place.

SUGGESTIONS FOR FURTHER READING, THINKING, AND WRITING

print

Mailer, Norman. *Ancient Evenings*. Boston: Little, Brown, 1983.

———. *Harlot's Ghost*. New York: Random House, 1991.

———. *Tough Guys Don't Dance*. New York: Random House, 1984.

web

www.albany.edu/writers-inst/mailer.html   New York State Writers Institute web page includes a biography, a bibliography, and a list of resources.

Links for the selections in this chapter can be found at www.seeingandwriting.com.

Miranda Lichtenstein, *Untitled #9*

GENERATING CLASS DISCUSSION AND IN-CLASS WRITING

Lichtenstein's picture has been constructed in such a way as to recall images of suburban homes in films. The mass of trees in front of the house, the suggestive red glow on the street, the centrality of the house—these details are likely to remind students of the houses featured in horror films. Before you begin discussion, you might ask students to write down five words that describe this photograph. Then put the students into groups to discuss the words they chose and to examine the picture together. Have them write a list of the details they see (as they did for Richard Estes's *Central Savings* in Visualizing Composition, Ch. 1).

At first, students will probably be drawn to the house because it is the central image of the picture. The glow from the windows will also draw their attention, but they may not consider why this detail might have factored into Lichtenstein's choosing this house. Students will also observe the slanting roof and the leaning tree, but they will probably have to take a second look before noticing the sidewalk and the red glow on the street. After you feel they've noticed enough details, ask them to list the words the picture evoked. Some students might find the picture to be "scary" whereas others describe it as "peaceful." If such differences exist, ask students why similar details elicited different responses. If students interpreted the same details differently, discuss why that might have happened. This could be a good way to bring up context. Some students might see a horror film in this picture only if they are familiar with the genre. Others, however, might not because this picture lacks the context of a horror film (e.g., the eerie music, the plot, etc.).

An effective way to help students examine an artist's technique is to ask them to imagine how the piece could have been arranged differently. Have them imagine the photograph from another angle or in different lighting. You could get them started by asking how the photograph would be different if several houses were included. Some students might find the picture less eerie with other houses in it, but the single house suggests isolation. Ask them about the effects of the red glow, which is most visible in the bottom right corner. If the picture had been taken from the other side of the street—at the edge of or inside the yard—the point of view might seem less intrusive and, therefore, less suggestive of an image in a horror film.

ADDITIONAL WRITING TOPICS

1. Ask students to retitle the photograph and create a plot for a movie around the context of the picture. Students might do their best work in groups. However, if group work for this topic seems unproductive, you could keep students in their individual seats and have them pass their writings around after each paragraph. Each student would start a plot on his or her own, and then pass it on to another student who would build upon that.

2. Put students into pairs—students whose interpretations differed during discussion would be best—to co-write an expository essay in which each student explains his or her interpretation of the photograph. Then the pair collaborates on a section that attempts to explain the similarities and differences of opinion.

3. Ask students to do a freewrite based on the feelings evoked by the photograph.

CONNECTIONS WITH OTHER TEXTS

1. Lichtenstein's photograph recalls images from horror films. Ask students to examine James Nachtwey's photograph of a crushed car (p. 274). In the essay, "Ground Zero," that accompanies the photo, Nachtwey said the scene "seemed like a movie set from a science-fiction film" (para. 4).

Discuss why we are so quick to make associations with film.

2. Direct students to Edward Hopper's painting *House by the Railroad* (p. 130). Discuss their first impressions of the house. Ask them to compare the techniques used by Hopper and Lichtenstein to create these impressions.

SUGGESTIONS FOR FURTHER READING, THINKING, AND WRITING

 web

www.members.aol.com/dadaloplop/GanisSite/
    Lichtenstein.html   E-Anthology *Iconophilia*'s

review provides insight into the techniques used by Lichtenstein in her "Danbury Road" series.

Links for the selections in this chapter can be found at www.seeingandwriting.com.

audio/visual

Scream. 111 min. 1996. Videocassette, color, rated R. Distributed by Miramax Films. Director Wes Craven and screenwriter Kevin Williamson manage to mock horror film conventions while making a genuinely scary film. It might be useful to compare the footage of the protagonist's house to Lichtenstein's photo.

VISUALIZING CONTEXT: **Defining One Place in Terms of Another**

GENERATING CLASS DISCUSSION AND IN-CLASS WRITING

In the Visualizing Context section of Chapter 1, students examined the complete installation of Pepón Osorio's *Badge of Honor* and compared it to their experience of seeing only one section of the installation—the son's bedroom—in the previous reading. Through this activity, they learned how different contexts can shape meaning. In this selection, students are asked to view Miranda Lichtenstein's photograph within the context of film.

Before you begin this discussion, you might ask students to recall the class's discussion of Lichtenstein's image. As they examine the images from *E.T.*, *American Beauty*, *Pleasantville*, and *The Ice Storm*, ask students whether they read Lichtenstein's photograph differently when viewed with these other images of suburbia. How are these images similar to and different from Lichtenstein's photograph?

Discuss how the classroom setting affects the way in which students view the still images from these films. When they saw the films in theaters or on video (most students probably have seen *E.T.* and *American Beauty*), did they consider how each film portrayed suburban life? How do horror films such as *Friday the 13th* and *The Nightmare on Elm Street* depend upon films that feature suburban homes as places of safety? And how does viewing the *Scream* series depend upon having knowledge of such horror films?

ADDITIONAL WRITING TOPICS

1. Ask students to consider Miranda Lichtenstein's photograph of an isolated house in different contexts: in a friend's collection of pictures, in a museum, and in this text. Have the students write an expository essay showing how their reading of the photograph changes in each context. How would their expectations be shaped by each situation?

2. Direct students to consider Lichtenstein's photograph as an advertisement. What product is it promoting? Students could write a brief description of the product and explain why they associate the picture with the product.

3. Students could then consider the photograph as the cover of an album. Ask students to freewrite about the type of music suggested by the photograph.

CONNECTIONS WITH OTHER TEXTS

1. Students could research the films mentioned above and write an expository essay about how each uses the context of suburbia for different purposes. For example, in *Pleasantville,* modern teenagers are transported into a black-and-white television show that recalls the idyllic suburban life of *Leave It to Beaver.* The teens' actions bring modernity into their surroundings, adding color literally and metaphorically to the lives of those around them. The changes that occur show how much was missing from the supposedly idyllic town.

2. Put students into groups to examine Raghubir Singh's photographs of India (pp. 198–99) in different contexts: as art, as movie stills, as travel brochure pictures, and as a friend's personal photographs. Ask each group to report what they noticed to the class. How did the context shape what each group saw?

Ron Hansen, *Nebraska*

GENERATING CLASS DISCUSSION AND IN-CLASS WRITING

"Nebraska" requires slow, careful reading not only to understand how Hansen creates a changing portrait of rural America, but also to unpack and appreciate the author's rich imagery.

Many students will likely have problems reading this story. They might find its frequent changes in time as well as its lack of a central character somewhat unsettling. Although characters are present in the story, they appear in cameos, adding to the "character" of the place instead of developing as characters themselves.

Before you discuss this story, you might put students into groups and make each group responsible for noting different elements in the story: how time passes through the mentioning of months and name-brand objects; how time passes through Hansen's use of punctuation; and how place is developed through characters' names and actions.

The story opens with the description of the land being settled and sod houses being built. The second paragraph depicts the arrival of the twentieth century in Americus: "And then the Union Pacific stopped by . . . and then a supply store, a depot, a pine water tank, stockyards, and the mean prosperity of the twentieth century." The second paragraph also marks the beginning of a seasonal rhythm that develops over several subsequent paragraphs. Hansen describes the heat of the "August noonday" (para. 2), the Democrat river frozen in winter (para. 3), and Billy Awalt "peppered and dappled with hay dust" in July (para. 4). (A similar rhythm can be observed in paragraphs 5 to 7.)

Hansen uses punctuation to give the story a sense of momentum. The first six paragraphs (most of them contain fewer than four sentences) seem to rush by with their long sentences strung together with commas that do not allow the reader to stop. An example is the fourth paragraph, which contains ninety-six words in its two sentences, eighty-five being in the first sentence. You might ask students to read such sentences aloud to get the sense of momentum. Hansen uses similar sentence structure later in the story, but the paragraphs slow down noticeably after the seventh. For comparison, you might ask students to read any of the first six paragraphs out loud, and then do the same with paragraphs 8 to 10, which use shorter sentences.

Hansen also uses names to show the passage of time. Names such as *Emil* and *Orin Jedlicka* (para. 3) suggest an earlier America than do *Victor Johnson* (para. 8) and *Donna Moriarity* (para. 9). The Ford truck and the Dairy Queen mentioned in paragraph 4 bring Nebraska closer to the present. And the bowl of Cheerios (para. 6) and Victor Johnson's "high-topped shoes" (para. 8) bring it even closer.

After students become accustomed to the rhythm of the first seven paragraphs, they should be prepared to read them more closely for their rich imagery. You might ask them to unpack the imagery in sentences such as: "And below the silos and water tower are stripped treetops, their gray limbs still lifted up in alleluia, their yellow leaves crowding along yard fences and sheeping along the sidewalks and alleys under the shepherding wind" (para. 5). If students have trouble articulating what they see, ask them to write it out first. How would they describe the trees' limbs that are "lifted up in alleluia"? Why "alleluia"? Is the assonance more aesthetically pleasing than "lifted up to the sky"? Is Hansen also trying to suggest something about nature through his personification of it? Similarly, ask students to describe the movement of the leaves "sheeping along the sidewalks . . . under the shepherding wind." What connections and consequences do students see in how Hansen personifies the trees, the leaves, and the wind? Ask them to look for other instances of personification and discuss the effects of its use.

Students are not likely to have many problems with the rest of the story, which focuses on the stores and people in the town. The groups that focused on Hansen's use of characters should be able to provide points of discussion. You might direct the class to paragraphs that describe a large number of people. What does Hansen suggest about the pickup truck drivers who "speak about crops or praise the weather or make up sentences whose only real point is their lack of complication" (para. 9)? Ask how the actions of the high-school boys and girls add to the character of the small town.

In paragraph 11, the narrator describes how an "outsider" would only be "aware of what isn't." As outsiders, how do students view this town that lacks, among other things, a hotel, a hospital, a bookstore, a "picture show," and "extreme opinions"? What, in your students' view, is the narrator's view of this town?

ADDITIONAL WRITING TOPICS

1. Ask students to experiment with shorter and longer sentences to create a rhythm and a sense of momentum. You could ask them to develop their own paragraphs, or they could choose some of Hansen's to alter. They could slow down the first six paragraphs and speed up later paragraphs by changing the use of periods and commas.

2. Have students write an essay that explains how Hansen portrays technology and nature in this story. What does this portrayal suggest about the narrator's attitude toward each? Students must cite specific passages to support their statements.

CONNECTIONS WITH OTHER TEXTS

1. Tillie Olsen's "I Stand Here Ironing" (p. 73) is carried by its strong characterization, Hansen's "Nebraska" by its strong evocation of place. Ask students to write an essay that explains how the narration by Olsen's protagonist develops a sense of place and how the description of place in "Nebraska" develops the characters within it.

2. Have students write an essay that compares the narrator in "Nebraska" to the narrator in Eudora Welty's "The Little Store." They should observe how the narrator's descriptions in each develop a sense of place and reveal the character of the narrator.

SUGGESTIONS FOR FURTHER READING, THINKING, AND WRITING

print

Hansen, Ron. *Atticus*. New York: HarperCollins, 1996.

———. *Hitler's Niece*. New York: HarperCollins, 1999.

———. *Nebraska*. New York: Atlantic Monthly Press, 1989.

———. *A Stay against Confusion: Essays on Faith and Fiction*. New York: HarperCollins, 2001.

[www.] *web*

www.mockingbird.creighton.edu/NCW/hansen .htm   Nebraska Center for Writers web site includes a brief profile, a bibliography, an interview, and critical reviews.

www.leaderu.com/marshill/mhr06/ hansen1.html   A particularly insightful interview regarding the subject of religion in Hansen's fiction.

Links for thes selections in this chapter can be found at www.seeingandwriting.com.

PORTFOLIO: **Richard Misrach**

GENERATING CLASS DISCUSSION AND IN-CLASS WRITING

In order to get students talking about Misrach's photos, you might want to ask them a simple question: Where is the horizon line in each photo, and what is above and below it? Once students have effectively divided the photos into two parts, have them classify the elements above and below the horizon. The horizon line determines where the viewer's eye is initially leveled and sets the composition center. This horizon might be natural, as in *Waiting* (p. 177); artificial, as in *Diving Board* (p. 178); or obscured, as in *Desert Fire* (p. 179). In each case, the horizon offers a clue to the photo's meaning. For example, in *Diving Board,* the decaying swimming pool has superseded the natural sea behind it, even though the pool is empty and useless; thus, it sets the visual center of the photo. What does this tell us? Perhaps one of Misrach's points is to emphasize what we lose when we choose the manmade over the nature-made, or how quickly we tend to abandon our manmade creations.

Next, move to a discussion of the way in which the viewer's eye is directed in each photo and how this is achieved. For example, in both *Wind Mill Farm* and *Waiting* the viewer's eye moves diagonally, following the lines in the sand that guide her vision. In the photo emphasizing the Air Force base, an American flag is nearly dead center of the picture, reinforcing the connection (Air Force = America); in the photo spotlighting a desert fire, a lurid orange spot of fire is the center point.

Finally, you might want to discuss how a photo achieves tone. Whereas an author has connotative and figurative language at her disposal, the photographer does not. Instead, she has other elements of her trade, such as lighting. To illustrate this, you could compare the lighting in *Waiting* (a natural scene) with that in *Palm Oasis* (an artificial scene). Which one looks warmer and more inviting? Why?

ADDITIONAL WRITING TOPICS

1. Ask students to pick up a travel magazine (e.g., *Travel and Leisure, Condé Nast Traveler,* or *National Geographic*) and analyze several of the photos within for the elements mentioned above (horizon, center point, movement, and tone). Students should write an essay analyzing one photo, structuring the essay around the tone of the photo and the way in which the photographer conveys the tone to the viewer.

2. The headnote accompanying the photos lists one of Misrach's goals as trying "to determine what makes the desert the desert" (p. 175). Ask students to choose another place, a product of either nature or man, and write a definition essay in which they explain what makes that place unique. They might choose a forest or a mall or even an online community.

3. The majority of your students are probably not from the town in which they're attending college. Ask them to venture out—beyond the college campus—to gather a portrait of their new "home." What do people do for a living in this city? Is there an economic divide? What are current local issues? How do the residents feel about college students? Students could research the topic by interviewing people, watching the local news, or reading the local newspaper (*not* the student newspaper), getting information from the Chamber of Commerce, and so on. Assign them a research essay focused on a particular aspect of their discoveries.

CONNECTIONS WITH OTHER TEXTS

1. Ask students to compare the way the desert is treated in Misrach's photos with the way Albert Bierstadt presents *Among the Sierra Nevada Moun-* *tains, California, 1868* (pp. 142–43). Have the class brainstorm a list of adjectives that describe Misrach's desert and Bierstadt's mountains, and then discuss what might account for the different words the students come up with and what larger categories they might represent.

2. Ask students to find other examples of Misrach's work in the library or on the web. Using the images from the book and the additional images they find as evidence, have them write a two- to three-page paper that starts with a strong thesis identifying the defining quality of Misrach's style.

SUGGESTIONS FOR FURTHER READING, THINKING, AND WRITING

print

Misrach, Richard. *Violent Legacies: Three Cantos.* New York: Aperture, 1992. Photographs by Misrach, fiction by Susan Sontag.

 web

www.blindspot.com   This online photography magazine includes a gallery with photo-graphs by, among others, Richard Misrach, Chuck Close, William Eggleston, and Wolfgang Tillmans.

Links for the selections in this chapter can be found at www.seeingandwriting.com.

Tony Hiss, *The Experience of Place*

GENERATING CLASS DISCUSSION AND IN-CLASS WRITING

Hiss's essay is based upon the idea that our surroundings affect us, and that when we change our surroundings, we also change ourselves. Not only can these changes harm the environment, but they can also harm us. Although Hiss does express concern for the environment, he is more interested in the close relationship between people and places. You might begin discussion by asking students how they think they are influenced by the places they inhabit. You could ask them to think about how the university affects them: Is a certain classroom more conducive for learning than another? Do students find studying easier in the library, in a classroom, or at home? What makes each place better or worse for studying? Or you could ask students to think about a place that evokes anxiety. Hospitals and dentistry offices will be likely responses; try to move students beyond the notion that these places cause anxiety because they involve pain. Ask them to list specific details that engage the five senses.

Hiss begins the essay by stating that we "react, consciously and unconsciously, to the places where we live and work, in ways we scarcely notice or that are only now becoming known to us" (para. 1). He does not provide any personal examples or hard evidence for his claims about how the environment affects people. He states that people and places have a "close bond" and that changing our surroundings risks "cutting ourselves off from some of the sights or sounds, the shapes or textures, or other information from a place that have helped mold our understanding and are now necessary for us to thrive" (para. 2). Ask students to think of examples that would back up this claim. Also ask how they read the last sentence of the second paragraph: "Overdevelopment and urban sprawl can damage our own lives as much as they damage our cities and countryside." To what extent are they convinced of the possible damage to their own lives? If so, what kind of damage would this be? Some students will probably supply reasons or examples that they think are implied by Hiss. Ask them to explain where and how Hiss convinces them. If they cannot find any examples, point out that as they write their essays, they need to provide the examples and the evidence for their readers.

Hiss urges that we consider ourselves and the environment when we change a place (para. 3). A mechanism he calls "simultaneous perception" can help us as we negotiate this balance. Simultaneous perception is an "underlying awareness" that "drinks in whatever it can from our surroundings" (para. 5). As Hiss states, it "allows any of us a direct sense of continuing membership in our communities, and our regions, and the fellowship of all living creatures" (para. 6).

You should ask students to carefully examine Hiss's evidence as he explains how experiences of places are becoming painful. Hiss states: "These days people often tell me that some of their most unforgettable experiences of place are disturbingly painful and have to do with unanticipated loss" (para. 7). He then gives examples of familiar places being changed: curved roads being straightened and trees being cut down. Do students share Hiss's experience? If some students have had the opposite experience—that people more often associate a place with "a magic moment" than with "unanticipated loss"—then students should be made aware of how unreliable Hiss's evidence is here because it is solely personal and can be contradicted by other personal accounts.

In paragraphs 8 to 10, Hiss notes how much we've transformed our surroundings, and he expresses concern over the state of the environment. Ask students how they feel about the following observation: "Until recently, a large majority of the world's population lived in villages. Less than a decade from now, a small majority of the world's population (52 percent) will live in cities" (para. 9). Many students will probably agree with Hiss's concern regarding the "epidemic of extinctions," but they may not understand how preserving the environment will "[help] us toward the next boost in our understanding" (para. 10). It should be noted that Hiss's concern for the environment in and of itself makes up a small part of this essay. His focus is on how people and places affect each other. As he ends the essay, he states that the experiences provided by places "are an inheritance that has been entrusted to our care. Guarding these experiences and championing them, as we're also learning, are skills that are natural to people" (para. 13). Ask students to discuss how we've managed to allow the endangerment of places and experiences if, as Hiss states, preserving and appreciating places are "natural" skills.

ADDITIONAL WRITING TOPICS

1. Have students write a descriptive essay about a place that affects them in a certain way. The place can be scary, comforting, enlightening. The essay should engage the five senses and should include some exposition as to why details have certain effects. For the conclusion, students could describe how the place would have the opposite effect if certain details were to change.

2. Ask students to research what Hiss refers to as the "brand-new science of place" (para. 7). Based on this research, they could write an expository essay for an audience unfamiliar with this science.

3. Ask students to respond in writing to one of Hiss's "experiential checklists" (para. 12).

CONNECTIONS WITH OTHER TEXTS

1. David Guterson's essay is also concerned with how communities are constructed. Ask students to assume the role of either Guterson or Hiss in a letter in which they write to the other about his essay. Students should carefully read the essay of the author whose identity they are going to assume.

2. Direct students to Martin Parr's picture of *Kalkan, Turkey* (p. 296), in which a tourist is completely oblivious to his surroundings as he looks through his camera. Discuss how our sense of place is possibly lessened by the increase in technological distractions.

SUGGESTIONS FOR FURTHER READING, THINKING, AND WRITING

print

Duany, Andres, Elizabeth Plater-Zyberk, and Jeff Speck. *Suburban Nation: The Rise of Sprawl and the Decline of the American Dream*. San Francisco: North Point Press, 2000.

Hiss, Tony. *Building Images*. San Francisco: Chronicle Books LLC, 2000.

———. *Experience of Place*. New York: Vintage Books, 1991.

Jacobs, Jane. *The Death and Life of Great American Cities*. New York: Vintage Books, 1993.

Langdon, Peter. *A Better Place to Live: Rebuilding the American Suburb*. Amherst: Univ. of Massachusetts Press, 1997.

[www] *web*

www.newurbanism.org/   New Urbanism is devoted to creating "livable spaces." Students wishing to research the "new science of place" referred to by Hiss might find this web site of interest.

Links for the selections in this chapter can be found at www.seeingandwriting.com.

Joel Sternfeld, *Taylor Hall Parking Lot*

GENERATING CLASS DISCUSSION AND IN-CLASS WRITING

If possible, you might ask students to examine the picture before they read Sternfeld's note. Encourage them to analyze the photo in regard to its angle, lighting, and outstanding details. Most of what they notice will emphasize the ordinary nature of the parking lot. After they read Sternfeld's text, ask them to look at the picture again. How has it changed? Do any students imagine the event happening?

You should let students know that Kent State University has several memorials on its campus. Ask students why they think Sternfeld chose to photograph this parking lot instead of one of the memorials. Some students might observe that the ordinariness of the parking lot suggests that this event could have happened at any university. (You might tell students that a similar event did happen at Jackson State University in which two people were killed and dozens were injured by police gunfire that left a college dormitory riddled with bullets.) Some students might claim that this is more effective than a photograph of a memorial; others will believe the opposite. Encourage the opposing sides to discuss their reasons and to explore the implications of each.

Sternfeld's photo depicts a normal parking lot—one that could be any parking lot at any university. The normality of the image drives home the reality of the event in a different way when compared to locations that feature memorials. Elaborate memorials sometimes risk turning tragic events into legendary symbols that overshadow the real human loss. Sternfeld captures the place, not the legend surrounding it.

ADDITIONAL WRITING TOPICS

1. Students could write an essay that compares and contrasts the effects of Sternfeld's photo to those of the photographs featured in the Kent State online gallery (web address is provided in the Suggestions section).

2. Students could take the first topic a step further by writing an argument essay that takes a position as to whether the simplicity of Sternfeld's photo and text is more powerful than the actual memorials.

3. Have students research the incidents at Kent State and listen to "Ohio" by Crosby, Stills, Nash, and Young. Then ask students to write an essay that examines how well the music and lyrics of "Ohio" capture the event.

CONNECTIONS WITH OTHER TEXTS

1. Direct students to examine Edward Hopper's painting *House by the Railroad* (p. 130). Ask them to compare the use of light in Hopper's painting to its use in Sternfeld's photograph.

2. Sternfeld's photograph captures the distant aftermath of a memorable moment. Without the text, some people would not know the events that made the place memorable. Ask students to view the photographs by Patrick Witty and Jeff Mermelstein (p. 221), which capture the beginning and the immediate aftermath of the World Trade Center's destruction. Discuss the feelings elicited by these photographs and Sternfeld's. Compare the different views on tragedy provided by these photographs.

SUGGESTIONS FOR FURTHER READING, THINKING, AND WRITING

print

Casale, Ottavio M., and Louis Paskoff, eds. *The Kent Affair: Documents and Interpretations.* Boston: Houghton Mifflin, 1971.

Eszterhas, Joe, and Michael D. Roberts. *Thirteen Seconds: Confrontation at Kent.* New York: Dodd, Mead, 1970.

Sternfeld, Joel. *On This Site: Landscape in Memoriam.* San Francisco: Chronicle Books, 1996.

 ### web

www.citypaper.net/articles/032097/article016 .shtml   Philadelphia *City Paper*'s online article on Sternfeld's *On This Site.*

www.library.kent.edu/exhibits/4may95/   Kent State University web site dedicated to the 1970 tragedy. Includes a chronology of events, a gallery of memorials (at Kent State and other universities), and links to other web sites.

www.ccaix.jsums.edu/~www/gg02.htm   Jackson State University web site dedicated to a similar tragedy that occurred ten days later in 1970 on its campus in which two people were killed and dozens injured by police gunfire.

www.clarkson.edu/~winklebh/vietnam2/ohio.html   Provides a photo taken during the Kent State shootings and lyrics to "Ohio" by Crosby, Stills, Nash, and Young, which was written to commemorate the tragedy. Links for the selections in this chapter can be found at www.seeingandwriting.com.

audio/visual

So Far. Crosby, Stills, Nash, and Young. Audio CD. 1994. Distributed by Atlantic. Contains a studio version of "Ohio," which was written immediately after the tragedy at Kent State. You might let students listen to this song before they examine the photo.

Pico Iyer, *Why We Travel*

GENERATING CLASS DISCUSSION AND IN-CLASS WRITING

In this essay, Iyer gives a number of reasons for why we travel, most of them effectively encapsulated in the first four sentences. However, he does more than list reasons—he makes a subtle argument for how we *should* travel.

You might ask your students to think about their own reasons for traveling. Unless they have been involved in international travel, they may not identify with many of Iyer's reasons because the "we" in his essay mainly refers to Americans who travel outside of the United States (although, at times, the "we" refers to people in general when Iyer speaks of personal journeys). At this time, you might bring up an important point of context—"Why We Travel" was first published in *Salon Travel* for a specific audience of travelers, not a broad audience of students. Iyer is writing "Why We Travel" for travelers and readers of travel literature, just as Stephen King wrote *Danse Macabre* for writers and readers of horror literature.

You might ask students to locate Iyer's reasons and compare his to theirs. According to Iyer, one reason for traveling is to have our assumptions and judgments unsettled. For him, the distinction between travelers and tourists is in whether they take their assumptions with them to their destinations. Iyer's discussion of tourists and travelers is easy to misread, so you might want to ask students for their interpretation. Students might state that Iyer is defining *traveler* and *tourist*: "a tourist is just someone who complains, 'Nothing here is the way it is at home,' while a traveler is one who grumbles, 'Everything here is the same as it is in Cairo'" (para. 4). However, Iyer's definitions depend upon how assumptions are managed. A tourist who assumes the sameness of home is disappointed by difference, whereas a traveler who assumes difference everywhere becomes disappointed by sameness. Iyer concludes: "It's all very much the same" (para. 4). In reality, Iyer is not interested in the differences between tourists and travelers.

In a subtle way, Iyer is arguing that the best way to travel—the way we *should* travel—is to leave our assumptions behind. He states: "But for the rest of us, the sovereign freedom of traveling comes from the fact that it whirls you around and turns you upside down, and stands everything you took for granted on its head" (para. 5). Ask students what they think of his example: "When you drive down the streets of Port-au-Prince, for example, where there is almost no paving and women relieve themselves next to mountains of trash, our notions of the Internet and a 'one world order' grow usefully revised" (para. 6). Does this example of extreme difference give students an idea of how the world isn't a "global village," despite the contrary claims of politics and cyberspace?

By allowing us to see difference, traveling saves places like Port-au-Prince from "abstraction" (para. 6). In turn, by engaging in a cultural exchange of items, ideas, and appreciation, we save ourselves from abstraction. Iyer states: "I find that I always take Michael Jordan posters to Kyoto and bring woven ikebana baskets back to California" (para. 7). He considers conveying ideas to be even more important than the transportation of items: "we carry values and beliefs and news to the places we go" and become "the only channels that can take people out of the censored limits of their homelands" (para. 8). Traveling also enables people to learn about other cultures, which in turn enables cultures to appreciate what they can teach others. As Iyer states, tourism "obviously destroys cultures," but this mutual exchange of appreciation "can also resuscitate or revive them" (para. 9).

The most important reason for traveling, though, is to learn about the self. We learn about ourselves, in part, from the anonymity of travel: "freed of inessential labels, we have the opportunity to come into contact with more essential parts of ourselves" (para. 12). Freed from our usual roles, we are "ourselves up for grabs and open to interpretation" (para. 13). Being open to interpretation, we have the opportunity to remake ourselves: "since no one I meet can 'place' me—no one can fix me in my résumé—I can remake myself for better, as well as, of course, for worse (if travel is notoriously a cradle for false identities, it can also, at its best, be a crucible for truer ones" (para. 15). What have your students learned about themselves through travel?

Although most of Iyer's examples involve world travel, he observes that the internal journey is most important. Movies, friendships, and novels can be journeys (para. 29). Referring to the ideas of Emerson and Thoreau, Iyer observes that we invent our own reality from what we project: "we invent the places we see as much as we do the books that we read. What we find outside ourselves has to be inside ourselves for us to find it" (para. 32).

For this internal journey to take place, it is crucial to leave assumptions behind. By being open to the experience, a journey can feel like a love affair. The travel-as-love-affair theme runs throughout Iyer's essay. He observes: "all good trips are, like love, about being carried out of yourself and deposited in the midst of terror and wonder" (para. 19). The complex interactions with foreigners that balance honesty and discretion resemble those experienced with lovers (para. 23). As the essay concludes, Iyer states: "And if travel is like love, it is, in the end, mostly because it's a heightened state of awareness, in which we are mindful, receptive, undimmed by familiarity and ready to be transformed" (para. 35).

ADDITIONAL WRITING TOPICS

1. Ask students to write an essay similar to Iyer's, titled "Why We _____" the blank being a subject students believe they could examine and explain. Some subjects you might suggest: *read, write, paint, draw, play, laugh, sing.*

2. "These days a whole new realm of exotica arises out of the way one culture colors and appropriates the products of another" (para. 26). Ask students to research how American products are treated by different cultures. Based on this research, they could write an essay that explains why each culture regards the products differently.

3. Iyer notes that novels, movies, and friendships take us on journeys (para. 29). Invite students to choose a novel, movie, or friendship that has transported them and write a narrative essay that shows how this occurred.

CONNECTIONS WITH OTHER TEXTS

1. Ask students to recall David Guterson's essay "No Place Like Home" (p. 157), in which Guterson vilifies Green Valley. Students could write a comparison/contrast essay on the word choice and tone used by Guterson and Iyer.

2. Ask students to examine Nikki S. Lee's photograph *The Tourist Project* (p. 375). How does Lee seem to define *tourist*?

SUGGESTIONS FOR FURTHER READING, THINKING, AND WRITING

print

Iyer, Pico. *The Global Soul: Jet Lag, Shopping Malls, and the Search for Home.* New York: Knopf, 2000.

———. *Tropical Classical: Essays from Several Directions.* New York: Knopf, 1997.

 web

www.powells.com/authors/iyer.html   Interview with Iyer on the Powells' City of Books web site.

www.dir.salon.com/topics/pico_iyer/index.html
    This web site features twelve articles by Iyer, including "Why We Travel."

Links for the selections in this chapter can be found at www.seeingandwriting.com.

audio/visual

Falling Off the Map. Pico Iyer. 7 (60 min.) cassettes. 1994. Recording. Read by David Case. Distributed by Books on Tape.

VISUALIZING COMPOSITION: **Tone**

GENERATING CLASS DISCUSSION AND IN-CLASS WRITING

This section introduces students to the concept of *tone*. As the text notes, "tone refers to the quality or character of communication" (p. 196). The selected editorials highlight words and phrases that illustrate how a certain tone is created by each writer. The editorials cover the same story: Citizens failed to call the police as they watched a man stalk and kill a young woman. Both express outrage and stress civic responsibility, but each does so in a different tone.

You might begin discussion by asking students to examine the title of each editorial. How does each title signal the tone? "What Kind of People Are We?" implies a tone of indignation and suggests a personal connection with the reader; "Civic Duty" suggests less emotional investment. As students read each editorial, they should note how the tone of the text reflects that of the title. You should note that students should be just as cognizant of tone when they title their own essays. To illustrate the point, you might read the titles from some of your students' essays and ask them to guess the subject matter and tone of each. This is an exercise that most students find fun— and slightly embarrassing, especially when a student learns that he was the fourth person to title an essay "My Definition of Success." As you quickly describe the subject matter and tone of each essay (without giving away the author's identity), students will not only learn to consider tone in their titles, but they will also try to create more interesting titles in the future.

Turning back to the text of each editorial, students might note that each expresses outrage and calls for responsibility. You should point out how each editorial establishes a personal distance from the event through the use of certain words and phrases. The first levels criticism at the irresponsible citizens but does not judge them as harshly as the second. Note how the first seems bewildered at how citizens could be so careless: "How incredible is it that such motivations as 'I don't want to get involved' deterred them from this act of simple humanity" (p. 196). The second editorial, on the other hand, hands down a judgment: "But it is cowardly and callous when anyone in a position to summon help fails to do so" (p. 197, para. 3).

The first seems emotionally closer to the event and shares responsibility: "Who can explain such shocking indifference on the part of a cross-section of our fellow New Yorkers? We regretfully admit that we do not know the answers" (p. 196). The second seems emotionally distant in its matter-of-fact tone: "Citizens have an obligation to the law as well as a right to its protection" (p. 197, para. 3).

Put students in groups and ask them to draft editorials about a recent event. For their editorials, they should attempt to achieve a distinctive tone. You might even suggest a certain tone for each group. Then ask each group to exchange its editorial with another group's and analyze it for effective, consistent tone.

ADDITIONAL WRITING TOPICS

1. Ask students to freewrite about the different tones that can be used in writing. After they've come up with a decent list, ask them to associate topics with each tone. What are some topics that cannot be written about with a humorous tone? Should an angry tone ever be used? When is an informal tone appropriate?

2. Students can choose one essay from this chapter to analyze for its use of tone. How is the author's tone reflected in word choice and details? How does the tone support the author's purpose?

3. Ask students to read the letters to the editor in the student newspaper. Have them write a brief essay that assesses whether the authors of the letters used the appropriate tone in order to fulfill the purpose of their letters.

CONNECTIONS WITH OTHER TEXTS

1. Ask students to examine Miranda Lichtenstein's photograph and Edward Hopper's painting. Both feature houses and create similar feelings of sinister isolation, but they evoke these feelings in different ways. Ask students to describe how these different images create similar feelings. How would students describe the tone of each? How is this tone achieved?

2. Ask students to compare Scott Russell Sanders's tone in "Homeplace" to David Guterson's in "No Place Like Home." Students could write an essay comparing and contrasting the tone of each essay and explain how the tone is crucial to the author's purpose.

Raghubir Singh, *Durga Puja Immersion, Where the Ganges and the GT Meet, West Bengal; Diwali Day Pilgrims at the Golden Temple*

GENERATING CLASS DISCUSSION AND IN-CLASS WRITING

The first Seeing question quotes a critic saying that Singh's photographs show "'the rich palette of India's landscapes and peoples'" (p. 200). Ask students to examine each photograph for a few minutes and write observations about each. You might divide students into groups and have them make notes about their observations, which they would then report to the class. If they have difficulty making their own observations, you might ask them to tailor their observations to the Seeing questions in the text.

As you discuss the photographs, you might begin by asking students to comment on the perspective of each. Students might note that the first picture is taken from the top of a set of steps and takes the golden temple as its focus. Other students might find that they locate the temple as the focus, but only briefly due to the colorful activity in the foreground. They might also notice that the clusters of people wear colorful clothing and are headed in various directions. If students were to look at the background of the photograph, they might observe that the buildings look similar to those seen in America; it is only when they look at the foreground that they get a sense of the foreign. As they make these observations, discuss how the clothing, the movement, the color, and the buildings compare to their counterparts in the United States.

As you move the discussion to the second photograph, you might ask students to compare it to the first. Ask them to apply their observations about clothing, movement, color, and buildings to this photograph. Students should consider this photograph from different angles. How would different angles have changed its narrative? Whereas the first photograph had a possible focus with the temple, this picture has no outstanding object at its center. Students might find that the three statues draw their attention. If this is so, ask how the multiple focal points create a sense of movement. Did students first focus on the statue in the picture's bottom left or in the middle? Whatever the answer, ask students to describe how their eyes next moved. Did they follow the crowd to the third statue by the river? If students look to the left side of the picture, they might notice the familiar buildings they also observed in the first photograph. Some students also might notice the bicycles, especially since they were absent in the previous picture. Ask students to consider why most of the people are clustered at the edge of the river. Are they observing the statue or something outside the picture's frame?

ADDITIONAL WRITING TOPICS

1. Using these pictures as inspiration, ask students to imagine themselves in the scene. Have them write a few paragraphs of description that engage the five senses and speculate on the lives of the people in the photograph.

2. Ask students to write an exploratory essay that considers why such colorful dress is largely absent in the United States. If the exploratory essay generates interesting ideas, you might direct students to write a research essay comparing and contrasting how each culture perceives and uses color.

3. Students could write a short essay that explains why they find one picture more appealing than the other. As students supply their reasons, they should compare and contrast the photographs and the effectiveness of the techniques used to create each one.

CONNECTIONS WITH OTHER TEXTS

1. Ask students to examine Albert Bierstadt's painting of scenic beauty, *Among the Sierra Nevada Mountains,* and compare his use of color and light to Singh's. Both artists are trying to capture a sense of place. What are the effects of their techniques? How do their different techniques capture dissimilar scenes?

2. The second Seeing question quotes the observation that Singh's photographs "reveal an Indian way of seeing" (p. 200). Ask students to look back through the text for photographs taken by Americans. Do the photographs create a sense of an "American way of seeing"? Can students articulate what that might be?

SUGGESTIONS FOR FURTHER READING, THINKING, AND WRITING

print

Singh, Raghubir. *Ganges.* New York: Aperture, 1992.

———. *The Grand Trunk Road: A Passage through India.* New York: Aperture, 1995.

———. *River of Color: The India of Raghubir Singh.* London: Phaidon Press, 1998.

———. *A Way into India.* London: Phaidon Press, 2002.

 web

Links for the selections in this chapter can be found at www.seeingandwriting.com.

 Re: Searching the Web

If students are not familiar with the World Wide Web, you might want to initially take them to a site, such as iVillage.com or About.com, that is structured like a community. About has "guides" that lead users through the web and point out important web locations. Ask students to consider how their exploration of the web is like an exploration of a foreign country or unfamiliar city. Visitors use maps (search engines), retrace their steps (via the history functions of their browsers), and so on. If students do choose to participate in a chat room or MUD, you may want to warn them that these verbal communities are often close knit and don't necessarily welcome strangers.

For an additional assignment, you might ask students to work in groups to go on the web and search out several personal homepages. They should write a collaborative analysis of one or two sites, keeping in mind Welty's statement, "The thing to wait on, to reach for, is the moment in which people reveal themselves" (p. 140). Students' analysis should address how the people who are constructing these pages reveal themselves by creating a place in virtual space.

Students can complete Re: Searching the Web exercises online at www.seeingandwriting.com. Additional tips and links for each exercise are also available.

Looking Closer:
Going Home

GENERATING CLASS DISCUSSION AND IN-CLASS WRITING

We are increasingly able to take home along with us in our travels. Items once inherently connected with the home have become portable. Not only do we have mobile homes, but we can buy vans that come with VCRs, televisions, video game systems. Cell phones make us available anywhere. You might ask students how many places they've considered their home. What essential qualities make a place "home"?

Marita Golden, A Sense of Place

Golden associates a sense of place with her roles as a writer, an American, and an African American. As a writer, she sees home as the first and the final sentence. As an American writer, she feels that her sense of place is "fluid," which has allowed her to claim "everyplace" as her home (para. 1). In the second paragraph, Golden manages to express—with an impressive economy of language—awe, disgust, pride, and even a touch of humor regarding the slavery of her ancestors. You might ask students how they read Golden's tone when she describes Africans' being enslaved as "grand theft . . . Part of a perverse, stunning, triangular trade-off of culture and identity" (para. 2). Do they sense pride when she states how her people "have indelibly stamped, reshaped, and claimed each place we have called ours" (para. 2)?

What do students think of Golden's description of America's heart as "a stubborn, wrenching, rainbow"? Can they explain how this metaphor works? In the last two lines, Golden brings an apt sense of closure to the essay. In the second-to-last sentence, she repeats the first sentence, which students will probably notice. However, they might interpret the last line in different ways: "The best of us embrace and rename it when we get there" (para. 4). You might ask students whether she is referring to writers, African Americans, or both.

Margaret Morton, Mr. Lee's House, the Hill, 1991

Morton's photo depicts a house held together by cardboard, wire, and straps. Ask students to describe the structure in the picture. What would they call it? Some will be stumped trying to classify it, and few would call it a house. Then ask them to consider how its owner might see it. Students may settle on the idea that it merely provides shelter, but such a notion is challenged by the smaller details—the calendar, the pictures, and various other ornaments.

Ericsson, *You Are Everywhere*

This Ericsson ad features the striking image of a map displayed on a man's face. The slogan promises a phone that will meet the needs of the traveler: "You are everywhere. Now there's a phone that works everywhere too." Ask students to think about the evolution of the phone and how the idea of the "home" phone has changed. Applications have traditionally had spaces for home and work numbers. Answering machine messages often begin with the phrase "I'm not home right now . . ."; yet only lately have they added "You can reach me on my cell phone."

Chang-rae Lee, *Coming Home Again*

"Coming Home Again" shows us that physical distance breeds emotional distance. In contrast to the pleasant phone call that AT&T's ad suggests, the initiating action that brings Lee's family back together is the news of his mother's impending death. He is brought back to his cultural home by returning to his physical home. In Lee's house, the home is the kitchen because it holds what he loves. After his mother dies, he attempts to re-create this home for his father by making the old family meals, but he fails.

Carmen Lomas Garza, *Tamalada*

Garza's painting calls forth the same nostalgia for the simple, the direct, in its evocation of folk art—its primitive one-dimensionality. The family in the painting gathers around the table, like Chang-rae Lee's. Garza, though, seems to bring the family together in communion, in an activity in which *all* participate. Ask students to note the use of red in the painting: The movement in the painting follows the reds—from the shirts to the tablecloth roses to the dress to the sweater to the handkerchief to the crate to the stove. The color forms a lifeline within the kitchen: It is the family's lifeblood, the place of their communion.

Lucille Clifton, *When I Go Home*

Clifton's poem defines home as "where the memory is" (p. 213, line 16). In this, she agrees with Lee and similarly ties her memories to her mother and to food. The house itself is just a hard, physical space ("linoleum" and "splintered floorboards") that cannot be called a home without her mother's lyrical voice and the perfume of her baking. Thus, Clifton need not move one inch physically to go home; she need only summon the memory of her mother. Clifton's poem raises the same tone of nostalgia we have seen before in this chapter, not just in Lee's work but also in Welty's—and to a certain extent in Sanders's. All long for something physically lost and search for a means of regaining this sense of security, this sense of self.

Erica Jong, from *Coming Home to Connecticut*

Erica Jong suggests that the ability to appreciate a sense of home is one that comes with age. She remarks, "As a child, not knowing there is an alternative, you never really appreciate home," for example (para. 2). Her piece concludes this chapter with the thought, "Home is the place where you feel safe" (para. 1), and she seems to share the sense of the casual, the comfort of being relaxed at home that Barney's photograph elicits. Jong rejoices in her "old terrycloth bathrobe" and "muddy clogs" as images that speak of home to her. But the concept of home goes beyond creature comforts and touches on spiritual comfort when she says, "Home is where you get out of bed at 3 A.M. . . . knowing no demons can follow you here" (para. 3).

Tina Barney, *Family in the Kitchen*

The casual intimacy of Barney's photo forms a similar lifeline. The people in this photo are rumpled and barefooted, informal and unrehearsed. You might ask students to turn back to Welty's photo of the shopkeeper (p. 139) for a contrast. You could begin discussion by asking the class to list the various items in Barney's photo that suggest "family" or "home" to them, or to sketch out the relationships they believe exist among these people and why. In Barney's work, the connecting color is white—it ties the scene together (the shorts, the dress, the cupboard, the chair, the bottle, the table leg) and moves the light and the viewer through the photo. You might lead a discussion on how the feeling viewers get from Barney's photo differs from the impression they get from Garza's painting—and why.

 For an interactive visual exercise for this selection, go to www.seeingandwriting.com.

ADDITIONAL WRITING TOPICS

1. Ask students to examine the portrayal of home in ads, particularly those that stress the notion of bridging distances or supplying a home away from home. You could suggest the following types of ads: telephone, automobile, Internet, hotel. Students could focus on one category (e.g., telephone ads) or could compare and contrast two categories (e.g., telephone and automobile ads).

2. In "A Sense of Place," Golden writes: "When all places fingerprint the soul, which grasp is judged to be the strongest?" (para. 3). Ask students to write an essay in which they describe the places that have left significant fingerprints on them, and then to explain which place has had the strongest grasp and why.

3. Have students research the history of the telephone. They can use this research as the basis of an essay that explains and analyzes how phones have reflected and influenced our culture.

CONNECTIONS WITH OTHER TEXTS

1. Ask students to compare Golden's "A Sense of Place" to Mailer's (p. 165). Have students point to specific textual evidence that indicates whether Golden and Mailer would agree on how to define a sense of place.

SUGGESTIONS FOR FURTHER READING, THINKING, AND WRITING

print

Golden, Marita. *Migrations of the Heart.* New York: Ballantine Books, 1996.

———. *A Woman's Place.* New York: Ballantine Books, 1990.

web

www.ericsson.com/index.shtml   Ericsson's homepage.

www.maritagolden.com/   Marita Golden's official web site.

Links for the selections in this chapter can be found at www.seeingandwriting.com.

Chapter 3

Capturing Memorable Moments

Introduction

You might begin discussion by asking students to talk about their memories of September 11, 2001. You should note how students recount their memories. Some might say that the first thing they did that morning was to turn on the television, only to see the nightmare being played and replayed on screen; others might say that they heard about the event from some other source—radio, the Internet, a friend—and then turned on the television. You might ask students whose first experience of the event wasn't visual to comment on how the experience of *seeing* it was different from the first experience. Some have observed that they did not comprehend the event or even feel an emotional response to it until they witnessed the television footage of the planes crashing into the towers and of the towers crumbling to the ground.

This might be an effective way to raise the topic of how we attempt to capture most of our memorable moments by visual means. You might ask students to consider the pictures in their photo albums. How many of their most memorable experiences have they captured on film? Major events are often visually recorded: birthdays, graduations, weddings, and the like. However, these may not necessarily be the most memorable moments to some. Indeed, some students observe that the experiences of certain events have sometimes been overshadowed by the recording of these experiences.

Ask students to comment on whether they identify with these lines from the text: "Often the most memorable experiences occur when we least expect them or are difficult to capture in a picture frame on a mantel" (p. 223). Ask students to freewrite about such memorable experiences.

 For additional resources for the selections in this chapter (including exercises and annotated links), go to www.seeingandwriting.com.

Patrick Witty, *Witnessing a Dreadful Moment in History* Jeff Mermelstein, *Here is New York*

GENERATING CLASS DISCUSSION AND IN-CLASS WRITING

The photographs by Mermelstein and Witty provide different angles on the destruction of the World Trade Center: Witty captures the expressions of onlookers as they witness the event; Mermelstein focuses on the immediate aftermath in a deserted area filled with debris covering a man. You might begin discussion by asking students to describe the September 11 photographs they are familiar with. Most likely students will describe pictures involving the twin towers.

Because this subject is understandably difficult to deal with, you might consider giving students a chance to express some of their feelings through freewriting. You might ask students to examine Mermelstein's picture, note outstanding details, and then freewrite about the feelings evoked by those details. Not only does this exercise give students an opportunity to vent, but it also provides them with details for discussing the first Seeing question. In the foreground, a few trash cans and boxes can be seen amidst the paper covering the ground. Students might note that the trash cans, boxes, and reams of paper were blown out of the offices of the twin towers, showing that the targets of this attack were men and women involved in business, not war. Indeed, the person in the center of the picture appears to be looking through his briefcase—a person of business, like the thousands of people in the towers. This photograph, then, reinforces the notion that soldiers abroad are not the only Americans at danger in this time of war: Everyday citizens were targeted in this attack and will probably be targeted again in the future. However, some students might see a symbol of resilience in the man. After all, the figure appears to be unscathed, surviving rock-solid amidst the aftermath of terror.

You might ask students to imagine Witty's position in the photograph: He is facing away from the twin towers, watching New Yorkers' reactions to the destruction behind him. Have your students consider why Witty thought this would be an important image to capture. Why wasn't he photographing the towers?

ADDITIONAL WRITING TOPICS

1. Ask students to write a brief narrative about how they learned of the events of September 11. They should describe the moments before they found out, but they should focus on the discovery and on their feelings associated with it.

2. Have students write an essay that explains how these photographs work through *not* showing the familiar images of destruction—the burning, falling towers. How do the angles and the images chosen by Mermelstein and Witty affect viewers?

3. Have students consider the very idea of studying this subject in a classroom. Ask them to freewrite about the effects of studying a recent tragedy through images and essays in a textbook. Studying a subject normally involves an attempt at being objective and finding some personal distance. If students have some success with the freewriting exercise, the subject could be turned into an expository or even an argument essay.

CONNECTIONS WITH OTHER TEXTS

1. In "On Photography" Susan Sontag writes "A way of certifying experience, taking photographs is also a way of refusing it—by limiting experience to a search for the photogenic, by converting experience into an image, a souvenir" (p. 293, para. 5). Students are probably aware of the plethora of photographic books devoted to the subject of September 11. To what extent can these photographs limit the experience, particularly when they are placed in a book of images that sits on a coffee table?

2. Regarding photography, James Nachtwey states, "There is power in the still image that doesn't exist in other forms" (p. 277, para. 17). Ask students to comment on the power of these photographs by Mermelstein and Witty. In what ways do the photographs affect students that the televised footage did not?

SUGGESTIONS FOR FURTHER READING, THINKING, AND WRITING

print

Mermelstein, Jeff. *Sidewalk*. Stockport: Dewi
    Lewis Publishing, 2000.

📰 *web*

www.nytimes.com/slideshow/2001/09/23/
    magazine/23MERMELSTEIN-SS_1.html

Slide show of Mermelstein's September 11
    photographs.

www.untitledmagazine.com/   Web site
    designed, published, and edited by Witty.
Links for the selections in this chapter can be
    found at www.seeingandwriting.com.

PAIR: Joe Rosenthal, *Marines Raising the Flag on Mount Suribachi, Iwo Jima* (photo and essay)

GENERATING CLASS DISCUSSION AND IN-CLASS WRITING

Rosenthal's photograph is not only one of the most famous images of World War II, it is also one of the most recognizable images in American history. This was not the only photograph taken by Rosenthal that day. He also took a picture of a large group of soldiers posed around the flag. But that picture remains largely unknown to the general public, whereas this candid shot has widepread recognition. What is it about this image that makes it so affecting, so lasting? Although Rosenthal's essay does not touch upon this question, you might begin discussion with it. Students will probably note that it represents American victory and pride. If responses remain at this general level, ask students to be more specific. You might tell them that the original photograph was wider horizontally; the image became famous only after it was cropped so that the flag runs diagonally throughout the entire frame. How does knowing about this change influence the viewer's perception? Ask students to imagine differences in the picture so they can see the importance of details. Couldn't an image of an already-raised flag be as moving? What if different timing had enabled Rosenthal to capture the faces of the soldiers? What if the shrapnel had been cleared from the ground?

   Alternatively, you might begin discussion by having students examine the photograph before they read the essay. Ask whether they know the circumstances surrounding the photograph. If they have not heard or read much about the battle or the photograph, ask them to infer the circumstances from the details of the image. Then you could direct them to read the essay and note the parts that affect how they view the photograph.

In his essay, Rosenthal explains how he rushed to the site once he heard that a flag was going to be placed on Iwo Jima. Students might be surprised to learn that a flag had already been raised and photographed. When Rosenthal arrived, he found the Marines had taken down the first flag to put up a larger one that could be seen by more soldiers. Rosenthal did make some preparations for the photograph: "Because there were some chewed-up bushes in the foreground that might cut off the bottom half of these Marines that were going to raise the flag, I grabbed a couple of rocks and a couple of old sandbags left from a Japanese outpost that had been blasted there, to stand on." However, he was interrupted by the arrival of Bill Genaust, a Marine movie cameraman, so both he and Genaust were barely able to capture the raising of the flag.

ADDITIONAL WRITING TOPICS

1. Ask students to freewrite about a personal photograph that has had a lasting effect on them. Why has this photograph, out of the countless number of photos they have seen, stayed with them for so long?

2. Although Rosenthal's photograph captures an image of victory, the victory signals only a turn in the battle. Ask students to imagine that the United States had lost the war. Then have them write a short description of Rosenthal's picture with this imaginary history in mind. How does this different history affect their reading of the photograph?

3. If the first writing topic prompted interesting responses, you might have students use it as the basis for an essay that analyzes how historical context plays into our readings of photographs.

CONNECTIONS WITH OTHER TEXTS

1. In "On Photography" Susan Sontag writes "A way of certifying experience, taking photographs is also a way of refusing it—by limiting experience to a search for the photogenic, by converting experience into an image, a souvenir" (para. 5). The image of this scene has been reproduced many, many times. Ask students whether the popularity of the image—the possibility of its being a souvenir—lessens the importance of the experience it captured.

2. Ask students to examine Shirin Neshat's photograph (p. 322), which features a woman who seems to represent Muslim women. Ask how this photograph—in the facelessness of the soldiers—might represent other soldiers or Americans.

SUGGESTIONS FOR FURTHER READING, THINKING, AND WRITING

print

Bradley, James. *Flags of Our Fathers*. New York: Bantam, 2001.

Ross, Bill D. *Iwo Jima: Legacy of Valor*. New York: Random House, 1986.

Thomey, Tedd. *Immortal Images: A Personal History of Two Photographers and the Flag Raising on Iwo Jima*. Annapolis: Naval Institute Press, 1996.

[www] web

www.iwojima.com/ Comprehensive web site about Iwo Jima. Includes description of battle, and photographs and film clips of the flag raising.

www.nps.gov/gwmp/usmc.htm National Park Service's picture and description of the Marine Corps War Memorial, a statue based on Rosenthal's photograph.

Links for the selections in this chapter can be found at www.seeingandwriting.com.

audio/visual

Heroes of Iwo Jima. 100 min. 2001. VHS videocassette. Distributed by A&E. Presents the battle of Iwo Jima through the photographers' viewpoints and includes interviews with nearly fifty people. Rosenthal's famous photo is discussed in the interviews.

VISUALIZING CONTEXT: **Raising the Flag**

GENERATING CLASS DISCUSSION AND IN-CLASS WRITING

This selection invites students to examine not only how Rosenthal's photograph of the flag raising at Iwo Jima has been used in different contexts, but also how it echoes throughout other images. Ask students to examine the different contexts in which Rosenthal's photo appears. How does each one change its meaning? Do other stamps or Super Bowl pre-game shows come to mind as your students look at these images? By now, they should know that an image's meaning is dependent upon its context. But can the original image's meaning be affected by being, as Rosenthal states, "the most widely reproduced photograph of all time"? Many people have probably seen the original photo only after seeing some of its countless reproductions.

Ask whether students see echoes of Rosenthal's image in the Associated Press photograph of the flag raising at ground zero. Have them freewrite about the feelings they associate with the A.P. photograph. Then ask them to look at the *Newsweek* cover. How does the text affect their reading? You might point out that the photo has been cropped for the *Newsweek* cover, just as Rosenthal's photograph was cropped before it became a famous image. How does the cropping change the viewer's focus? In the A.P. photo the men and the flag can be points of focus, but the wreckage above and behind them also draws the eye. However, the *Newsweek* photo leads the eye directly to the flag, centered in the picture and surrounded by text.

ADDITIONAL WRITING TOPICS

1. Ask students to write about how the feelings evoked by the Associated Press photograph compare to those inspired by Rosenthal's picture.

2. Students can analyze the contexts presented here for how they create meaning and change the meaning of the original image. Encourage students to research the Internet for other contexts in which Rosenthal's photograph has been presented. How do the different contexts of each affect the meaning of the original? When an image becomes an icon, is its original meaning lost?

3. Have students compare and contrast Rosenthal's photograph with the Associated Press photograph of the flag raising. Students can argue whether the popularity of the A.P. photo is dependent upon Rosenthal's picture.

CONNECTIONS WITH OTHER TEXTS

1. Another famous photograph is that of an astronaut standing next to an American flag on the moon. Patriotism seems to run through famous American images. Ask students to research famous images from other countries. Does a common theme of national pride run throughout them all?

2. Ask students to research the history of an iconic figure. How has it changed over the years? For what purposes has it been used? They should examine some of its many contexts and explain how the icon takes on different meanings in these contexts.

Sarah Vowell, *Shooting Dad*

GENERATING CLASS DISCUSSION AND IN-CLASS WRITING

Sarah Vowell's essay paints an amusing and touching portrait of her relationship with her father. Vowell and her father have ideals that exist on different ends of the political spectrum, which caused arguments during her teenage years. As she grew older she wanted to become a better daughter, which culminated in her helping her father test his homemade cannon. The cannon experiment drew the two closer together and made her realize that she's more like her father than she thought.

As you take students through the essay, you should ask them to study how Vowell's humor works. You might begin discussion by having them name authors they find humorous. Students might list Dave Barry, David Sedaris, Douglas Adams, P. J. O'Rourke, Joe Queenan, or various other writers with a unique way of crafting humor. Ask students if they can characterize the humor of the writers they named. You might point out that Vowell uses irony throughout the essay, mainly through forms of understatement and hyperbole. You could then lead the class through the essay, asking students to identify instances of irony.

With its playful use of Lincoln's phrase "A house divided against itself cannot stand" (found originally in the Bible), the opening line sets a lighthearted tone for the essay: "If you were passing by the house where I grew up during my teenage years and it happened to be before Election Day, you wouldn't have needed to come inside to see that it was a house divided" (para. 1). Vowell's politics and her father's differ, mainly on the issue of guns: "About the only thing my father and I agree on is the Constitution, though I'm partial to the First Amendment, while he's always favored the Second" (para. 2).

Their disagreements were more serious than Vowell lets on in the essay. Students should note that she could have written a serious essay had she chosen different memories and a different tone. She describes their arguments as "bickering" (para. 5), yet this description is probably an understatement, given her feelings on his profession: "There were times when I found the fact that he was a gunsmith horrifying" (para. 6). She also states that they "were incapable of having a conversation that didn't end in an argument" (para. 6). But Vowell's purpose here is to write a humorous account of her relationship with her father, so her tone and examples must match.

Vowell usually creates humorous sentences through irony and word choice. She uses hyperbole when she refers to her teenage home as a "Civil War battleground" (para. 1) and the safe areas of the house as the "DMZ" (para. 7). Understatement is apparent in her concern over her father's desire to fire a cannon in the mountains: "I was a little worried that the National Forest Service would object to us lobbing fiery balls of metal onto its property" (para. 21). Her specific attention to detail can be seen in her recollection of how prominent guns were in her household: "I had to move revolvers out of my way to make room for a bowl of Rice Krispies on the kitchen table" (para. 3). She chooses *revolvers,* not *guns,* and *bowl of Rice Krispies* instead of *bowl of cereal* or *food.*

Even though Vowell and her father seemed most at odds during her teenage years, her descriptions signal similarities that she would later realize. They shared a tendency to be single-minded: "All he ever cared about were guns. All I ever cared about was art" (para. 6). The areas in which they practiced their hobbies were cluttered: "Dad's shop was a messy disaster area, a labyrinth of lathes"; Vowell's music room was "also a messy disaster area, an obstacle course of musical instruments" (para. 7). You might note Vowell's wonderful use of alliteration as she describes her father's workshop as "a labyrinth of lathes" and "a makeshift museum of death" (para. 7).

Vowell's eventual decision to become a better daughter led to her helping her dad fire his homemade cannon, a nineteenth-century reconstruction that took two years to build. Her description of the event helps readers to see it by making familiar comparisons. She likens the lit fuse and sound of the cannon to the imagery and sounds of cartoons: "When the fuse is lit, it resembles a cartoon. So does the sound, which warrants Ben Day dot words along the lines of *ker-pow!*" (para. 23). Her description of the smoke is familiar and funny: "There's so much Fourth of July smoke everywhere I feel compelled to sing the national anthem" (para. 23). Vowell was surprised by her reaction, which was similar to her father's. Her ultimate description of the event is simple: "It's just really, really cool. My dad thought so, too" (para. 24).

Vowell recorded the event with her tape recorder and foot-long microphone. She was surprised that the recorder's sound measurement needles did not break from the noise, which she admits was painful to hear: "The cannon was so loud and so painful, I had to touch my head to make sure my skull hadn't cracked open" (para. 26). As Vowell and her father fired the cannon again, two hikers became spectators and commented on her tape recorder and foot-long microphone. Upon hearing this comment, Vowell realized how similar she is to her father: "Oh. My. God. My dad and I are the same person. We're both smart-alecky loners with goofy projects and weird equipment" (para. 29).

Near the end of the essay, Vowell explains how her father wants his ashes to be shot out of the cannon. The last paragraph ends on a genuinely touching note as Vowell reminds us of when she covered her ears from the loud, painful cannon shot earlier in the essay. She says she will not cover her ears when she shoots her father's ashes from the cannon. The final paragraph works through the repetition of "I will" at the beginning of the second through the sixth sentences. The surprise of the different beginning in the seventh sentence accentuates the importance of her decision: "But I will not cover my ears. Because when I blow what used to be my dad into the earth, I want it to hurt" (para. 34).

ADDITIONAL WRITING TOPICS

1. Ask students to freewrite about a time when they noticed striking similarities or differences between themselves and their parents.

2. Have students write a personal narrative about a time when they realized they were more like their parents (at least one of them) than they had originally thought. Or students could write about a time when they realized they were becoming less like their parents. The impetus for the realization does not have to be similar to Vowell's. Students could write about a habit, a belief, a mannerism, and so on. Ask students to write this narrative in a humorous tone.

3. Use the same topic from item 2, but ask students to write the narrative in a serious tone. You could assign items 2 and 3 to show students how a writer's choice of tone changes the presentation and inclusion of information.

CONNECTIONS WITH OTHER TEXTS

1. Vowell's essay avoids detailing the heated arguments between herself and her father. In "This Is Our World," Dorothy Allison states, "Art is not meant to be polite, secret, coded, or timid. Art is the sphere in which that impulse to hide and lie is the most dangerous" (p. 264, para. 41). What do your students think of Vowell's essay in light of Allison's view of art? Do they think Vowell's essay is artistic? Do they think humor can be an art form? Ask them to back up their arguments with specific examples.

2. Have students read Joe Queenan's essay "The Skin Game" (p. 366), which is a humorous piece on the subject of tattoos. Queenan's essay also involves his father, but primarily as a means to discuss how the perception of tattoos has changed in our culture. Then ask students to write a comparison and contrast of the two essays in terms of their tone, purpose, and humor.

SUGGESTIONS FOR FURTHER READING, THINKING, AND WRITING

print

Vowell, Sarah. *Radio On: A Listener's Diary*. New York: St. Martin's Press. 1998.

———. *Take the Cannoli*. New York: Simon & Schuster, 2000.

www. web

www.hearingvoices.com/sv/ RealAudio clips of Sarah Vowell reading her work—including "Shooting Dad"—on *This American Life*.

dir.salon.com/topics/sarah_vowell/index.html Includes over seventy articles Vowell has written for her column at Salon.com.

Links for the selections in this chapter can be found at www.seeingandwriting.com.

Barry Lopez, *Learning to See*

GENERATING CLASS DISCUSSION AND IN-CLASS WRITING

In this essay, Lopez explains why he abandoned the profession of photography for writing. Many reasons played into his decision, but most of them involved the portrayal of animals in nature photography. He also expresses concern over how memory has been regarded by his generation and how the photographer's authority has increased. You might begin discussion by asking students to comment on Lopez's shift from photography to writing. Which ethical concerns raised by Lopez especially surprised them?

One of the factors that caused Lopez's shift from photographer to writer was his unhappiness with the perception of memory in his generation. The practice of preserving memories through photography "had become so compulsive, that recording the event was more important for some than participating in it" (para. 39). Lopez notes that his generation was "storing memories that would never be retrieved, that would never form a coherent narrative" (para. 39). This is a disadvantage of photographs: They "tend to collapse events into a single moment," leaving out critical details (para. 34). This lack of coherency could also be seen in the way his pictures were being used to create an "entertaining but not necessarily coherent landscape of wild animals (images that essentially lied to children)" (para. 40).

These images "lied" in how they misrepresented the lives of animals. Lopez notes that in the 1970s animals were often reduced to caricatures in wildlife magazines: "Promoted as elegant, brave, graceful, sinister, wise, etc., according to their species, animals were deprived of personality and the capacity to be innovative" (para. 36). Images that would have expanded people's understandings of wildlife were often found too disturbing to publish: "A female wolf killing one of her pups, or a male bonobo approaching a female with a prominent erection, was not anything magazine editors were comfortable with" (para. 36). Lopez felt these wildlife images were similar to those of women in *Playboy*: "Both celebrated the conventionally gorgeous, the overly endowed, the seductive" (para. 38).

Lopez was also concerned that the "authority of the image" has changed in photography. Due to the "modern emphasis on the genius of the individual artist" and the advent of computer manipulation, the photographer has become the authority, which has resulted in "fabricated images of wildlife" (para. 13).

In addition to these problems, Lopez had concerns about how his photography was affecting his writing process. Photography inclines him to get the "clean, fixed image right away," which he does not want to do in his writing: "I want, instead, to see a sentence fragment scrawled in my notebook, smeared by rain" (para. 41).

However, he seemed to be most influenced by an encounter he had while involved with scientific research in the Arctic, which brought him into contact with a polar bear. As he followed the bear, Lopez missed details that were important to him as a writer because he was distracted while trying to ready his camera (paras. 28–31). More important, though, was the way the bear affected him: "In some way the bear had grabbed me by the shirtfront and said, Think about this. Think about what these cameras in your hands are doing" (para. 33).

Britta Jaschinski's photograph "Malayan Tapir" accompanies the essay. Ask students whether this photograph reflects any of Lopez's concerns about the portrayal of animals in photography. Would he be bothered by it, or does it support his views?

ADDITIONAL WRITING TOPICS

1. Lopez notes some of photography's shortcomings that influenced him to switch to the writing profession. Ask students to write an essay comparing and contrasting the advantages and disadvantages of photography and writing.

2. Lopez discusses how part of the research designed to protect seals also involved shooting them (para. 26). Deer are dealt with in a similar fashion. One argument in favor of hunting is that it helps keep deer populations from expanding beyond their habitats. Students could research the subject and write an essay in which they either defend hunting or promote an alternative.

3. In paragraph 54, Lopez gives his definition of a photographer: "A photographer seeks intimacy with the world and then endeavors to share it. Inherent in that desire to share is a love of humanity." Ask students to write a definition of another profession (something in the arts would probably be best) and then write an essay that defends the definition.

CONNECTIONS WITH OTHER TEXTS

1. Lopez notes that authority over a picture now belongs to the photographer. One reason for this change in authority is the advent of digital manipulation. How does the Kodak Picture Maker, which allows for the enlargement and enhancement of pictures, change a picture's context, removing some of its narrative spine?

2. Tony Hiss (p. 182) and Barry Lopez share concerns about the natural environment. Ask students to examine how each author makes statements about preservation. Who makes explicit statements? Who makes implications? Does the nature of the statements support each essay's tone and purpose?

SUGGESTIONS FOR FURTHER READING, THINKING, AND WRITING

print

Lopez, Barry. *About This Life: Journeys on the Threshold of Memory*. New York: Knopf, 1998.

———. *Arctic Dreams: Imagination and Desire in a Northern Landscape*. New York: Vintage, 2001.

———. *Crossing Open Ground*. New York: Vintage, 1989.

———. *The Rediscovery of North America*. New York: Vintage, 1989.

web

www.barclayagency.com/lopez.html   Includes a profile of Lopez and links to interviews and an essay by Lopez.

www.capitolabookcafe.com/andrea/lopez.html Interview with Lopez about his book *About This Life*.

Links for the selections in this chapter can be found at www.seeingandwriting.com.

audio/visual

About This Life. 1998. Read by Barry Lopez. 2 audio cassettes. Published by Audio Literature.

Crossing Open Ground. 2000. Read by Barry Lopez. 2 audio cassettes. Published by HighBridge Company.

RETROSPECT: *Some Enchanted Evening*

GENERATING CLASS DISCUSSION AND IN-CLASS WRITING

This Retrospect offers images of proms from 1954 to 2001. Although they all capture the same event, the images differ in striking ways: black and white versus color; couples versus parties; semi-casual versus formal versus costumed; professional versus amateur. You might ask students to use these distinctions to initially classify the images. How are students able to distinguish professional photos from amateur snapshots, for example? They might look at the lighting or the backdrops. How can students distinguish couples who seem to be close from those who seem to have been thrown together at the last minute? They might look at body language. Have students compare the photos from the 1950s and 1960s to those of the early 1990s. What differences are evident in the posture of the couples, in their proximity to each other? On the basis of these differences, what can students infer about the changes in youth culture over time? What has changed about proms so that more of the later pictures show groups of young women rather than couples only? What do these images capture? You might ask students to compare their own proms to those pictured.

Prom night is a significant ritual that young adults participate in—or may refuse to participate in. Why is the prom so significant in our culture? What does it represent? In some ways, with its emphasis on dresses, tuxes, and limos, the prom is a wedding rehearsal. This is especially evident in the earlier photos. All the photos reveal that both young women and men spend a significant amount of money on prom night—for outfits, flowers, limos, and so on. What are they buying? The promise of romance is one possibility. Another is simply a memory. If students feel fine about their own proms, you might ask them to bring in their prom night photos and an estimate of how much they spent; this could generate a lively class discussion. You might also ask students to list other examples of rituals of memory within our culture (e.g., weddings, graduations, bar and bas mitzvahs).

ADDITIONAL WRITING TOPICS

1. Ask students to do a short freewrite that reflects their memories of a prom—or why they did not go to a prom. This may be a sensitive subject for some students, so you might encourage them to move forward from this memory to an assessment of how important, or how memorable, the prom is for some people.

2. Have students choose a couple in any of the Retrospect's prom photos and write a brief narrative that imagines the prom date of this couple.

3. Prom is big business, and many sectors of the economy are involved in marketing memories to teens. Ask students to research the prom business and write an essay that gives a specific type of analysis of this phenomenon (e.g., economic, sociological).

CONNECTIONS WITH OTHER TEXTS

1. The Retrospect title is "Some Enchanted Evening." Like the theme for many proms, this is a song title. You might have students research the lyrics for this song or for a song that served as their own prom theme. Then ask them to write an essay that offers a close reading of the song lyrics as they relate to the chapter's theme of capturing memorable moments.

2. In "On Photography," Susan Sontag notes how photographs do not merely capture moments anymore. According to Sontag, a photograph can "interfere with" or "invade" the moment to the point of becoming an event in itself (para. 8). Do these prom photos support Sontag's view?

Sherman Alexie, *The Joy of Reading and Writing: Superman and Me*

GENERATING CLASS DISCUSSION AND IN-CLASS WRITING

Alexie's essay, as the title states, is about the joy of reading and writing, but it is also about the power of literacy. In this essay, Alexie explains how he learned to read and how reading became a way to save himself from the poverty and negative expectations he faced on an Indian reservation. You could begin discussion by asking students how literacy has figured in their own lives. Do they recall their first reading experience? You could also ask if students have shared Alexie's experience in terms of their education being influenced by cultural stereotypes—stereotypes created and reinforced by members as well as nonmembers of the culture.

Alexie opens the essay with an interesting hook: "I learned to read with a *Superman* comic book" (para. 1). Readers are pulled in by the essay's title and lead sentence, thinking that the work will largely concern Alexie's love of a comic book character.

Since he devotes only one paragraph to Superman, he needs to direct readers away from the comic book hero to avoid disappointing them. He does this by using negative statements that not only take the focus off of the comic book but also intrigue readers to read further: "I cannot recall which particular Superman comic book I read, nor can I remember which villain he fought in that issue. I cannot remember the plot, nor the means by which I obtained the comic book" (para. 1). At this point, readers wonder what Alexie does remember; then they find out personal information about the author: He is a Spokane Indian who was three years old when he learned to read while living with his impoverished family on an Indian reservation.

His father's love of books inspired Alexie to read. Before he could even understand most of the words in his father's books, Alexie grasped the concept of the paragraph. As he states, "I didn't have the vocabulary to say 'paragraph,' but I realized that it was a fence that held words. The words inside a paragraph worked together for a common purpose" (para. 3). This knowledge inspired him to "think of everything in terms of paragraphs" (para. 3). His "reservation was a small paragraph within the United States" (para. 3). He saw that each member of his family "existed as a separate paragraph but still had genetics and common experiences to link us" (para. 3).

Alexie's paragraph-as-a-fence metaphor structures his essay. You might put students in groups and ask them to locate and list the main idea of each paragraph, telling them to use the third paragraph's subject—paragraphs as fences—as a guide. Because Alexie's prose is clear and organized, most groups should arrive at the same answers. However, a few groups are bound to disagree. If this happens, asking each group to justify its answer should sort out possible discrepancies.

You might also ask students to examine how the eight paragraphs come together as a unified essay. After all, Alexie touches on a number of subjects such as literacy, personal history, and cultural stereotypes, to name a few. How does he make these subjects work for a common purpose? He unifies the essay by using transitions that involve key words or concepts from the last sentence of the previous paragraph. The end of the second paragraph, for example, relates how Alexie learned to love books through his father's example; the third paragraph begins with Alexie reading his father's books. The fourth paragraph opens with a transition phrase that refers to his fascination with paragraphs in the third paragraph: "At the same time I was seeing the world in paragraphs" (para. 4). The last sentence of the sixth paragraph states that failure was expected of Indians by both Indians and non-Indians; the seventh paragraph opens with the statement "I refused to fail."

The last three paragraphs focus on the educational stereotypes Alexie faced as an Indian. His classmates wanted him to fit the stereotype—quiet, ignorant, and submissive. Most of his Indian classmates "lived up to those expectations inside the classroom but subverted them on the outside" (para. 6). As he observes, there was a kind of acceptance for those who failed: "Those who failed were ceremonially accepted by other Indians and appropriately pitied by non-Indians" (para. 6). Ask students if they have ever been treated as an outcast for not fulfilling a cultural expectation.

Alexie refused to fulfill the expectations of others and "read anything that had words and paragraphs" with a love made of "equal parts joy and desperation" (para. 7). Some students might not understand why Alexie's situation was so desperate, why he states with such gravity: "I was trying to save my life" (para. 7). You might encourage students to research what life is like on an Indian reservation.

ADDITIONAL WRITING TOPICS

1. Ask students to write a personal essay in which they recount how their education was encouraged or discouraged by family, friends, community, or culture.

2. Using Alexie's paragraph-as-fence metaphor as an example, students could write an essay that explains other features of writing through metaphor. They could write about essay structure, grammar, or punctuation. Or they could write an essay on punctuation, with each paragraph devoted to a certain mark in which they explain the mark and use it at the same time.

3. Ask students to freewrite about how education has helped and hindered them.

CONNECTIONS WITH OTHER TEXTS

1. In his essay, Alexie talks about how he "grows into a man who often speaks of his childhood in the third-person, as if it will somehow dull the pain and make him sound more modest about his talents" (para. 5). In "Why We Travel" (p. 189) Pico Iyer says something similar about travel: "All of us feel this from the cradle, and know, in some sense, that all the significant movement we ever take is internal" (para. 29). Read these statements to your students, and ask them to freewrite in response to each.

2. In this essay, Alexie explains how reading and writing saved him. In "Learning to See" (p. 238), Barry Lopez explains how he came to see photography as "a conscious exercise in awareness, a technique for paying attention" (para. 16). Ask students to write an expository essay on how images and words have significantly affected their lives.

SUGGESTIONS FOR FURTHER READING, THINKING, AND WRITING

print

Alexie, Sherman. *Indian Killer*. New York: Atlantic Monthly Press, 1996.

———. *The Lone Ranger and Tonto Fistfight in Heaven*. New York: Atlantic Monthly Press, 1993.

———. *Reservation Blues*. New York: Atlantic Monthly Press, 1995.

【www.】 *web*

www.fallsapart.com/ The official Sherman Alexie web site. A comprehensive site that details Alexie's books, movies, interviews, recordings, and reviews.

Links for the selections in this chapter can be found at www.seeingandwriting.com.

audio/visual

Smoke Signals. 88 min. 1999. VHS videocassette. Distributed by Miramax Films. Directed by Chris Eyre. Written by Sherman Alexie. Based on stories in *The Lone Ranger and Tonto Fistfight in Heaven*.

Lauren Greenfield, *Ashleigh, 13, with Her Friend and Parents, Santa Monica*

GENERATING CLASS DISCUSSION AND IN-CLASS WRITING

By now, students should be tuned in to the apparently authentic, spontaneous, or informal nature of the photographs in this chapter. They may have begun to evaluate the sincerity or "truth" of the photographs in terms of the elements of the photographic composition and tone. Ask students to make observations about the elements in this photograph that signal, "I am not posed." (Consider the colorful disorder of the bathroom, the inattention of the individuals in the frame to the camera, the casual and intimate nature of the 13-year-old subject dressing for a grown-up date.) Greenfield's photograph invites us right into the bathroom of a contemporary California nuclear family; like the prom pictures, it demonstrates our passion to record events in our family lives through snapshots, photographs, and videotape.

Greenfield's photographs are "colorful and disquieting" (p. 254). At first glance we can see the colorfulness; however, the disquieting elements may be more difficult for students to discern. Ask them to comment on the central figure in the frame. What do we know about her, and how do we know it? You might point out the tight, black clothing and the pearls, for example, as visual cues that she is seeking to look adult—although the caption informs us that she is merely 13 years old. However, the fact that she is standing on a scale, looking down at the record of her weight, dominates other impressions we might have of her. We understand that she is checking her image—but she is not doing so visually in the mirror. Instead, she is measuring herself against some abstract standard to see if her weight is acceptable. This is both a public and a private moment. No one else in the photograph can see the numbers on the scale. The mother and father and friend all maintain a respectful distance as Ashleigh puts the finishing touches on her image by stepping onto the scale.

ADDITIONAL WRITING TOPICS

1. You could ask students to catalogue the visual objects in the frame that characterize this American family, then to build a short paper from these observations. Ask students to group the objects by category and explain how they support the students' inferences about the family.

2. Ask students to write a brief character analysis of Ashleigh based entirely on the inferences they draw from this photo of her.

3. Suggest that students read this photograph in terms of the role of the teenager in our culture, especially the role of the female teenager.

4. Greenfield's photographs offer "unremitting criticism of a culture that measures success by how closely individuals conform to stereotypical images of power, wealth, and beauty" (p. 254). Direct students to write an explanation of what stereotypic "images of power, wealth, and beauty" are being categorized here.

CONNECTIONS WITH OTHER TEXTS

1. Have students read Dorothy Allison's essay, "This Is Our World" (p. 259), and take notes on the statements Allison makes about class. What do they think Allison would say about Greenfield's photograph? Would it meet her criteria for what constitutes art?

2. Tina Barney also documents the lives of the middle class (*Family in the Kitchen,* p. 215). Ask students to compare the photographs by Barney and Greenfield. How are they alike? What differences can students identify?

SUGGESTIONS FOR FURTHER READING, THINKING, AND WRITING

print

Greenfield, Lauren. *Fast Forward: Growing Up in the Shadow of Hollywood.* New York: Knopf/Melcher Media, 1997. Introduction by Carrie Fisher.

[www.] *web*

Links for the selections in this chapter can be found at www.seeingandwriting.com.

New York Times, September 11, 2001

The ancillary image is the front page of the *New York Times* that was printed on September 11 before the attacks on the World Trade Center and the Pentagon. You might ask students how this could be an example of the following quotation by Allison: "The world is meaner than we admit, larger and more astonishing. Strength appears in the most desperate figures, tragedy when we have no reason to expect it" (para. 37). Students might respond that events later in the day made many see how astonishingly cruel the world can be. Indeed, the front page shows an American society unconcerned with terrorism—and certainly not expecting it on American soil. The headlines that stand out the most involve school dress codes, stem cell research, television ratings, the economy, and local electoral campaigns. Compared to the headlines that would be printed later in the day, these reflect a kind of innocence.

However, looking closely at these early September 11 headlines reveals another way to interpret this page in the context of Allison's quotation. This alternate view suggests innocence and ignorance. The smallest headline on the page is "Violence in Mideast, Despite Plans to Talk," and the story contains the least amount of front-page text. The two paragraphs of text report on conflicts that could ruin the truce negotiations between Israelis and Palestinians. At the bottom of the page, under the "INSIDE" heading, the headline "Afghan Rebel's Fate Unclear" is followed by news about an assassination attempt on the leader of the opposition to the Taliban. Although neither story suggests any reason to expect imminent danger in the United States, each reveals conflicts and issues that we would become irrevocably linked with later that day, that we would soon see commanding bigger print and more space on the front page. These stories involve places in the world that experience acts of terrorism on a daily basis. What these smaller headlines suggest is how dependent our worldview is upon the media. Ask students how knowledgeable they were of the Taliban and of the violence in Israel when this front page was being printed. In "This Is Our World," Allison collects news clippings to prove the cruelty in the world—"the woman who drowned her children, the man who shot first the babies in her arms and then his wife" (para. 37). In a way, these small headlines raise the following question: If the cruelty of the world is hidden in the margins of the morning paper, what other reaction to terror could there possibly be but naïve shock?

 Re: Searching the Web

You might want to offer students some direction on where to start researching the assignment. For example, they could start with the online archives of CNN or another news service. Alternatively, they may wish to begin in the archives of the *Washington Post* or *New York Times*. Part of this assignment requires them to assess the validity of the sources they find. Most English composition handbooks have materials on evaluating online sources, and increasingly college libraries are offering short courses and web sites on how to evaluate such materials.

The headnote about Nick Ut indicates that Kim Phuc eventually visited the Vietnam Veterans Memorial. More than any other monument in this country, the Vietnam Memorial has become a touchstone for the memories of a generation. Ask students to research the Memorial on the World Wide Web by assigning them one of the following topics: the controversy surrounding the design of the monument by Maya Lin, the rationale behind Lin's design, or the National Park Service catalogue of objects left at the Memorial. Students should then write an essay on the Memorial based on their research, using as their starting point Phuc's statement, "We cannot change history, but we should try to do good things for the present and for the future to promote peace" (p. 165).

Students can complete the Re: Searching the Web exercises online at www.seeingandwriting.com. Additional tips and links are also available.

Dorothy Allison, *This Is Our World*

GENERATING CLASS DISCUSSION AND IN-CLASS WRITING

Allison's work is structured around the rhetorical device of the fragment, which opens up the essay in thought-provoking ways. This structure encourages active participation from the reader, who is forced to draw connections between the sections of the essay.

However, it may also confuse students who are more comfortable with a standard presentation. To initially engage students, you may want to break the class into groups and assign each one a fragment of the whole essay. Ask them to answer basic questions: What is Allison's point in this section? How does she support it? What figurative language does she use? Then bring the class back together to discuss the work as a whole. Ask students to identify recurrent themes or ideas that have appeared in the groups' analyses of the different fragments. Shortly after the essay's midpoint, Allison writes, "I think that using art to provoke uncertainty is what great writing and inspired images do most brilliantly. Art should provoke more questions than answers and, most of all, should make us think about what we rarely want to think about at all" (para. 35). You might ask students to discuss how the very structure of this essay forces a reader to think, to ask questions, and to feel less than certain about his or her conclusions.

The narrative elements in Allison's essay share a common thread in that they are forcing us to look at life as an ongoing testament to the power of art. Allison's childhood memory of her fascination with the overly beautiful image of Jesus and its ability to calm her with "genuine sympathy" meets its mirror in the ability of her own writing to comfort its readers with her truth (paras. 37–38). Her friend Jackie, the painter, holds the same "'bit of magic'" (para. 27) that Allison accords to the painter of Jesus. Actions and works—even simple ads—that we might think of as commonplace are true art to Allison. They hold the power to lay bare "our emotional and intellectual lives" (para. 39). The power of art is to sustain and reveal our lives or—in the language of this chapter—to capture our most memorable moments.

In leading students through the essay, you might want to ask them to focus on Allison's vocabulary. They could construct a glossary of the terms she uses to discuss "art" and draw from these terms a working definition for art as Allison sees it. You might also have students consider why Allison so often links art with children. In some ways she is deploying a standard cultural association: Children are innocent and pure. She uses this association to bolster her definition of art as a place of "revelation" and "personal truth." Ask students to consider their own definition of art in relation to Allison's.

ADDITIONAL WRITING TOPICS

1. Ask students to write a short in-class piece in which they respond to Allison's contention that art holds a "'bit of magic.'"

2. Have students write an essay in which they delineate Allison's definition of art and then apply it to a nontraditional type of art. They might select one that Allison mentions—murals, ads, folk art—or choose one of their own. The key is that they cannot choose a traditional, recognized "high" art form.

3. Allison writes, "Sometimes, I imagine my own life as a series of snapshots taken by some omniscient artist who is just keeping track—not interfering or saying anything, just capturing the moment for me to look back at it again later" (para. 16). Ask students to buy a disposable camera and document their lives for one day, taking at least twenty-four pictures (one for each hour of the day). Then have them construct a visual essay of that day on the basis of their photos, writing a fragment for each one and modeling the fragments on Allison's structure of the shared theme.

CONNECTIONS WITH OTHER TEXTS

1. You might ask students to consider the images and texts from this chapter and how they apply to Allison's criteria of art: "Art should provoke more questions than answers and, most of all, should make us think about what we rarely want to think about at all" (para. 35).

2. Allison writes that she believes in "the nobility of the despised, the dignity of the outcast, the intrinsic honor among misfits" (para. 37). Ask students to look back at Pepón Osario's *Badge of Honor* (p. 90) in relation to this observation and to Allison's contention that artists have a special perspective that is not shared by the "sheltered and indifferent population" (para. 37).

SUGGESTIONS FOR FURTHER READING, THINKING, AND WRITING

 web
Links for the selections in this chapter can be found at www.seeingandwriting.com.

audio/visual
Bastard Out of Carolina. Directed by Anjelica Huston. BMG Video, 1997. Rated R. Performers include Jennifer Jason Leigh, Ron Eldard, Glenne Headley, Lyle Lovett, Christina Ricci, Michael Rooker, Grace Zabriskie, Diana Scarwid, and Susan Taylor.

Dorothy Allison. 23 March 1998. Recording. Distributed by WHYY, Philadelphia. Terry Gross, host of National Public Radio's *Fresh Air,* interviews Allison about *Bastard Out of Carolina* and her other books.

Visualizing Composition: Structure

The photographs of the river and the train rails invite students to observe how they reveal a similar pattern. The text's discussion of *pattern* introduces students to the similar term *structure* and how it is used in the arts and sciences. You should have students read the text before you focus on the topic of essay structure. After students finish reading, direct them to the sentences that involve essay structure, concluding with the following line: "In an essay, structure can usually be mapped by following the organizing pattern of topics that the writer presents" (para. 4).

You can use this line as the springboard for a discussion on how vital organization is in writing essays. You should note how outlines can assist students in planning their essays, but be sure to encourage students to find their own methods of organization and to be willing to change the essay's pattern when necessary. Many students resist using outlines because they often feel bound to follow their first outline or because they're intimidated by the formal examples sometimes used in grammar handbooks.

If students have had difficulty following some of the readings in the text, you might divide the class into groups to write outlines for those readings. Because they recently read Barry Lopez's "Learning to See," you might suggest that essay. Direct them to begin by noting each paragraph's subject in the margins or on a separate piece of paper. As they make notes for each paragraph, they should notice that paragraphs can also be grouped together by subject.

If you have noticed haphazard organization in your students' essays, you can have them perform a similar exercise with their own essays. In the previous class session, ask each student to bring an essay to class on the day this reading will be covered. Since many students have difficulty with critically reading their own work, have them exchange essays, make marginal notes for each paragraph, and group the paragraphs together by subject. While many essays might contain one subject per paragraph, most essays will probably not link the paragraphs together in an effective order. By the end of the exercise, the students should recognize the pattern—or lack thereof—in their writing.

Alternatively, you might ask students to use a word processor to randomly rearrange the paragraphs in their essays by cutting each paragraph and pasting it in a different place. They could then print their essays for class and exchange them with other students. By observing transitional clues, which may or may not be there, each student figures out the essay's organization and numbers each paragraph to reflect its original order. If you happen to be in a computer classroom, ask students to bring an essay on disk, so they can use a word processor to disassemble and reassemble each other's writing.

If students have had difficulty analyzing images, you could practice finding patterns with the class. You might start with images they've already come across in the text. For instance, you could direct them to Tina Barney's photograph from the previous chapter's Looking Closer section (pp. 201–17). Ask them to consider how Barney uses color to tie the photograph together and to draw the reader's eye through the photo. You could also have them examine how the horizon structures Richard Misrach's photographs (pp. 176–80).

ADDITIONAL WRITING TOPICS

1. Don DeLillo's "In the Ruins of the Future" is separated into sections. Ask students to analyze each section of the essay and to explain how each one operates as a part of the whole.

2. Have students write a brief analysis of the structure of an essay they previously wrote for class. Tell them to pay particular attention to paragraph order and transitions.

CONNECTIONS WITH OTHER TEXTS

1. Sherman Alexie's essay is easy to follow because of its effective transitions and unified paragraphs. You might photocopy the essay, cut apart each paragraph, and put students in groups to reassemble the essay on the basis of its transitions. Or, if a scanner is available, you could scan the essay and disassemble it before you print it out.

2. Ron Hansen's short story "Nebraska" (p. 171) is difficult to understand until readers grasp how the passage of time creates the story's structure. You might ask students to reread the story and write an essay that explains how its structure is vital to reading the story and understanding its purpose.

PORTFOLIO: **Andrew Savulich**

GENERATING CLASS DISCUSSION AND IN-CLASS WRITING

This series of photographs represents moments of "'spot news'—spontaneous photographs of the violence and accidents, the humorous and odd events of everyday life, especially in urban areas" (p. 267). You might ask students to begin by discussing what constitutes "news" in our culture. As they begin to read these photos as news, what kinds of inferences can they draw about the nature of the news that is being presented? For example, each of these photographs is concerned with some kind of violent or life-threatening event. Is that what makes them a type of news? Ask students if they recognize the people in the photos. Does celebrity have anything to do with news in these photographs?

Have students make a series of observations that culminate in a short definition essay about the composition of these photos and what is—and what is not—news-like about them. For example, you might suggest that the black and white format itself is generally coded for "documentary" and therefore suggests "real." Also, the apparent spontaneity of the photographs seems to support the idea that these are unposed and, therefore, contain the "truth" of the instant in which the picture was snapped. In short, what do the photos suggest about our ability to read certain types of images in certain ways, often without consciously acknowledging the aspects of the image that lead us to stereotype it before we even analyze the content? (The events depicted are potentially violent, the photos have a grimy urban feel, they are shot at night, they are in black and white—they look like newspaper photos; they therefore promise truth or objectivity.) None of the photos, however, features political figures, such as JFK, or political situations, such as the Vietnam War. Each one seems to be about the private plight of an individual in an extraordinary situation. Is this today's idea of news, or would we want to argue that these photographs are art, although using a news-like approach? Ask students to write an in-class paragraph (to practice their skills at making concrete observation and writing concrete details) that depicts a black and white snapshot moment in their own lives.

ADDITIONAL WRITING TOPICS

1. In order to continue developing your students' awareness of the relationship between seeing and writing, ask them to write a short piece in which they discuss the visual elements that construct a meaning for each of these photos. Which photos would work without a caption?

After the students have written entirely different captions for each of the photographs in the series, ask them to analyze the particular visual elements that prompted their new captions.

2. Ask students to write an essay that compares and contrasts two of Savulich's photos with two color photographs from the web that also depict "spot news" moments. Students should also consider the importance of the captions in their essay.

CONNECTIONS WITH OTHER TEXTS

1. Students' readings of these pictures are influenced by each photograph's text. Refer students to other news photographs from the chapter—by Witty, Mermelstein, Rosenthal, Nachtwey—and ask them to generate a number of captions for each picture and consider how those captions might change their perceptions of the events.

2. People have a passion to collect memorable moments by capturing an image of those moments. Ask students to classify the kinds of memorable moments that are regarded as significant in the many images in this chapter and to define the characteristics of each one represented here—private versus public, celebrity versus anonymous, political versus apolitical, historical versus ahistorical, and so on.

SUGGESTIONS FOR FURTHER READING, THINKING, AND WRITING

 web

Links for the selections in this chapter can be found at www.seeingandwriting.com.

audio/visual

The Killing Screens: Media and the Culture of Violence. 1 cassette (41 min.). 1994. VHS videocassette. Distributed by Media Education Foundation.

Talking Pictures

Ask students to spend some time watching and analyzing the types of television shows that reflect Savulich's fascination with capturing images of urban violence. What shows deal with urban street violence? Are they staged or are they "real"? What happens to the promise that documentary "tells the truth" when the events in these shows are re-created, cast, and scripted yet presented as if they were "happening now"?

James Nachtwey, *Ground Zero*

In this essay, Nachtwey relates his experiences of seeing the twin towers burn and crumble, of avoiding the falling debris from the second tower, and of taking pictures of the aftermath at ground zero. A good point of discussion in this essay involves the subject of visible versus invisible suffering. You might begin discussion by asking students to examine Nachtwey's photo and discussing the thoughts and emotions it elicits.

Nachtwey's unaffected tone—particularly in the first few paragraphs—might surprise some students. As he recounts his first reaction to the tragedy, he does not describe feelings of dread or loss; instead, he matter-of-factly states: "When I saw the towers burning, my first reaction was to take a camera, to load it with film, go up on my roof, where I had a clear view, and photograph the first tower burning" (para. 2). It might be important to point out that his lack of emotion here is not due to a lack of empathy. As he explains, in a situation like this his actions are based upon instinct: "Documenting a crisis situation that's clearly out of control is always very instinctual. There's no road map. No ground rules. It's all improvisations" (para. 4). Later in the essay, he explains how his long experience documenting war zones played a part in his surviving and working by instinct: "I don't fold up in these situations. I've been in them enough times to somehow have developed the capacity to continue to do my job" (para. 7).

His instincts led him to the site of the fallen tower, which "seemed like a movie set from a science-fiction film" (para. 4). Many viewers of televised images of the planes striking the towers said that they looked like scenes from a movie. However, Nachtwey had a live perspective and still compares the scene to something made by Hollywood.

You might ask students to look at the "Crushed Car" photograph taken by Nachtwey and compare it to his description of the area: "Very apocalyptic—sunlight filtering through the dust and the destroyed wreckage of the buildings lying in the street" (para. 4). Do students see how this picture could resemble the set of a science fiction movie?

Nachtwey often compares his experiences at the World Trade Center to his experiences in war zones. The level of danger was familiar enough to cause Nachtwey to act instinctually (para. 7). However, this experience was different because the falling towers were the only danger: "It wasn't as if people were shooting at us or we were being shelled or there were [landmines] there" (para. 12). Another element that made this experience different was that the "frontline troops" were firemen, and their job wasn't to kill people, but to save them (para. 13).

Probably the most important difference between this event and his war-time experience involves the aspect of visible suffering. Nachtwey hasn't been able to fully process this experience because of its lack of visible suffering. As he states, "I didn't witness people suffering, because they were invisible. I didn't feel it as strongly as when I witnessed people starving to death or when I've seen innocent people cut down by sniper fire" (para. 15). Students might claim that to see two towers burn and crumble is to witness visible suffering. However, students most likely have not had Nachtwey's experiences of seeing death up close. You might ask students to recall their own first experience with the events of September 11. Was their first experience visual or aural?

If some students first heard about the event and later saw images, ask them which had a stronger effect. If students found the images to have more of an impact, ask why they think this is so. Are visual images naturally more powerful than other stimuli? Or have we been conditioned by an increasingly visual culture? If students doubt the power of visual images, ask how often they think about the Pentagon or Flight 93 (which crashed into the ground in Pennsylvania) when they think of September 11. The images of these events only presented the aftermath of each and were not shown as often as those involving the twin towers.

If this discussion is hampered by students' being understandably too close to the subject, you might suggest that they examine past events in similar terms. Have them think about the most tragic events in history. (Avoid naming a specific branch of history, such as American, European, or world.) Ask them to list the first few events that come to mind. Most likely, the Holocaust will be near the top of the list. Some students might focus on American history, which will lead to most of the following being named: the bombing of Pearl Harbor, the assassinations of John F. Kennedy and Martin Luther King Jr., the Vietnam War, the explosion of the space shuttle *Challenger*, and the recent spate of school shootings. Of course, others will be listed, but most—if not all—will have connections with visual images. As students list events, think about possible visual connections, particularly those made through film (*Pearl Harbor; Schindler's List; Platoon; Saving Private Ryan; JFK*). Although these events are certainly tragic, many others are often overlooked because they do not have strong visual ties. For example, many students will think of the Holocaust because of *Schindler's List*. Fewer students will think of slavery in America, and even fewer will think of the treatment of Native Americans.

ADDITIONAL WRITING TOPICS

1. This essay raises an interesting issue regarding the importance of vision in how we mentally and emotionally process events. As Nachtwey states, "I didn't witness people suffering, because they were invisible. I didn't feel it as strongly as when I witnessed people starving to death or when I've seen innocent people cut down by sniper fire" (para. 15). Ask students to write an argument essay in which they take a position on whether visible suffering has more of an emotional impact than invisible suffering.

2. Using Nachtwey's quotation from item 1, ask students to write an expository essay on why vision is—or has become—vital in mentally and emotionally processing events. You could suggest that students research aural cultures and the blind for more insight.

3. In his essay Nachtwey states, "There is power in the still image that doesn't exist in other forms" (para. 17). Ask students to write an essay that compares and contrasts still images (photographs) with moving images (film). Do they agree or disagree with Nachtwey's assertion?

CONNECTIONS WITH OTHER TEXTS

1. Regarding the reality of September 11, Don DeLillo states, "It was bright and totalizing, and some of us said it was unreal. When we say a thing is unreal, we mean it is too real, a phenomenon so unaccountable and yet so bound to the power of objective fact that we can't tilt it to the slant of our perceptions" (para. 67). Many observers of the televised footage noted how it seemed like something out of a film. Nachtwey notes that the site of the fallen tower "seemed like a movie set from a science-fiction film" (para. 4). Have students consider whether we turn to film because we cannot, as DeLillo states, fit the event into our perceptions.

2. Nachtwey states that photographers need to document tragedies with "compassion and in a compelling way" (para. 19). Ask students to look at Joel Sternfeld's photograph of the parking lot at Kent State (pp. 186–87), which years earlier had been the site of a national tragedy. To what extent do your students think that Sternfeld's photograph fits Nachtwey's criteria?

SUGGESTIONS FOR FURTHER READING, THINKING, AND WRITING

print

Nachtwey, James. *Inferno*. London: Phaidon Press, 2000.

(www.) *web*

www.digitaljournalist.org/issue0110/interviews
_intro.htm   The Digital Journalist web site

features video interviews with several September 11 photographers, including Nachtwey.
www.johnpaulcaponigro.com/dialogs/dialogs_n-z/james_nachtwey.html   Interview with Nachtwey regarding his views on journalistic and collective responsibility.
www.pbs.org/newshour/gergen/jan-june00/nachtwey_5-16.html   Interview with Nachtwey regarding his book *Inferno*.
www.september11news.com/AttackImages.htm   A large resource that features, among other things, timelines, international and U.S. news web archives, international and U.S.

magazine covers, and images of the attack and the aftermath (the latter category contains four pictures by Nachtwey).
www.time.com/time/photoessays/shattered/ *Time's* exclusive collection of Nachtwey's September 11 photographs.
Links for the selections in this chapter can be found at www.seeingandwriting.com.

audio/visual

Ground Zero America: First Response. 50 min. 2002. Videocassete. Distributed by The History Channel.

Don DeLillo, *In the Ruins of the Future*

GENERATING CLASS DISCUSSION AND IN-CLASS WRITING

In this sorrowful essay, DeLillo attempts to understand the causes and effects of the terrorist attacks on September 11. He sees this event as a meeting of the past and the future. America represents the future through its technology; the terrorists represent the past. DeLillo breaks his essay into eight sections, each covering a different subject related to September 11. Much of the essay focuses on the effects of the attacks. You might begin class discussion with the effects of this tragedy. Early in the essay DeLillo states, "This catastrophic event changes the way we think and act, moment to moment, week to week, for unknown weeks and months to come, and steely years" (para. 3).

Ask students how much their lives have changed as a result of this event. Some students' relatives or friends might be among those who died—or those who survived; some students may have witnessed the event in person. Others, though, may not have experienced such dramatic upheavals. If students state that they no longer take their lives for granted or that they appreciate each moment life has to offer, you might ask for specific examples of how their lives were before and after the attacks. Such responses are typical—and often exaggerated—when a tragic issue is raised. Although many students might have experienced life changes in the weeks and months following September 11—and the subsequent anthrax scares—most students' lives have probably returned to a sense of normalcy. If this seems to be the case, an interesting question is raised: How can people resume normal lives after such an event?

You might then direct the discussion toward the causes of the attacks. Ask students why they think we were attacked. Most will probably list reasons similar to those offered by DeLillo—the terrorists hate our modern culture and our status as a superpower. According to DeLillo, the terrorists want to stop the future and "bring back the past" (para. 5). He explains the causes of the attacks in a general way. He states that the terrorists did not target the global economy in their attacks on the Pentagon and the World Trade Center. Instead, America itself "drew their fury" through our technology, our modernity, our pervasive culture, as well as the "blunt force of our foreign policy" (para. 2). Ask students whether these explanations seem satisfying.

In the second section of his essay, DeLillo compares the closed world of the terrorist to the open world of the Americans, and he explains how the terrorist's separate way of life gives him an edge. As DeLillo states, "Plots reduce the world. He builds a plot around his anger and our indifference. He lives a certain kind of apartness, hard and tight" (para. 7). This way of life allows the terrorist to see Americans not as human beings, but as objects of "judgment and devastation" (para. 7). Ask students if they can think of other times in history in which mistreatment and murder were rationalized by others being viewed as less than human. Students are likely to name the Holocaust, slavery, and the treatment of Native Americans. Some students might even note that some Americans responded to the September 11 attacks by violently lashing out at Muslims. How do people learn to make such judgments?

DeLillo uses the terms *narrative* and *counter-narrative* several times throughout the essay. These references are likely to confuse students because they are never clearly defined. DeLillo introduces the term *narrative* early in the essay, ascribing it to the actions of the terrorists: "Today, again, the world narrative belongs to terrorists" (para. 2). He introduces *counter-narratives* in the third section of the essay: "The narrative ends in the rubble, and it is left to us to create the counter-narrative" (para. 13). Some students might have the following interpretation: The terrorists' actions have caused the destruction at ground zero, and we have a duty to respond to those actions (presumably with violence). Another reading—and this seems more plausible—is that the counter-narratives are the stories that have come out of the terrorists' narrative.

DeLillo tells a number of stories in the essay's third section and devotes all of the fourth section to a story involving his nephew. As he states, "There are a hundred thousand stories crisscrossing New York, Washington, and the world. Where we were, whom we know, what we've seen or heard" (para. 14). These are the counter-narratives, a fact that becomes clearer when he repeats a phrase—"left to us"—from his first reference to counter-narratives: "People running for their lives are part of the story that is left to us" (para. 15). These stories don't have to be true, though. As he notes, false memories and the rumors spread on the Internet also make counter-narratives (paras. 22–23). These counter-narratives have a use in our reaction; they help us in our attempts to gain some perspective on this unimaginable event: "We need them . . . to set against the massive spectacle that continues to seem unmanageable, too powerful a thing to set into our frame of practiced response" (para. 25).

A theme that unifies DeLillo's essay involves the past and the future—the terrorists' religious beliefs and America's technology, respectively. The terrorists fear the future represented by America's technology: "It brings death to their customs and beliefs" (para. 65). DeLillo observes that we make our own future through technology, not through God or miracles. Through the terrorists' actions, "the future has yielded, for now, to medieval expedience, to the old slow furies of cutthroat religion" (para. 55). DeLillo represents the fall of the towers as the reversal of the future: "there was the huge antenna falling out of the sky, straight down, blunt end first, like an arrow moving backward in time" (para. 67).

DeLillo believes that the event has affected our sense of time: "We seem pressed for time, all of us. Time is scarcer now. There is a sense of compression, plans made hurriedly, time forced and distorted" (para. 68). This distortion results from our hope being taken from the future. As DeLillo states, the psychological effect of witnessing so much death has influenced us all: "We are all breathing the fumes of lower Manhattan, where traces of the dead are everywhere, in the soft breeze off the river, on rooftops and windows, in our hair and on our clothes" (para. 73).

ADDITIONAL WRITING TOPICS

1. DeLillo states that the terrorists were able to kill because their "righteous fever" (para. 9) made them not see the "humanity and vulnerability" (para. 8) in Americans. Ask students to write a short essay that considers the possibility that the "righteous fever" did allow them to see such qualities. What other explanations can students offer?

2. In several instances, DeLillo implies that America was targeted largely because of its technology (paras. 63, 57). In paragraph 58 he clearly states: "They want what they used to have before the waves of Western influence." What evidence does DeLillo provide for these claims? Ask students to research other possible explanations. This research could be the basis of an argument essay in which students offer different explanations and take a position on which one seems most likely.

3. Ask students to elaborate on DeLillo's notion of the Internet as a counter-narrative. For in-stance, some web sites show pictures and make claims about people seeing the Devil's face in the smoke pouring from the struck towers. (How they know what the Devil's face looks like is a question in itself.) A photograph was spread over the Internet that was claimed to have been taken on top of Tower 1, showing a plane heading toward the building. Students could research these false stories and other instances of mysticism that surround the event and write an essay that analyzes these counter-narratives and offers an explanation as to why some people need or want to believe in them.

CONNECTIONS WITH OTHER TEXTS

1. Ask students to reread some of DeLillo's more touching, sorrowful statements. Then direct them to Mermelstein's haunting photo of the aftermath. Which evokes more feeling in your students? Have them consider each composition as a whole. If some students feel that DeLillo's touching statements were lost due to the essay's length, then point out that Mermelstein's photograph could have lost some of its edge had it been taken from a different angle.

2. Time and tragedy link DeLillo's essay and Sternfeld's photograph (pp. 186–87). Time is an important theme that runs throughout DeLillo's essay. Sternfeld photographed Kent State's Taylor Hall parking lot years after the fatal shootings there. Ask students whether they think Sternfeld waited too long in taking the picture. Did DeLillo not wait long enough?

SUGGESTIONS FOR FURTHER READING, THINKING, AND WRITING

print

Armstrong, Karen. *Islam: A Short History*. New York: Modern Library, 2000.

Bergen, Peter. *Holy War, Inc.: Inside the Secret War of Osama bin Laden*. New York: Free Press, 2001.

Carr, Caleb. *The Lessons of Terror*. New York: Random House, 2002.

DeLillo, Don. *The Body Artist*. New York: Scribner, 2001.

———. *Underworld*. New York: Scribner, 1997.

———. *White Noise*. New York: Viking, 1985.

www.9-11-2001.org/ A memorial site for the victims of September 11.

www.counterpunch.org/wtclinks.html This web site for the political newsletter *Counterpunch* features numerous Internet links on September 11 and the war in Afghanistan. A good source for students wanting to see both American and nonAmerican viewpoints.

www.perival.com/delillo/delillo.html A DeLillo web site created by a fan in 1996. Probably the most comprehensive DeLillo web site on the Internet.

www.september11news.com A large resource that features, among other things, timelines, international and U.S. news web archives, international and U.S. magazine covers, images, and "mysterious coincidences" (what DeLillo would call false counter-narratives). Links for the selections in this chapter can be found at www.seeingandwriting.com.

audio/visual

Biography: Osama bin Laden: In the Name of Allah. 50 min. 2002. VHS videocassette. Distributed by A&E Home Video.

Investigative Reports: Portrait of a Terrorist: Mohammed Atta. 50 min. 2002. VHS videocassette. Distributed by A&E Home Video. Provides background on the terrorist who flew the first jet into the World Trade Center.

Looking Closer:
Taking Pictures

GENERATING CLASS DISCUSSION AND IN-CLASS WRITING

These visual and verbal texts display how cameras are not only practical tools for the capturing of moments, but also artistic implements that make us look at the world differently. Some of these texts urge us to take pictures and to be taken in by them. Others warn us to not rely too heavily on photographic images.

Shizuka Yokomizo, *Strangers*

Even though Yokomizo asked these individuals for permission to photograph them through a window in their home, her pictures raise issues of privacy. You might ask students how the people seem to react in these pictures. What does their body language suggest? Students might point to the girl's crossed arms as a sign of discomfort. The young man's face is difficult to read: Does it show disinterest or contempt? In the picture obscured by the screen, the girl's reaction cannot be seen, but she clearly has the most relaxed pose. You might ask students why these strangers would agree to be photographed in this way. Would any of your students pose for Yokomizo?

N. Scott Momaday, *The Photograph*

Momaday's narrative piece, like Canin's, cautions us about relying too much on the photographic image. He describes the disillusionment of an old Navajo crone who inhabited the beautifully described landscape of the Navajo reservation, "so remote as to be almost legendary in the mind" (para. 7). The old woman wanted to have Momaday's father take her picture, yet when she saw the photograph she was disturbed and would have nothing to do with it. Momaday theorizes that in this remote place she had probably never seen her image before and that the photograph "was a far cry from what she imagined herself to be" (para. 8). Thus, we must not rely too heavily on the photographic apparatus to bring us true visions of ourselves, Momaday suggests. He says, "in its dim, mechanical eye it had failed to see into her real being" (para. 8).

Susan Sontag, *On Photography*

Sontag's essay begins with the family and then moves to a broader look at the role of the photograph in our culture. In the beginning, she mentions how "each family constructs a portrait-chronicle of itself—a portable kit of images that bears witness to its connectedness" (para. 3). That is, photographs are the witnesses; they provide evidence that there was a family event (e.g., a vacation, graduation, wedding, or reunion) and that *we were there*. Sontag goes further, however, when she says that a photograph is more than "an encounter between an event and a photographer" (para. 8). She suggests that taking photographs has begun to take on "peremptory rights—to interfere with, to invade, or to ignore whatever is going on" (para. 8).

Duane Hanson, *Tourists*

Hanson's life-sized sculptures of human figures show us another way in which we demonstrate our passion to examine ourselves and the American experience. These are not idealized images of our culture. Instead, like Greenfield's photographs, Hanson's sculpture offers a criticism of the image of the American traveler. The figures—the man clothed in a palm tree shirt, undignified bermudas, and rubber sandals, with a camera and binoculars strapped around his neck; and the woman in black and white beads, fussy hair cover, big sunglasses, tacky clothes—offer a familiar and colorful (yet disquieting) stereotype of the "ugly" American tourist couple.

Martin Parr, *Kalkan, Turkey*

In this photograph we are given another vision of the tourist—this time, in search of an image to take home to prove he has been to Turkey on vacation. Like Hanson's tourist, this man is clothed in childish shorts and encumbered by a camera strapped around his neck and even held up before his eyes. In this vision of the tourist, he is unable to see what is around him—he can only see through the lens of his camera. He seems oblivious to the man walking beside him, to the mule he is riding, and to the landscape he is traversing. He is focused on getting the shot of Turkey, not being in Turkey.

Ethan Canin, *Viewfinder*

Canin's brief written piece demonstrates a different way in which a photograph can be an icon of family life. In this case the feeling elicited by the photograph is genuine, but the image itself does not correspond to the memory Canin associates with it. The photo is supposedly a snapshot that he treasures of his mother, whom he feels he remembers clearly. Yet he later discovers that his memory of the event and the objects the photograph captured were faulty. In this photo the blankets he remembers so clearly are not blankets, and the woman he recalls so fondly is not his mother—it is his grandmother! Thus, the emotion summoned by the memory the photo evokes is real, but the representation of it is not.

Kodak, *Keep the Story with a KODAK*

This old-fashioned magazine advertisement (April 1923) indicates that Kodak was fully cognizant of the role that photography could, and would, play in the life of the family. The image of the grandmother reading to her grandchildren illustrates how to "keep the story" and provides a nostalgic vision of the family's generations and harmony. This advertisement bears out Sontag's assertion that "cameras go with family life" (para. 2).

Kodak, *Share Moments. Share Life*

This ad for the Kodak Picture Maker shows a small picture of two women—most likely daughter and mother—sitting on a patio swing. You might ask students to carefully examine the ad for overstated language and its intended audience. The three checked boxes to the right of the picture suggest not only how simply the Picture Maker can be operated, but also how easily moments can be "shared forever." The text below the enlarged picture refers to pictures as "gifts"; the tagline "Share Moments. Share Life" equates the sharing of pictures with the sharing of life. Some students might notice that women are featured prominently in each Kodak ad. How might Kodak think its appeal to "share life" will be more effective with women than with men?

ADDITIONAL WRITING TOPICS

1. Students could research the portrayal of women in Kodak ads. They should analyze a group of ads that cover at least two decades (or that include some of the oldest and newest ads) and explain how Kodak uses women to sell cameras. Students should also be alert for and explain portrayal changes in the ads that reflect social changes.

2. Invite students to research the history of photography. How did people initially view it? How has it changed over time? Based on this research, ask students to write an essay that compares and contrasts early and modern perceptions of photography.

CONNECTIONS WITH OTHER TEXTS

1. Shizuka Yokomizo and Peter Rostovsky (pp. 325–27) received permission from their subjects. Rostovsky based his portraits on written descriptions, whereas Yokomizo took photographs through windows in the dark of night. Which artist would your students feel more comfortable working with? Which experiment do they think turned out more artistically interesting?

2. Ask students to consider Susan Sontag's assertion that "photographing is essentially an act of non-intervention" (para. 9). Ask them to imagine the role of the photographer in Mark Peterson's photograph, *Image of Homelessness,* in Chapter 2 (p. 155). What are the ethics involved with taking such a picture?

SUGGESTIONS FOR FURTHER READING, THINKING, AND WRITING

print

West, Nancy Martha. *Kodak and the Lens of Nostalgia.* Charlottesville: University of Virginia Press, 2000.

www. *web*

www.photoarts.com/gallery/kodak/ This web site's images of Kodak ads date from 1900 to 1926 and cover six categories: travel and leisure, women, Christmas, family, outdoors, and packaging.

www.kodakgirl.com/kodakgirlsframe.htm This impressive site maintained by Martha Cooper contains images of Kodak ads—all featuring women—that date back to 1890.

Links for the selections in this chapter can be found at www.seeingandwriting.com.

Chapter 4

Embodying Identity

Introduction

GENERATING CLASS DISCUSSION AND IN-CLASS WRITING

You might want to start discussion by asking students to consider the two different kinds of bodies discussed in the chapter introduction: public and private. Make sure they understand what it means to say that the public body is the one created by consumer culture, the body "on billboards . . . on computer and TV screens, on the pages of magazines and newspapers, in museums, galleries, and libraries" (p. 304). How else does this culturally created body become part of public discourse? How often—and in what sources—do students encounter images of the body in their everyday activities? They probably see these figures so often that they cease to think of them as actual physical constructions.

In part, this occurs because these types of bodies are often not real. When artists and writers "reimagine" the body, and scientists and engineers design it, the public body becomes an artistic and a "social construction" (p. 308). You might ask students to consider the ways in which a body can be socially constructed: through culture, through media, and so on. They could bring in specific socially constructed images of the body to illustrate this concept.

The chapter introduction describes the private body as "something to be controlled and yet beyond control" (p. 305). Ask students whether they agree. Some students may be uncomfortable discussing their personal feelings about their private bodies, and it may help to keep the discussion general. How does our society view those who are physically different? How important is the discrepancy between our physical "real" body and the often idealized "public" body? What do trends like eating disorders, steroid addictions, piercings, and tattoos say about the way our public and private bodies are being constructed? You could also concentrate on the notion of "body language" addressed in the text and explore how this type of language creates meaning and may even have a grammar and syntax all its own—one that includes the public and private bodies.

 For additional resources for the selections in this chapter (including exercises and annotated links), go to www.seeingandwriting.com.

Mario Testino, *Doubles, Lima,* and *Shalom and Linda, Paris*

GENERATING CLASS DISCUSSION AND IN-CLASS WRITING

Because students will read these images in the context of the introduction, they may initially focus on the relative size of the bodies represented. The rotund shapes of the men from Lima are contrasted with the stick figures of the models from Paris. You might ask students to consider how the photos emphasize this difference. For example, the men's bellies are exposed, and their postures make their stomachs appear to thrust at the camera. The women are in sleek black wraps that cinch in at their waists. The robes also form deep V-shapes that normally would reveal cleavage but do not in this case. The men are exposing the flesh they have in abundance; the women are hiding the flesh they do not.

Make sure that students move beyond the issue of body size and concentrate on body language. Both photos seem to capture real joy. Shalom Harlow's broad, open-mouthed smile is the same as those on the men's faces. Linda Evangelista's arm position is much like that of the man on the left in the photo—open and exuberant. The context of both photos (the men in beach trunks, the women in backstage wraps and wig caps) seems to indicate candid shots. To a viewer, neither shot seems overly posed. You might ask students to think about both photos in the context of Patrick Kinmouth's comment: "'[In his book, Testino's] role is immediately to trap [the image] as it flashes by'" (p. 309).

ADDITIONAL WRITING TOPICS

1. Ask students which photo appeals to them more. They should write a brief in-class piece explaining why, being very specific about elements of the photo's content and style that capture their attention.

2. The chapter introduction instructs students to think about the body "as a locus for expressing ourselves and fashioning an identity" (p. 308). Ask students to write an essay that explains how each of the images "fashions an identity" for the bodies represented within it.

3. One element revealed in these contrasting images is the fact that body image differs across cultures. Have students research the differences in body images in at least two different cultures—neither of which can be American. You might cluster students in groups so that their research can be more extensive. Then, ask them to write individual essays based on their findings.

CONNECTIONS WITH OTHER TEXTS

1. You might put students into groups and assign a different image from the chapter for each group to analyze. If a group ends up with an image of a man, that image should be compared to Testino's *Doubles, Lima* photograph; a group assigned an image of a woman will compare it to *Shalom and Linda, Paris*. As the groups consider these images, they should focus upon both body language and size. One person in each group should take notes about the group's discussion, which will then be presented to the class for larger discussion.

2. You might ask students to compare the second photo, *Shalom and Linda, Paris*, with Lauren Greenfield's photo in Chapter 3, *Ashleigh, 13, with Her Friend and Parents, Santa Monica* (pp. 254–55). Students could write an essay on the public bodies constructed in both images. What ideal of beauty is being expressed?

SUGGESTIONS FOR FURTHER READING, THINKING, AND WRITING

print

Testino, Mario. *Any Objections.* New York: Phaidon Press, 1998. Contains previously unpublished photographs of fashion models and ordinary people.

Wolf, Naomi. *The Beauty Myth.* New York: William Morrow, 1991. A modern classic on cultural standards of beauty and their effects on women; fits well with the overall theme of the chapter.

web

www.monash.edu.au/health/pamphlets/ BodyImage/index.htm   This site from Monash University in Australia provides a "body image" self-test for both men and women.

Links for the selections in this chapter can be found at www.seeingandwriting.com.

PAIR: Jacinto Jesús Cardona, *Bato Con Khakis*
César A. Martinez, *Bato Con Khakis, 1982*

GENERATING CLASS DISCUSSION AND IN-CLASS WRITING

Martinez's painting is based upon Cardona's poem. You might keep this information from students until after they've examined the painting. As students examine Martinez's painting, ask them to comment on how the artist uses shape and color to create a personality. How does the figure's position also suggest character? Have students make a list of the character traits they find in the painting.

Then turn the discussion to Cardona's poem. Even though they won't know the meaning of *bato,* ask them to write a brief description of the character depicted in the poem. You should then have them read and discuss the Seeing questions, which define *bato* and lead the discussion back to Martinez's painting. If students cannot guess the meaning of *Spanglish,* you can tell them that it is what the word suggests: Spanish mixed with English (more specifically, untranslated or incorrect English terms).

As students compare Cardona's poem and Martinez's painting, ask them to look at the lists they made earlier. Do the character traits they saw in the poem match those seen in the painting? Have students discuss and possibly argue their interpretations of each piece.

Martinez's painting is made of indefinite outlines and scribbles of color, enhancing the figure's coolness as well as his insecurity. The jagged lines and scribbles reflect the desired carelessness of the poem's character: "looking limber in a blue vest, / laidback in my dark shades." The indefinite outlines show that he is too cool to be concerned with how he is represented, but the fact that they are not defined reflects the insecurity revealed in the third stanza: "Alas! I'm the bifocals kid; /cool bato I am not." The dark blues and purples represent the coolness of the "blue vest" and the "dark shades" seen in the poem. The figure is leaning back, hands in his pockets, showing that he is "laid-back" like the character in the poem.

ADDITIONAL WRITING TOPICS

1. Ask students to write an expository paper about the strategies used by Martinez to represent Cardona's poem.

2. You could reverse the second Writing topic in the student's reader. Students could write an argument essay in which they support or challenge the claim that Martinez's painting would be ineffective had it not been accompanied by Cardona's poem.

CONNECTIONS WITH OTHER TEXTS

1. Have students compare Martinez's interpretation of Cardona's poem to Rostovsky's interpretations of the descriptions he received from strangers. How different are the prose descriptions from poetry? Ask students to write a prose description of Martinez's painting.

2. Direct students to examine Chuck Close's *Self-Portrait* (p. 118) and write a poem that would serve as its description.

3. Ask students to write a short essay explaining which piece appeals to them more. Tell them to be specific as to why the other piece is not as appealing.

SUGGESTIONS FOR FURTHER READING, THINKING, AND WRITING

print

Cardona, Jacinto Jesús. *Pan Dulce*. San Antonio: Chili Verde Press, 1998.

Quirarte, Jacinto. *Mexican and Mexican American Art in the United States, 1920–1970*. Austin: University of Texas Press, 1973.

 web

www.saalm.org/martinez.html   San Antonio Art League Museum's announcement of Mar-

tinez as its Artist of the Year. Provides a brief profile and an image of his "Bato Rojo."

www.artarchives.si.edu/oralhist/martin97.htm Smithsonian Art Archives Institute interview with Martinez.

Links for the selections in this chapter can be found at www.seeingandwriting.com.

Judith Ortiz Cofer, *The Story of My Body*

GENERATING CLASS DISCUSSION AND IN-CLASS WRITING

Cofer's memoir begins with a quote from Victor Hernández Cruz, "Migration is the story of my body," that sets the tone for the piece. Her story reflects her ethnic heritage and the way in which her ethnicity is read differently as she moves from place to place. To open a discussion, you might direct students to consider how and why Cofer's skin color "changes" when she moves from Puerto Rico to the United States (para. 3). For example, she is "*blanca*, white" in Puerto Rico but becomes "'colored'" and "dirty" after her move to Paterson, New Jersey. The positive and negative values assigned to Cofer's body shift according to the ideal public body within the culture where she lives. In the United States, this ideal is symbolized by "Susie, the schoolteacher doll" (para. 5) with pure white skin and "fine gold hair" (para. 7). Cofer cannot possibly measure up to this ideal, no matter how much she scrubs. Her skin will never be "pink like [her] friend Charlene and her sister Kathy" and is instead read as "dirty brown" by the men in the grocery store (para. 6). This reading follows her throughout the essay, recurring in elementary school (where she will always fall third in the "pretty" hierarchy; para. 15) and later in high school (where she loses her date for the dance because his father "had seen how the spics lived. Like rats"; para. 17).

You might ask students to examine Cofer's essay for a sense of how the definition of beauty changes from culture to culture. Some of these changes might not be expected. The Latino standard for beauty is exemplified by Cofer's own mother: "long, curly black hair, and round curves in a compact frame" (para. 13). As a child, Cofer is rewarded for being "*bonita*" and learns the essence of beauty from her mother. She describes herself as being dressed up "like a doll" (para. 14); but as she grows older, she fits neither the Latino nor the American definition of beauty. She is judged too skinny by the Puerto Rican boys and is not white enough for the Americans.

Cofer's reaction is to drop out of the beauty game and opt for a self-definition of "'brain'" (para. 15). You might ask students to consider this reaction. Clearly, Cofer has thrived as an intellectual and an academic and ends her essay on a positive note, stressing that her "sense of self-worth" now comes from her "studies" and "writing" (para. 18). However, the tone of her essay and her ability to recall with such precise detail the definitions of beauty that excluded her suggest that there is some lingering pain attached to these memories.

You might ask students to consider the structure of Cofer's essay, specifically its division by headings—Skin, Color, Size, and Looks—and how these sections connect to each other and Cofer's overall purpose. Why does she use these headings? You could direct students to analyze how each heading comments on or reflects the information that follows. You might also divide the class into groups and assign each group one heading and its relationship to the essay as a whole. The groups could discuss the literal and figurative relationship between the head and the section; they could even select one sentence within each section that exemplifies the head and/or connects it to the others. For example, the condition of Cofer's "skin" as a result of her chicken pox leads to the statement "This was when I learned to be invisible" (para. 2), and the theme of invisibility repeats throughout the essay. For example, under the Looks heading, Cofer circles back to the Skin section, writing, "I was nearly devastated by what the chicken pox episode had done to my self-image . . . and I hid behind my long black hair and my books" (para. 15). The phrase "my books" moves the reader forward as Cofer's life heads toward a new self-definition.

ADDITIONAL WRITING TOPICS

1. Cofer ends with the statement, "My studies, later my writing, the respect of people who saw me as an individual person they cared about, these were the criteria for my sense of self-worth that I would concentrate on in my adult life" (para. 18). Ask students to write a short statement that explains their own criteria for establishing a sense of self-worth.

2. Cofer speaks at one point about "presentability" as a quality by which students at her school were judged (para. 15). Ask your class to flesh out a definition of "presentability" as defined within the essay. What is Cofer's attitude toward this quality?

3. Early in the essay Cofer writes, "I started out life as a pretty baby and learned to be a pretty girl from a pretty mother" (para. 2). Later she remembers, "My mother was proud of my looks, although I was a bit too thin. She could dress me up like a doll" (para. 14) and presents her mother as the living representation of Latino beauty (para. 13). Ask students to write an essay that analyzes how physical beauty and its consequences figure into Cofer's relationship with her mother.

CONNECTIONS WITH OTHER TEXTS

1. Cofer discusses how the concept of beauty varies among cultures. You might ask students to read Bruce Bower's essay "Average Attractions," which seems to offer evidence that beauty can be empirically defined and measured. Ask students to write an essay that supports their own view and responds to the essays by Cofer and Bower.

2. Both Cofer and Chang-rae Lee (in "Coming Home Again"; p. 205) offer memoirs that recount the difficulties of growing up as "other" in the United States. Ask students to write an essay in which they compare and contrast these writers' autobiographical works, paying close attention to the types of details and the tone of each.

print

Cofer, Judith Ortiz. *An Island Like You: Stories of the Barrio.* New York: Orchard Books, 1995.

Cofer, Judith Ortiz. *An Island Like You: Stories of the Barrio.* New York: Orchard Books, 1995.

(www) *web*

www.dive.woodstock.edu/~dcox/ohenry/cofer
.html   A Judith Ortiz Cofer page established

as part of an authors series by Montgomery College in Texas.

Links for the selections in this chapter can be found at www.seeingandwriting.com.

Shirin Neshat, *Grace under Duty, 1994*

GENERATING CLASS DISCUSSION AND IN-CLASS WRITING

Neshat's photograph presents a female Muslim touching her closed lips with her fingers. It's a subversive image in many respects. According to Islamic law, only a woman's hands and eyes are to be exposed. Most of the woman's face is obscured—seemingly in accord with Islamic law—yet her mouth is revealed and her eyes are hidden. The hands touching her lips might symbolize silence, and the Islamic writing on her fingers suggests the source of the silence. However, since the image seems to emphasize the power of Muslim women, the calligraphy could also suggest a voice against the imposed silence, the muted words spilling down her fingers. Neshat emphasizes the femininity and sensuality of Muslim women, which can be seen in the woman's touch of her full lips.

Ask students to examine the photograph and write notes about the details that stand out. Since the Seeing questions provide important information regarding Neshat, you should discuss them with the students in class. Before you discuss the Seeing questions, though, ask students their views of Muslim women. If they are familiar with the stereotypes being broken down by Neshat, from where did they learn them?

ADDITIONAL WRITING TOPICS

1. Ask students to do research on Muslim women. With their research as a guide, students could assume the role of a Muslim woman for a first-person narrative.

2. Ask students to write an expository essay about how this photograph suggests and then subverts the image of the subordinate Muslim woman. They should direct their essay to an audience unfamiliar with Neshat's photo and with Islamic law.

3. Neshat's images of powerful women are specific to her culture and the issues within it. Invite students to write a description of a photograph that would suggest and subvert the image of a subordinate woman from another culture.

CONNECTIONS WITH OTHER TEXTS

1. Ask students to examine Nikki S. Lee's photographs, which reveal Lee's ability to adopt the appearance of certain subcultures. Ask students to imagine what *The Muslim Women Project* might look like and to write a brief description. Do they still imagine the typical media portrayal of the powerless woman?

2. Neshat's picture subverts popular images of Muslim women. Chuck Close's *Self-Portrait* (p. 118) subverts self-portraits. Ask students to compare and contrast the ways in which each artist accomplishes this act of subversion.

SUGGESTIONS FOR FURTHER READING, THINKING, AND WRITING

print

Kahn, Shahnaz. *Muslim Women: Crafting a North American Identity*. Gainesville: University Press of Florida, 2002.

Neshat, Shirin. *Women of Allah*. Turino: Marco Noire Contemporary Art, 1997.

〔www.〕 *web*

www.alpertawards.org/archive/winner00/neshat.html   Includes brief profile of Neshat and list of exhibitions, awards, and publications. Neshat also comments on her own work and on how art has become more experimental due to technology.

www.filmmakermagazine.com/fall2001/reports/turbulent.html   *Filmmaker* magazine's web site features an essay on Shirin Neshat's film *Turbulent*.

www.gladstonegallery.com/neshat_01/sn01.html   The Gladstone Gallery includes production stills from Neshat's films.

www.iranian.com/Arts/Dec97/Neshat/index.html   *The Iranian* web site published by Jahanshah Javid features images from Neshat's *Women of Allah*.

Links for the selections in this chapter can be found at www.seeingandwriting.com.

The assignment asks students to consider "how identity is constructed and contested in virtual space. How do online environments help shape our sense of self?" (p. 324). You might help students generate ideas by discussing how virtual spaces are different from physical spaces, how virtual identities can be different from physical ones. When students meet other people on campus, they probably evaluate the looks of others as they worry about their own. Some students might identify with the feeling of being limited by how friends and family expect them to behave. Virtual reality can offer opportunities for people to break out of their usual roles.

You might suggest that students enter chat rooms, message boards, or visual chat environments under different identities, changing their user name and personality each time. Warn them not to treat the identity as a caricature; ask them to explore different personalities that interest them. They should consider not only how they felt assuming different identities, but how they ex-perienced the reactions of others to their different personalities.

For another assignment, you could suggest that students enter a chat room or a visual chat environment as a member of the opposite sex. Visual chat sites offer users the ability to create a visual alter ego (referred to as an "avatar"). Students can then write an essay that explains how this experience has affected their views on interactions between the sexes. Ask students to consider how members of the same and opposite sex treated them after their virtual sex change. They should include specific examples from their online experiences.

One limitation of such sites is that they are increasingly requiring users to pay. You might suggest that students use The Palace, www.thepalace.com, or find visual chat sites through a search engine.

Students can complete the Re: Searching the Web exercises online at www.seeingandwriting.com. Additional tips and links for each exercise is also available.

PORTFOLIO: **Peter Rostovsky**

GENERATING CLASS DISCUSSION AND IN-CLASS WRITING

Rostovsky's paintings play with the notions of how portraits are made and how realistic they are. Since his paintings are based upon descriptions sent to him, each portrait is dependent upon his interpretations of the descriptions, and his interpretations focus on some words more than others and are influenced by cultural stereotypes.

You might begin discussion by preparing a description of yourself in a style similar to those featured in these portraits. (If you think students will guess that you are the basis of the description, then describe someone else—perhaps a student). Ask students to write a description of the portrait they would draw for this description. (If any students are artistically inclined and can draw quickly, they should feel free to draw the portrait.) Or you could put students into groups of two and ask each person to come up with a description and then to describe a portrait based upon the other's description. The description should be written in a style similar to those in this selection and should apply to a friend or a family member. Advise your students to describe as many details as possible—the angle, expression, and features of the face; the length and style of hair; and the color of the background. Ask several students to describe their portraits to the class and to explain how certain words of the description influenced them.

After this exercise, students should be prepared to discuss the Seeing questions. As they examine the paintings, you might ask how they are different from traditional portraits. Some students might observe that apart from the color in the background, the portraits have no context. Two of the paintings (the man in *I work for a government agency* being the exception) resemble candid snapshots, not planned portraits, which seems fitting because the two people represented seem to be more active. The energy is palpable in *HAIR: fire and cognition* as the man practically shakes with the anger present in his steely gaze and clenched teeth. The woman's head in *Slim as a beanpole* is slightly tilted, accentuating her "too big" nose, and her lips are slightly parted as though she is about to speak (fitting in with the description: "like to talk a lot, big mouth").

You might ask how the background color works in each portrait. The colors are not merely in the background but can be seen reflecting off the figures, surrounding them like auras. The man in *HAIR: fire and cognition* is surrounded by a bold red, whereas the less abrasive man in *I work* is softened by a dull green. *Slim as a beanpole* is surrounded by a pale yellow.

Ask students how each writer's syntax affects Rostovsky's interpretations. For instance, the man pictured in *HAIR* writes with short, bold words. He uses capitalization as titles ("HAIR," "HEAD") and to punctuate a point: "No HAT." The man pictured in *I work* seems timid and reserved, which comes across in his uncertain description: "I work hard; can't tell you much."

After students look at the *Cabinet* ad, ask them how closely they think Rostovsky's portraits fit the descriptions.

ADDITIONAL WRITING TOPICS

1. If students performed the group exercise in the Generating Class Discussion section, ask them to write an essay explaining how they composed the portrait based upon the other person's description. Which words influenced them most and why? How were stereotypes involved in their portrait?

2. Ask students to generate alternative descriptions for Rostovsky's paintings.

3. If the discussion went well regarding the factors that influenced Rostovsky's interpretations, you might have students write an essay that analyzes and explains the phrases and the syntax of the descriptions in relation to Rostovsky's paintings.

CONNECTIONS WITH OTHER TEXTS

1. Moyra Davey's photograph of a desk invites viewers to make inferences about the person who owns it. Ask students to describe the contents of a desk for each of Rostovsky's figures.

2. Ask students to find passages from Sarah Vowell's essay "Shooting Dad" (p. 231) that could be turned into a description similar to the ones used by Rostovsky.

SUGGESTIONS FOR FURTHER READING, THINKING, AND WRITING

print

Smith, Michael C. *Personals: Portraits of Real People and Their Personal Ads!* North Hollywood, CA: Universe Publishing, 2001.

web

www.publicartfund.org/pafweb/projects/
rostovsky_detail.htm   An image and description of a mixed-media work by Rostovsky.

Links for the selections in this chapter can be found at www.seeingandwriting.com.

VISUALIZING CONTEXT: **Advertising the Self**

GENERATING CLASS DISCUSSION AND IN-CLASS WRITING

The four personal ads presented in this selection connect with those that Rostovsky interpreted for his portraits. There are several ways context can be discussed through this selection. First, you might consider how these ads present personalities in a certain context. You might begin discussion by reading the ads as a class and then asking students whether they have a good grasp of the personalities involved. Which ad, in a sense, paints the clearest picture? Do students find that more personality is revealed in what each ad writer seeks in the other person?

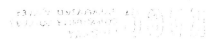

Then ask each student to follow the style of the ads in the text and write a personal ad with a limit of forty words. Tell them that you will read the ads to the class and ask students to guess who wrote each ad. Knowing that their ads will be dissected by other students, most will write an ad that is either obvious or fraudulent. Whether the ads are read out loud or not, you can engage students in a discussion about the context of the assignment. Then have them write another ad that will not be read by anyone else. When they have finished, ask them to compare the two ads they have written. Was the second one more honest? Which elements did they present more honestly in the second? Assure the students that they can speak generally in response to these questions; they don't have to cite specific instances from their ads. Some students might raise the point that even the second ad isn't a genuine reflection since it, too, was written for this class. To close out this area of discussion, you could ask students to discuss how writing essays for a teacher changes the way they write. How does the context of the writing situation affect their writing?

Next you might ask students to consider the context of this reading. These personal ads would normally appear in a newspaper, but students are encountering them in a textbook. How does that difference change the way your students approach these ads? If students were reading these ads in a newspaper, they would probably be more familiar with their style and syntax. Since they are encountering the ads in this text, some students might have difficulty with interpreting some of the abbreviations—"ISO SW/H/A/M" (para. 2).

ADDITIONAL WRITING TOPICS

1. Although students were probably resistant to the idea of your reading their ads to the class, they will most likely be open to the idea of incorporating them into an essay that only you will read. Ask students to write an essay that analyzes the different contexts created in the writing exercise involving the two ads. How did each context change their writing? Why did they change certain elements? Ask them to consider the different audiences imagined for each ad: in the first, their classmates and instructor; in the second, strangers who read personal ads. If students stated in discussion that they could not truly imagine the second audience for the second ad, encourage them to analyze why this occurred.

2. Ask students to locate essays written for two different classes. Have them write an essay that analyzes the context of each writing situation and how they approached this context. How is their writing different in each? In their essay, they should consider the subject, the instructor, and the assignment itself.

3. Instruct students to analyze the personals section of a newspaper. Ask them to write a brief ex-

pository essay about how they view the ads in the newspaper differently from those in the text.

They should explain how the different contexts affect their readings.

CONNECTIONS WITH OTHER TEXTS

1. Ask students to consider Rostovsky's paintings. If they had encountered these paintings in a museum—and not in a textbook that prompts them with questions—how would they regard them? What if they saw them as personal ads on the Internet?

2. Instruct students to bring product advertisements to class and discuss how they could also be used artistically.

Bruce Bower, *Average Attractions*

GENERATING CLASS DISCUSSION AND IN-CLASS WRITING

Bower's essay seeks to answer one question, "What constitutes physical beauty?" (para. 2). The answer he finds is based on the work of two psychologists, Judith H. Langlois and Lori A. Roggman. Their research reveals that viewers prefer a "prototypical face" that is the composite, or average, of at least sixteen other faces. Langlois goes as far as to suggest that humans have "a built-in 'beauty-detecting' mechanism that averages facial features" (para. 15). The appeal of prototypical faces is that they "most readily yield social information through such facial expressions as happiness or disgust" (para. 15). In other words, the faces are appealing because they are easily read.

You might ask students to consider the ramifications of the psychologists' findings. Traditionally, beauty has been seen as a subjective, aesthetic quality. Prior to this research, Bowers notes, those studying physical attraction assumed that "physical beauty was unmeasurable. Good looks were assumed to be perceived as a unified whole" (para. 5). Yet Langlois and Roggman suggest that beauty can be defined empirically and measured. Students might discuss how these findings could be applied to other academic disciplines (e.g., art history and theory) or to professions (e.g., advertising and marketing).

Bower ends with the thought that some beauty may "lie beyond the bounds of an absolute measure" (para. 19). His examples include celebrities such as Cher. These people have other appealing qualities (e.g., fame, money, lifestyle) that may supersede average composite beauty. You might ask students to think of additional examples in which an aspect other than physical appearance affects their appraisal of someone's attractiveness. Students could chart some of these aspects on the chalkboard to see if certain qualities reappear frequently. They might discuss how these qualities could be factored into future research by Langlois and Roggman.

If your students are used to doing research, you could ask them to consider how Bower builds up his authority within this short essay. For example, he explains the research done by Langlois and Roggman and describes their academic affiliations and publications. He also cites another psychologist, Ellen S. Berscheid, who believes these findings are significant. You might direct students to think about using similar strategies in their own writing.

ADDITIONAL WRITING TOPICS

1. Ask students to review the photos that accompany this essay (p. 333). Which of the images do they find most appealing? Does their choice match the researchers' findings? Why did the students choose this photo?

2. Usually, describing someone as "average" is not considered a compliment. You might have students write a short essay in which they compare the definition of *average* put forward by Bower with their own working definition of *average*. Do the terms overlap at any points? Why?

3. Bower remarks, "Neither Langlois nor anyone else has the faintest idea how to quantify charisma" (para. 21). Ask students to offer their own definitions of *charisma* and to support this definition with at least three examples of charismatic public figures. These examples should help to illustrate and explain the students' definitions.

CONNECTIONS WITH OTHER TEXTS

1. Ask students to consider how the altered image of Cindy Jackson (p. 370) reflects a strategy of averaging similar to that described by Bower. How is Jackson trying to compose her physical image to reflect an accepted cultural average (in this case, Barbie)?

2. In assessing the theory put forward by Langlois and Roggman, Berscheid argues that "[m]ost exceptions [to these findings] may be individuals in the public eye, such as movie stars, whose appeal sometimes lies largely in perceptions indirectly linked to facial beauty, such as glamour and fame" (para. 17). Have students analyze the photos of Madonna (pp. 508–09) in light of this statement. How do the photos reveal some of the elements of her attractiveness? What elements of her attractiveness rest outside the photographs?

print

Schefer, Dorothy, and Bruce Weber. *What Is Beauty? New Definitions from the Fashion Vanguard*. New York: Universe Publishing, 1997.

[www] *web*

www.psych.st-and.ac.uk:8080/research/ perception_lab/prototyping/   The web site of the Perceptions Lab at the University of St. Andrews in Scotland links to more information on the research behind Bruce Bower's article. The site also offers visitors the opportunity to participate in a research experiment on their perception of facial attractiveness by using the type of digitized prototypes described in the essay.

Links for the selections in this chapter can be found at www.seeingandwriting.com.

audio/visual

Mr. Skeffington. Directed by Vincent Sherman. 147 min. 1944. Videocassette. Distributed by Warner Brothers. An old-fashioned melodrama with a moral in which Bette Davis portrays Fanny Skeffington, a young beauty who marries an older man to save her brother from an embezzlement charge. After her marriage she continues to trade on her beauty, gathering admirers and driving her husband to divorce her. She gives up everything, including her daughter, in pursuit of her image as a public beauty, only to find in the end that she has nothing left at all.

Marge Piercy, *Imaging*

GENERATING CLASS DISCUSSION AND IN-CLASS WRITING

Piercy's poem addresses the conundrum of how we view our bodies from the perspective of the consciousness inside the body, rather than from the perspective of the spectator outside the body. In addition, as a poet and as a writer Piercy positions herself as a creator rather than as a subject. That is, she is creating the vision; she is not the object to be viewed.

Like Barbara Kruger, Piercy takes the body as a representational "battleground" as her topic. Her opening assertion, "I am my body," can be seen as a call for unity. She is not, like Cindy Jackson or Charles Atlas, ready to change her body as she might change clothing ("This is not a dress, a coat; / not a house I live in"). Instead, her poem is a plea to "glide down the ladder of bone" and to "enter and join to the body lying down as if to a lover."

Piercy is not denying her body as a misrepresentation of her self and making it her task to refashion it, surgically or otherwise. Instead, she notes that we are "estranged from ourselves to the point / where we scarcely credit the body's mind." She asks the reader to "[reclaim] what we once knew," which she names "the other, my lost holy self."

ADDITIONAL WRITING TOPICS

1. Ask students to examine Piercy's poem in terms of the progression of imagery that refers to the body. Then have students write an explication of the poem that highlights this imagery.
2. Direct students to write about the diction and resultant connotations in a comparison of the first and last stanzas of the poem. Students might consider shifts from "lump of meat" to "holy self," for example.
3. Invite students to choose three words from the poem and to write a brief report on the history of their meaning as reported in the *Oxford English Dictionary*.

CONNECTIONS WITH OTHER TEXTS

1. In the essay on p. 557, Susan Bordo discusses the contemporary conception of the body as an object to be formed and shaped by the self, and the underlying idea that the self is independent from the body. Have your students discuss the ways in which Piercy's poem is a refutation of this current cultural idea of the self and body, pointing to specific images in the poem to strengthen their argument.
2. Ask students to study the images of Cindy Jackson in this chapter's Looking Closer section: How might Jackson respond to this poem?

SUGGESTIONS FOR FURTHER READING, THINKING, AND WRITING

print
Piercy, Marge. *Circles on the Water.* New York: Knopf, 1982. Selected poems.

web
www.hubcap.clemson.edu/~sparks/piercy/ mpindex.html   Includes book summaries, biographies, and articles.

Links for the selections in this chapter can be found at www.seeingandwriting.com.

audio/visual
The Bride of Frankenstein. 75 min. 1935. VHS videocassette. Distributed by MCA Home Video. The ultimate tale of body construction in which Frankenstein finds a mate but still

does not live happily ever after. The film opens with a prologue involving Mary Shelley played by Elsa Lancaster, who does dual duty as the Bride.

Marge Piercy. 50 min. 1986. Recording. With host Kay Bonetti, Piercy discusses the political and social aspects of her work.

Talking Pictures

The assignment requires students to choose one TV show or film that helps set standards of physical beauty and to analyze this definition with reference to Bruce Bower's essay, "Average Attractions" (p. 332). Most students will be drawn to shows and films that define female beauty, so you may want to offer suggestions of recent examples that define male attractiveness—such as the TV programs *Dawson's Creek* and *Angel,* or the films *Forty Days and Forty Nights* and *Best Man.* Alternatively, you might want to point students to a film like *How Stella Got Her Groove Back,* which has male beauty as its focus.

As yet another approach, you might direct students to apply this assignment to a TV show or channel that should—ostensibly—have very little to do with physical beauty: for example, the evening news, the weather channel, or a financial news network. Then have students write an essay on how issues of physical attractiveness factor into these types of programming. You could suggest that they compare several newscasts or financial reports to see if there is a difference from network to network.

Gish Jen, *What Means Switch*

GENERATING CLASS DISCUSSION AND IN-CLASS WRITING

In this story the narrator/protagonist is Mona Chang, a Chinese "born-here" girl (para. 1) whose parents move from Yonkers to Scarsdale in order to ensure that their daughters have a good education. The narrative traces Mona's real education as she learns about class, social cliques, and boys. You might ask students to compare Mona's experience with their own and to consider how much of the agony of adolescence transcends race. In this journey, Mona's ethnicity seems to be a blessing. She cultivates a sort of Chinese mystique by claiming to be able to make her "hands like steel by thinking hard" (para. 5), by spouting random Chinese words in nonsensical order, and by announcing unusual facts: "I rush on to tell her I know how to get pregnant with tea" (para. 9). She describes Scarsdale, "a liberal town," as embracing the Changs because they are a rarity (para. 12). However, the older Mona warns that as more and more Asian families moved into suburbs like Scarsdale, they were not regarded favorably. You might ask students to consider Jen's description of the Changs as "permanent exchange students" (para. 12). Ask them to discuss how this characterization conveys a sense of both closeness and distance.

Mona's life is considerably complicated by the arrival of a new student, Sherman Matsumoto. At first glance she believes him to be Chinese, which means that he poses a threat to the identity she has fashioned for herself. However, he is Japanese and seems completely lost in America, knowing little of the language and even fewer of the customs. You might suggest that students examine the way in which Sherman is at first feminized through description: the kitty notebook, the "pretty-boy" looks (para. 68), his puppy-dog devotion to Mona. In all these descriptions Mona is able to keep the upper hand; she can remain in control. Once Sherman begins to act more like an American man (like the picture of John Wayne that he draws; para. 113), he becomes more distant from her. Students might discuss the moment in which Mona learns that Sherman knows judo and how this moment becomes pivotal to the story's direction and conclusion.

The story's title comes from a conversation between Mona and Sherman. Mona explains that she is not Chinese but American: "'Everybody who's born here is American, and also some people who convert from what they were before. You could become American.' But he says no, he could never. 'Sure you could,' I say. 'You only have to learn some rules and speeches'" (para. 107). Mona's use of the word *convert* could be interpreted both as the mistake of a young person unfamiliar with the term's proper usage and as a choice by Jen that reveals something at the heart of culture. To become American in the traditional, melting-pot sense means to give up one's ethnic identity. Sherman seems to understand this meaning, asserting, "'But I Japanese'" (para. 108) and refusing to accept Mona's statement. Mona's private thought, "I think maybe he doesn't get what means switch" (para. 111), forms the story's title. Unlike Mona's ethnic background, which is already altered by her "born-here" status, Sherman's ethnicity seems immutable in part because of his culture's ties to nationalism, as represented by his crayon-drawing of the Japanese flag.

You might ask students to consider how easy it truly is to "switch" cultures. How much of one's ethnic past can actually be dismissed through conversion to a new identity? Mrs. Chang's visceral reaction to the sight of the Japanese flag hanging on her refrigerator seems to suggest that some cultural memories are indelible. Further, the fact that immediately after this incident the family again discusses building a wall around their home may be read by students as a symbolic gesture to protect their culture, about which Mona seems to know very little.

The relationship between Mona and Sherman begins with brushed shoulders and then progresses to hand kisses and neck kisses, but it stalls there. Mona knows that American boyfriends kiss their girlfriends on the lips and desperately wants Sherman to give her these recognizable, and therefore meaningful, signs of affection, because having a boyfriend who will go to first and second base seems to be a necessary step to popularity. Mona seems to feel internally divided about her affections with Sherman. On the one hand, she wants the relationship to proceed according to her American expectations. But on the other hand, she is timid and perhaps feels that she is experiencing something more genuine with him. Sherman senses her wish to conform with the popular way of proceeding, and his final act of flipping her can be read as his statement that he is hurt by her rejection of his real feeling and his real culture, which she wants him to replace with American conventions. Although Mona used her difference and its novelties as a way to gain popularity, she fears nonconformity as much as any of the other students.

ADDITIONAL WRITING TOPICS

1. Ask students to write a short personal narrative in which they compare their adolescence with Mona's. What elements of this experience seem to be universal and independent of race?

2. A recurring image in Jen's story is the runaway automobile that almost crashes into the Changs' home. These incidents are often linked to Mona's interactions with Sherman. Direct students to write an analytical essay in which they explain the symbolic importance of this recurring motif.

3. Mona's ethnicity seems to be an asset throughout the majority of the story. Only near the very end does she seriously question her culture and its effects on her family's behavior. Have students write an essay in which they trace Mona's shift in attitude toward her Chinese culture.

CONNECTIONS WITH OTHER TEXTS

1. In his essay "The Joy of Reading and Writing: Superman and Me" (p. 251), Sherman Alexie also makes observations about problems of conversion and cultural allegiance. Ask students to compare Jen's feelings about cultural identity to Alexie's.

2. Jen's fictional character Mona in "What Means Switch" and Chang-rae Lee in "Coming Home

Again" (p. 205) share a desire to trade some of their Asian heritage for a chance to be American. Ask students to write an essay comparing the strategies used by each protagonist to assimilate into American culture.

SUGGESTIONS FOR FURTHER READING, THINKING, AND WRITING

print

Fong-Torres, Ben. *The Rice Room: Growing Up Chinese-American: From Number Two Son to Rock 'n' Roll.* New York: Plume, 1995. An experience similar to that of Mona in Gish Jen's story, but from a boy's perspective.

Jen, Gish. *Who's Irish?* New York: Knopf, 1999. Stories focusing on the immigrant experience in America.

Solomon, Barbara H., ed. *The Haves and the Have-Nots: 30 Stories about Money and Class in America.* New York: Signet Classic, 1999. Stories by Sandra Cisneros, Alice Walker, Ethan Canin, Gloria Naylor, Raymond Carver, Kate Chopin, and John Cheever, among many others.

www. web

www.mcdougallittell.com/disciplines/_lang_art/authors/jen.cfm   A bio of Gish Jen.

www.uiowa.edu/~commstud/resources/GenderMedia/asian.html   A site from the University of Iowa that provides links in categories ranging from Asian American to Indigenous.

Links for the selections in this chapter can be found at www.seeingandwriting.com.

audio/visual

The Joy Luck Club. Directed by Wayne Wang. 139 min. 1993. VHS videocassette, rated R. Distributed by Hollywood Pictures. Based on Amy Tan's novel. Performers include Kieu Chin, Tsai Chin, France Nuyen, Lisa Lu, Min-Na Wen, and Tamlyn Tomita.

RETROSPECT: *Building the Male Body*

GENERATING CLASS DISCUSSION AND IN-CLASS WRITING

This Retrospect invites students to look at advertising stereotypes of the public male body from the beginning of the twentieth century through the present. As the chapter's introduction suggests, Americans have an "obsession with weight and fat" (p. 305), and this series of photographs of the male body reflects their obsession; in particular, the focus is on the "athletic look" (p. 305). In each advertisement the physical body of the man is in the foreground—the actual flesh is revealed, with an emphasis on the muscles. The implication in each image is that the male body pictured has been created through the individual's discipline and will. Indeed, Americans "regard the body as something to be mastered and shaped" (p. 308), and these photographs feature stereotypical masculine body shapes that emphasize upper body strength and are the result of the men's efforts.

The first photograph suggests a relationship between physical health and cultural health. "Weakness A Crime; Don't Be A Criminal" (p. 350), the ad intones verbally, while the images show a "normal" male body shape (perhaps weak, and therefore criminal) and a more muscular, chiseled male body (stronger, and therefore not criminal)—probably after partaking of the advice or products featured in the magazine. Students in the 2000s may find it interesting that in this ad from 1900 both male figures are nude and are portrayed almost as if they were sculptures. There is no context other than a dark background, and the nudes are formally and identically posed in a side view with hands clasped behind their backs.

The message of the second ad is also explicit. The words tell us "How Joe's Body Brought Him FAME Instead of SHAME" (p. 351). In this case, a drama unfolds in the comic strip wherein the weakling, after being humiliated at the beach by a more "fit" man, goes home and reshapes his body by building his muscles (particularly his upper body, which is visible in the last frame of the comic). He then becomes the "Hero of the Beach" and draws admiring glances, most importantly from the woman who sees that he is a "real man after all." Thus, the ad lets us know that it is up to the male viewer to achieve the ideal masculine body shape—to be "A New Man . . . in Only 15 Minutes A Day"—by using the Charles Atlas body building method.

The third ad presents its messages about male attractiveness overtly in the photo of the seminude man and more implicitly in the paradoxical product name, "Relax-A-cizor." The effect of the ad depends upon several assumptions about what is attractive to a man and for a man. Ask your students to notice where their eyes go when looking at the ad. They will probably say their eyes go first to the full-body frontal photograph of the man, which conveys that an attractive man is trim and strong, with a tight waistline and muscled arms and legs. In case we doubted his attractions, the woman clinging to his leg and gazing up his body is our proof. The eye then goes to the text above the man, and we take in the appealing paradox of the name "Relax-A-cizor," which implies another assumption—that a man would like to look good without working for it. Ask your students what this might imply about cultural feelings about exercise. Does this ad reveal an attitude toward fitness different from the ones we now have? Perhaps the actual work of exercise was seen as unattractive at the time this ad was made, as opposed to today, when ads feature men (and women) engaged in grueling exercise. Or, working for an attractive body may have been seen as a kind of vanity—a quality considered effeminate. Or perhaps this ad was just designed for those who would rather not exert themselves physically. Either way, Relax-A-cizor is meant to be seen as offering a solution—it gives a man effortless fitness.

The last ad catches the male subject in a dilemma regarding his pursuit of fitness. He is between the light and the dark of the laundry closet and the darkened hallway—perhaps on his way to a pre-dawn run. The ad's question is, "Does it matter to you that if you skip a day of running, only one person in the world will ever know? Or is that one person too many?" The furrowed brow in the top third of the frame of the advertisement signifies that this is an important issue. Again, the message is explicit: The man has a responsibility to work toward maintaining himself as athletic, muscular, and fit—in sum, to not be criminal, to not be shamed, and to not lie to himself about the level of his commitment to bodily excellence.

ADDITIONAL WRITING TOPICS

1. Ask students to write a personal narrative in which they recount their first awareness of the ideal body shape for their gender. Who is the person they first admired as a physical ideal for themselves? Was it an actual person they knew, or an ideal or icon gleaned from their culture? Ask them to describe this person or image and to discuss why they felt it was ideal.

2. The chapter introduction points out that "the body has been so analyzed and scrutinized that it is at once an anatomical object and a social construction" (p. 308). Ask students to write an analysis of the progression of male body shapes presented in this series of photographs. Have them consider what their observations about the physical ideals presented suggest about the social construction of masculinity.

3. Direct students to collect images of male body shapes from current advertising media. Ask them singly, or in collaborative groups, to analyze the images they find. Direct them to consider:

- the size of the body in the frame
- the portion of the body that is dominant
- the context in which the body is pictured
- the lack of or the type of clothing the figure wears
- the product being advertised

What conclusions can the students draw from their observations? Have them write individual essays on their findings.

CONNECTIONS WITH OTHER TEXTS

1. Refer students to Mario Testino's *Doubles, Lima,* which depicts two large men who do not fit the masculine profile set forth in these ads. Do students consider these men to *not* be masculine? Ask students to consider how the men's open display of size and emotion might violate the standards shown in these ads.

2. Ask students to compare and contrast the male body ideal with the female body ideal exemplified by the Barbie Doll image that Cindy Jackson seeks (p. 370).

SUGGESTIONS FOR FURTHER READING, THINKING, AND WRITING

print

Gaines, Charles. *Yours in Perfect Manhood, Charles Atlas: The Most Effective Fitness Program Ever Devised.* New York: Simon & Schuster, 1982. Photographs by George Butler.

(www) *web*

Links for the selections in this chapter can be found at www.seeingandwriting.com.

Albert Bliss, *Homeless Man Interviews Himself*

GENERATING CLASS DISCUSSION AND IN-CLASS WRITING

In this selection Albert Bliss interviews himself, splitting into Mr. Bliss, the interviewer, and Al, the interviewee. He presents readers with a different perspective on homeless people, explaining why he sees them as "rugged individualists" (para. 14) and "fearless" (para. 28). Bliss also provides a typical day in his life, describing how he earns money and where he sleeps (para. 22).

You could start discussion by asking students how they view homeless people. Do they see homelessness as the result of choice, circumstance, or both? Some students might not have any experiences with homeless people, so their perceptions might rely completely upon the media's portrayal or upon the accounts of friends and family. If their perceptions are not based upon personal experiences, how have the homeless been presented to them—as "rugged individualists" or "city bum[s]"? What do they think of Bliss's equating the homeless with "great American pioneers . . . guys like Daniel Boone, Davy Crockett, and Jim Bowie" (para. 14)?

One of the most interesting aspects of this interview is the fact that it is a self-interview, and it is executed so well that readers can forget this fact halfway through. Mister Bliss, in stereotypical interviewer fashion, asks questions in a formal, unaffected tone: "Did you ever think you would be homeless?" (para. 6). In contrast, Al speaks informally and uses slang: "What's the plan for today? Same jig as yesterday. Moving luggage from bus to cab" (para. 22). Since Bliss handles these different tones so well, a question could be raised about the reliability of Al's statements. If Bliss assumes the interviewer's role so well, is it possible that he is also altering the interviewee's to fulfill a stereotype?

One area that might be probed during this discussion is the interviewee's explanation of the different types of vagrants. According to Al, there are two types of vagrants. Bliss finds vagrancy to be a choice. One type is the bored worker who became a vagrant: "These men got bored with the nine-to-five jig and now they drink and snort because there is nothing else to do" (para. 18). The other type seems to suffer from existential despair and "turns to substance abuse because life is pointless" (para. 18). Bliss fits into the latter category: "I tried to blot out the disturbing questions by working a full-time job. That did nothing to quell my anguish" (para. 26). Ask students if they agree with Bliss's reduction of vagrants into two categories. Do they believe him? What other reasons for vagrancy can they come up with?

ADDITIONAL WRITING TOPICS

1. Ask students to research Bliss's other writings. They could use examples from his other writings to compare and contrast with the views stated by himself in this interview to evaluate the reliability of his self-portrayal.

2. Direct students to imagine they are homeless. Have them write a narrative about a typical day. They should be specific about the city and the climate. Some suggestions for issues they should address: Where do they sleep? Where do they go to the bathroom? Where do they eat? How do they brush their teeth? What do they do with their time? How do they get clothes, and where do they change them? How do people walking by on the street treat them? How will they get a job?

3. Students could do research on homelessness and use it as the basis for an essay that either supports or disputes common perceptions.

CONNECTIONS WITH OTHER TEXTS

1. Bliss's interview is strikingly honest in places. Ask students to find the instances in which Bliss seems at his most revealing. Then direct students to Chuck Close's detailed self-portrait

(p. 118). How does each artist portray himself with honesty? How does each hide?

2. Ask students to recall Peter Rostovsky's portraits of strangers based upon their written descriptions. Rostovsky chose clothing, position, and color to depict personality. If he were to paint Bliss's portrait based upon this interview, how would he portray Bliss's clothing and stance? What color would fill the background?

SUGGESTIONS FOR FURTHER READING, THINKING, AND WRITING

print

Culhane, Dennis P., and Steven P. Hornburg, eds. *Understanding Homelessness: New Policy.* Washington, DC: Fannie Mae Foundation, 1997.

Liebow, Elliot. *Tell Them Who I Am: The Lives of Homeless Women.* New York: Penguin Group, 1993.

web

www.ssc.wisc.edu/irp/ University of Wisconsin—Madison's Institute for Research on Poverty web site. Good for research on U.S. poverty issues.

www.poormagazine.com/ POOR magazine's web site, the Poor News Network, focuses on issues of poverty, providing a perspective often ignored in mainstream media. Bliss's "Homeless in San Jose" can be found here.

www.realchangenews.org/pastissues/ Dec_13_01/features/christmas_story.html *Real Change News's* web site features a Christmas story written by Bliss.

Links for the selections in this chapter can be found at www.seeingandwriting.com.

VISUALIZING COMPOSITION: **Purpose**

GENERATING CLASS DISCUSSION AND IN-CLASS WRITING

In the cartoon, the floor is littered with different running-shoe brands: Adidas, Nike, New Balance, All Star, and so on. The woman's problem is not that she cannot decide whether the shoe fits or looks good, which would seem to be important criteria. Rather, the woman cannot decide which brand suits her: "I can't decide. I'm having a brand identity crisis." The author satirizes not only how our society is inundated by a proliferation of brands, but also how people are dominated by brand names to the point of being defined by them.

To help students create and find purpose in their writing, you should familiarize them with the writing process and have them write and rewrite drafts for clarity of purpose. First drafts of essays are often exploratory exercises for most students; they express ideas about the assigned topic, but they have not yet focused the ideas into a purpose. To help students develop a sense of purpose early in the writing process, you could have them generate ideas by doing brainstorming and freewriting exercises related to the essay's topic. Some students learn the benefit of such exercises after doing them often in class. If you have trouble coming up with freewriting exercises, you could consult creative writing guides; they often feature excellent exercises you could assign every few days to help students get into the habit of using them.

One of the most difficult aspects of the essay for students to grasp is the thesis statement—which, of course, is inextricably tied to purpose. Grammar handbooks supply helpful thesis statement exercises for students. However, after working through such exercises, many students still regard the thesis as something that has to be tacked on to the essay, and they continue to have trouble seeing how it is an integral part of the essay. Most students only get beyond this perception after doing a lot of writing. Assure students that they should feel free to adjust, revise, even completely change their thesis statement and goal throughout the writing process, especially if they come to doubt the reasons behind their initial writing impulse.

Asking students to search for thesis statements in the text might be a fruitless exercise because most professional writers do not use them. However, you could ask students to analyze essays for purpose. Have them search for the writer's purpose in an essay from the text; then have them do the same for a fellow student's essay.

You might begin discussion by asking students to talk about their understanding of purpose. You should point out that communication always has a purpose. Use simple examples: Letters between friends often inform; advertisements persuade; movies entertain. Then you could ask students to read the text and examine the cartoon. Students might have several different interpretations of the cartoon's purpose; ask them to cite specific evidence from the cartoon that proves the purpose.

ADDITIONAL WRITING TOPICS

1. Instruct students to freewrite about how they keep their intended purpose in mind as they write.
2. Have students write a brief essay that explains how *purpose* determines the *tone* and *details* of an essay. Their audience should be beginning writers who are unfamiliar with these terms.
3. Ask each student to exchange a previously written analytical essay with another student.

Each student should try to determine the essay's purpose and assess whether the writer fulfills that purpose. Ask students to explain how the organization and tone work or fail to work in achieving the purpose.

CONNECTIONS WITH OTHER TEXTS

1. Direct students to Albert Bliss's "Homeless Man Interviews Himself." What is the purpose behind Bliss's interview? How does he achieve that purpose by interviewing himself?

2. Ask students to examine Tim Gardner's paintings that re-create actual photographs (pp. 79–82). Ask what Gardner's purpose might be by re-creating photographs through watercolor paintings. To help students unpack this question, you should have them discuss the qualities they associate with paintings and photographs. How are Gardner's paintings different from the students' expectations?

SUGGESTIONS FOR FURTHER READING, THINKING, AND WRITING

print

Heffron, Jack. *The Writer's Idea Book: How to Develop Great Ideas for Fiction, Nonfiction, Poetry and Screenplays.* Cincinnati: Writer's Digest Books, 2000. Provides over 400 writing prompts.

[www.] *web*

Links for the selections in this chapter can be found at www.seeingandwriting.com.

Art Spiegelman, *Mein Kampf*

GENERATING CLASS DISCUSSION AND IN-CLASS WRITING

Mein Kampf is Spiegelman's struggle with memory and history. He specifically deals with his personal history of turning his father's memories of being a prisoner at Auschwitz into the Pulitzer Prize–winning *Maus*. Although students will most likely understand the reference to Auschwitz, they may not understand why Spiegelman represented Jews as mice in *Maus*; some might even be offended. However, Spiegelman based this representation upon Nazi propaganda, which portrayed Jews as mice and referred to them as vermin (Poles were similarly referred to as pigs). Even though a complete understanding of *Maus* is not needed to appreciate *Mein Kampf*, the image of the 5,000-pound mouse becomes richer with this knowledge of Nazi propaganda. With this viewpoint, the mouse represents the terrible weight of history—history that allowed humans to see and treat another group of people as less than human. Without this knowledge, the mouse might only be seen to represent Spiegelman's father and/or the success of *Maus*.

You might begin discussion by asking students to analyze the title. What is Spiegelman's struggle? *Mein Kampf* is also the title of Hitler's book—why did Spiegelman choose the same title? In the same panel as the title, he seems to imply that his struggle is following up on the success of *Maus*: "Remembering those who remembered the death camps is a hard act to follow." However, the struggle seems to be with memory and history, and the difficulty of passing each on. The entire comic takes place in "the murky caverns" of his memory and begins with Spiegelman recalling his childhood: "I was just another baby-boom boy." He follows this up with two typical statements in the second panel, but the third statement—"My parents survived Auschwitz"—reveals the opening line to be ironic.

You might also ask students to examine the different elements separately at first. Direct students to examine only the images, explaining the narrative of the text panel by panel. Students will find that the visual cues allow them to have a basic understanding of *Mein Kampf*; however, the panel of Spiegelman running from a large mouse might be an exception. Ask students how they would characterize Spiegelman based upon his self-rendering here. They should examine the doors in the cavern and the items on the shelves behind the door labeled "Childhood Memories." What do these details show about his personality? Ask students to list a few words that describe Spiegelman.

Next, tell students to read only the spoken dialogue, ignoring the images as well as the narrative boxes in the fourth panel and the last three panels. Does Spiegelman take himself seriously? Do your students believe him when he says "I don't really know anything!"? What does Spiegelman mean when he states that the comic book is "a great medium for artists who can't remember much anyway"?

Finally, students should read it again, connecting the visual to the verbal, and noting how the narrative boxes add to the text's purpose. How did students read the last three panels when they ignored the narrative boxes? How does the narration affect their reading? When the narration is read in those boxes, Spiegelman's struggle with personal history becomes apparent. The factual tone of the narration contrasts with the emotional dialogue between Spiegelman and Dashiell, stressing the differences between Spiegelman's childhood and his son's. The first piece of narration observes, "My parents died before I had any kids." Since his children never met their grandparents, they may not know about the horror of the Holocaust. You might point out the pleasure in Spiegelman's face as he tells his son that he shouldn't be scared of the movie *King Kong*: "It was only a story!" In the narration Spiegelman notes, "The knee on Dash's Superman pajamas is ripped," reminding readers of the hole in his Cisco Kid outfit and of the fact that his parents could not comfort him by saying "It was only a story."

ADDITIONAL WRITING TOPICS

1. Spiegelman comforts his son's fear of a movie by telling him "It was only a story!" In class you might have discussed whether Spiegelman told his children about their grandparents' experiences in Auschwitz. Ask students to write a letter to their child (real or imagined) in which they explain a horrific event—the Holocaust or September 11 would probably be examples of which students are most knowledgeable.

2. Ask students to write an essay that compares and contrasts the essay and the comic as media. What are the advantages and disadvantages of each? Your students are free to choose any essay they've read in the text to compare to *Mein Kampf*.

3. Instruct students to research the source of Spiegelman's title, *Mein Kampf*. Then ask them to write a brief essay that explains how they think Spiegelman intends the context of the title to be read and whether he succeeds. How does the title set a tone for the comic?

CONNECTIONS WITH OTHER TEXTS

1. Spiegelman states that photographs "only help me remember having seen the photos before." He is not the only writer in this text to criticize the usefulness of photographs. Barry Lopez (p. 238) also notes how his generation was "storing memories that would never be retrieved, that would never form a coherent narrative" (para. 39). Have students ever felt this way when looking at photographs? Does video solve the problem?

2. Direct students to examine Scott McCloud's "Show and Tell" (p. 637). Ask them to compare and contrast how each author represents himself. How does this representation reflect each text's purpose?

SUGGESTIONS FOR FURTHER READING, THINKING, AND WRITING

print

Hitler, Adolf. *Mein Kampf*. Boston: Houghton Mifflin, 1971.

Spiegelman, Art. *Maus*. New York: Pantheon Books, 1986.

———. *Maus II: A Survivor's Tale: And Here My Troubles Began*. New York: Pantheon Books, 1991.

Wiesel, Elie. *Night*. New York: Hill and Wang, 1960. Relates Wiesel's childhood experience of the Holocaust.

[www.] web

www.geocities.com/Area51/Zone/9923/ispieg2.html   In this interview, which mainly deals with his other work, Spiegelman provides some of his thoughts on *Maus*.

www.georgetown.edu/bassr/218/projects/oliver/MausbyAO.htm   Written for a class at Georgetown University, this is an interesting essay about *Maus*'s depiction of the Holocaust.

www.nmajh.org/index.htm   National Museum of Jewish History's web site includes information on Spiegelman's *Maus* in its exhibition section.

www.ushmm.org/   United States Holocaust Museum's official site.

Links for the selections in this chapter can be found at www.seeingandwriting.com.

audio/visual

Life Is Beautiful. Directed by Roberto Benigni. 118 min. 1998. VHS videocassette. Distributed by Miramax Films. When a Jewish man and his family are taken to a concentration camp, the man tries to protect his son from the horrors around them by turning the situation into a game. Much like *Maus*, the film *Life Is Beautiful* encountered controversy when it was first released due to its different portrayal of the Holocaust.

Schindler's List. Directed by Steven Spielberg. 197 min. 1993. VHS videocassette. Distributed by MCA/Universal Pictures. Based on the true story of Oskar Schindler, a German businessman who saved over 1,000 Jews from Auschwitz by turning his factory into a refuge.

Moyra Davey, *The City*

GENERATING CLASS DISCUSSION AND IN-CLASS WRITING

This twist on the self-portrait features a photograph of objects on a desk. Before you examine the picture, you might ask all students to place items on their desks for a group exercise in which you will borrow the items to create details for composites of the students. Gather enough items to arrange two composites, a "female" and a "male." As you gather items—keys, textbooks, pens, watches, cell phones, pagers, a purse, a wallet, and so on—think about how to sort and arrange the items to create an identity for each composite. Ask your students to make inferences about each personality based on the items you present to the class. The items should have plenty of details from which to draw inferences. Tell students to pay attention to the size, color, and condition of the objects as they make their inferences.

Now that they have had some practice with making inferences about people based on personal objects, separate the students into groups to analyze Davey's picture. As they examine her work, ask them to make notes of their observations and inferences; also have them note when they move from observation to inference. If students have difficulty with moving from observation to inference, you could direct them to the objects that stand out to you and explain how they seem to represent the owner of the desk. You might observe the photograph at the top of the image, the camera to the right of the newspaper, or the book—on the subject of photography, it seems—at the bottom left. All of these details suggest that the owner is involved in photography. You could also ask about the presentation of the objects on the desk. How would a different arrangement of the objects—a more organized one, for example—affect the students' view of the desk's owner? Which objects do they think are used most often by the owner?

ADDITIONAL WRITING TOPICS

1. Students could write a self-portrait by describing the contents of their own room or desk. They could turn this self-portrait into an expository essay about how the contents reflect personality and lifestyle.

2. Photography takes the photographed out of context. In this picture we see Davey's desk, but we cannot see her bookshelf or bed. We see one object from one moment in her life. Using Davey's picture as inspiration and a possible example, students could write a paper that supports or challenges the claim that photography cannot accurately represent reality.

1. Roe Ethridge's picture of a refrigerator (p. 39) allows inferences to be made about the family that owns it. Consider the perspective of Ethridge's and Davey's photographs. Which angle provides more information?

2. Based on Art Spiegelman's presentation of himself in *Mein Kampf,* ask students to write a brief description of his desk.

SUGGESTIONS FOR FURTHER READING, THINKING, AND WRITING

print

Davey, Moyra, ed. *Mother Reader: Essential Litera-ture on Motherhood.* New York: Seven Stories Press, 2002.

McCurry, Steve. *Portraits.* New York: Phaidon Press, 1999. You could pass this book around the room and ask students to examine some of the portraits within it. How much of a person's identity can students infer from a picture of a face? Although Davey's desk might seem limiting in terms of how much it reveals about its owner, a picture of her face might be just as limiting.

www. *web*

www.motherreader.com/ Provides information on Davey's book.

Links for the selections in this chapter can be found at www.seeingandwriting.com.

Looking Closer:
Self-Fashioning

GENERATING CLASS DISCUSSION AND IN-CLASS WRITING

The texts in this section suggest the fluidity of identity and show how cultural shifts and technological advances influence our ideas of who we can be.

Joe Queenan, *The Skin Game*

In this humorous essay, Queenan discusses the cultural shift in how tattoos are re-garded. He has been opposed to tattoos his entire life but is forced to reconsider by his father's ghost, who tells Queenan to get a tattoo. Queenan observes that tattoos used to be reserved for the unrefined, the criminal; tattoos were the "emblems of blue-collar lunacy, alcohol abuse, and temporary insanity" (para. 14). Today, he notes that tattoos have lost their power to shock. Queenan visits tattoo shops, only to find that housewives and schoolteachers have joined the tattooed ranks of bikers and criminals. As you discuss the essay, you might ask students to compare their views of tattoos with their parents'.

Cindy Jackson, 1973 and 1998

These two digitized photographs of Cindy Jackson demonstrate one woman's attempt to achieve an ideal female body shape. Unlike the Retrospect advertisements featuring male figures (pp. 350–53), Jackson's transformation is not through nutrition, body building, or exercise. Her efforts are implemented through extensive cosmetic surgery. Indeed, "shaping of the body . . . is commonplace; *toning, nipping, tucking, shaping,* and *figuring* are all terms in the public discourse" (p. 305). Cindy Jackson has modeled her body on the so-called physical perfection of the Barbie Doll.

Discuss with your students the characteristics of the Barbie Doll that Jackson evidently finds attractive, on the basis of their observations of her current image. What kind of identity has she constructed for herself through this restructuring of her body? Direct students to notice her change in posture and her change of clothing as well as her bodily characteristics.

You might also note that in the 1973 photo Jackson is associated with an accomplishment that exists outside of the frame and is not physical but intellectual—her graduation from high school. Moreover, she is placed against a landscape—she exists in a *place.* In the 1998 photo, however, she is a one-dimensional cutout against a white background. She is not associated with anything outside the visual frame; she is not *placed.* Now Jackson seems less a human individual and more a female abstraction.

Cindy Sherman, *Untitled #8*

This is one of Sherman's many self-portraits. Her appearance varies in each portrait, which raises the notion of how the self can be so easily captured. Do female students recognize themselves in this picture? You might ask students to compare this picture of Sherman to pictures of Cindy Jackson and Lynn Johnson in regard to femininity.

Rockport, *I'm Comfortable Being a Man*

RuPaul is advertising the comfort of Rockport dress shoes by advertising how at ease he is "being a Man." The irony is that his celebrity is based on being a famous drag queen. Evidently he is so comfortable being a man that he can also be a woman—by wearing women's clothes and exploiting his gender identity. Thus, although this image is traditionally masculine in that RuPaul is wearing a man's power suit and tie and is holding his cane in a position that calls attention to male anatomy, in fact his androgynous face and the small words "rupaul, drag superstar" under his cane may cause us to question his actual gender. The ad capitalizes on the androgyny of his image and his unconventional route to celebrity.

Lynn Johnson, *Nose Piercing*

The photograph of a woman staring with raised eyebrows into the hand-held mirror in order to get a better view of her pierced nose demonstrates a concrete desire to confront one's own self-image. Whether or not the woman finds herself pleasing is ambiguous. Probably all of us confront our "mirror selves" daily. Ask your students which parts of their own faces they are drawn to when they look in the mirror.

Nikki S. Lee, *The Skateboarder's Project (#8)* and *The Tourist Project (#9)*

Lee's photographs capture group identity. Lee alters her own identity to fit in with the subjects of her photographs. Ask students to describe the groups presented here— which details determine identity? If your students were to imagine the people against white backgrounds, would they still be able to identify them? Lee's photographs also raise notions of how fluid identity is, how much it can be changed by context. You might ask students to think about how their personalities change in different situations.

 For an interactive visual exercise for this selection, go to www.seeingandwriting.com.

ADDITIONAL WRITING TOPICS

1. Lee's photographs demonstrate the flexibility of identity. Ask students to write a narrative about a time in which they adopted the appearance and behaviors of others to fit in. For their conclusion, they should consider how that experience has had a lasting effect on who they are.

2. Ask students to write a research essay that documents the ideal female image that was characteristic of each decade of the twentieth century. Part of their research should note the parallels between the ideal female image and the cultural status of women at the time.

3. Direct students to form groups and to collaborate in creating lists of admirable human qualities. Then have them write a journal entry in which they group the qualities according to assumptions about the appropriate gender for each. You might want to conclude by inviting students to read their entries aloud to the class.

4. Put students in small groups of men and small groups of women. First, ask each group to generate a list of five qualities commonly associated with men and five qualities associated with women. When each group is done, a representative should write the group's list on the board. When all the lists are on the board, have students discuss whether each quality is innate or cultural. As you come across cultural qualities, cross them off. By the end, students will probably be surprised by the few remaining innate qualities listed.

CONNECTIONS WITH OTHER TEXTS

1. Refer students to the Retrospect in Chapter 3, and have them analyze the characteristics of male and female beauty that are presented in those photographs as compared to the ideals discussed in this chapter.

2. Ask students to consider how Madonna's image has changed over the years (pp. 508–09). Do they believe that Madonna changed her image to prolong her career—to successfully "reinvent" herself? Or do they believe that Madonna's changes have largely been personal and that those changes have been expressed through her work? Ask students to consider the people depicted in this chapter: How have their identities been fashioned? How much do personal changes depend upon social changes?

3. Direct students to consider Lauren Greenfield's photograph of Ashleigh at age 13 (p. 254–55). Compare the image of Ashleigh on the scale to the images of women in this section. Is she merely confronting her own image? Or is she obsessing over it?

SUGGESTIONS FOR FURTHER READING, THINKING, AND WRITING

print

Gilbert, Steve. *Tattoo History: A Source Book*. New York: Juno Books, 2001.

Hoffman, Katherine. *Concepts of Identity: Historical and Contemporary Images and Portraits of Self and Family*. New York: HarperCollins, 1996.

Kimmel, Michael S. *The Gendered Society*. New York: Oxford University Press, 2000.

Lee, Nikki S. *Projects*. Ostfildern: Hatje Cantz Publishers; New York: D.A.P, 2001.

Morris, Catherine. *Essential Cindy Sherman*. New York: Harry N. Abrams, 2001.

Queenan, Joe. *Balsamic Dreams: A Short but Self-Important History of the Baby Boomer Generation*. New York: Holt, 2001.

———. *Confessions of a Cineplex Heckler: Celluloid Tirades and Escapades*. New York: Hyperion, 2000.

———. *My Goodness: A Cynic's Short-Lived Search for Sainthood*. New York: Hyperion, 2001.

———. *Red Lobster, White Trash, and the Blue Lagoon: Joe Queenan's America.* New York: Hyperion, 1998.

www *web*

www.dir.salon.com/people/conv/2001/07/13/ queenan/index.html   Salon's web site features a profile and a two-page interview with Queenan.

www.tonkonow.com/lee.html   This site includes galleries of Lee's various projects.

www.masters-of-photography.com/S/sherman/ sherman.html   Includes a gallery of Sherman's work and links to articles about Sherman.

Links for the selections in this chapter can be found at www.seeingandwriting.com.

Chapter 5

Producing America

Introduction

GENERATING CLASS DISCUSSION AND IN-CLASS WRITING

The chapter's title is involved with the notion of how the "American experience" can be packaged "in order to make it replicable—and therefore purchasable" (p. 381). Before students read the introduction, ask them to make a list of specific people, places, and ideas that they associate with America. How many of the items listed have been replicated and sold? If students have a difficult time understanding how ideas can be replicated and sold, you could direct them to the paragraph that explains how phrases such as "life, liberty, and the pursuit of happiness" have become "co-opted by advertising slogans coined by marketers" (p. 381). Do students agree with the claim that the use of such phrases by corporations is a sign that originality has become less valued?

You could tell students that their notions of America might be challenged in this chapter. The last paragraph notes how America's identity is uncertain: "What America is, and what it does and should represent, are all questions under serious debate." Ask students to freewrite some answers to the questions raised above. After discussing their answers, instruct them to keep their answers until the end of the chapter to see if they've changed.

 For additional resources for the selections in this chapter (including exercises and annotated links), go to www.seeingandwriting.com.

Andreas Gursky, *99 Cent*

Gursky's photograph of the aisles in a 99 cent store gives an unrelenting image of consumer culture. Gursky is above the scene, suggesting the objective point of view of a security camera. Aisles of neatly organized food packages and juice containers stretch into the distance and reflect in the mirrored ceiling. The viewer can be overwhelmed by the color and the repetition, almost to the point that the products seem to lose their individuality and become swatches of color. In this way, the products are all surface yet create depth. The few people that appear in the picture are also lost among the products. Generally, a person is often the focus of a photograph. Gursky plays with this convention, making it hard for the viewer to focus on any one person for very long.

You might begin discussion by asking students to examine the photograph and write a paragraph on their first impression of it. If students ask for more direction, you should at first avoid the suggestion that they examine the photograph as a statement about American culture. Instead, ask them to describe the scene and their emotional reaction. Students will probably write very little about the people in the picture, or they will write about how they have difficulty focusing on the people. Some students might state that the seemingly endless packages of consumable products reflect the wealth and freedom of American society; others might see gluttony.

Gursky digitally enhanced certain parts of this image. You might make students aware of this and ask them which parts seem exaggerated, if any. How does this information change their view of the picture? You could also ask students whether it is good for cameras to "lie." Doesn't Gursky's picture—even with its digital manipulation—still tell a truth?

ADDITIONAL WRITING TOPICS

1. Ask students to freewrite on whether digital enhancement makes photography more or less artistic.

2. Ask students to go through a supermarket or department store and examine how product packaging appeals to consumers. For an expository paper, they should choose one product (e.g., a vacuum cleaner) and explain how the packaging of its different brands appeals to consumers.

CONNECTIONS WITH OTHER TEXTS

1. Throughout the text, students have encountered advertisements that have tried to appeal to the consumer as an individual (Chapter 1, bicycle ads; Chapter 2, Ericsson ad; Chapter 3, Kodak ads). Gursky's picture presents the ultimate goal of all advertising: to sell products. In ads, the product often gets lost. If you were to ask students about their favorite commercials, some students will probably be able to describe the commercial well but won't recall the product being advertised. You might ask students to examine some of the ads in the text: How prominent is the product in each ad?

2. Joel Sternfeld's *A Young Man Gathering Shopping Carts* (p. 408) presents—as the apt title states—a man gathering shopping carts in an empty parking lot. In Gursky's photo, viewers can barely focus on any individual since the colorful products draw the eye. Sternfeld's photo does not present products, but the eye is drawn away from the one person in the picture by the colorful carts, which once held the products. You might ask students to see the photos by Gursky and Sternfeld as "Before" and "After."

SUGGESTIONS FOR FURTHER READING, THINKING, AND WRITING

print

Galassi, Peter, and Andreas Gursky. *Andreas Gursky: Museum of Modern Art, New York*. New York: Museum of Modern Art, 2001.

[www] *web*

www.artcyclopedia.com/artists/gursky_andreas .html   Provides numerous links to Gursky's artwork.

Links for the selections in this chapter can be found at www.seeingandwriting.com.

PAIR: **Robert Pinsky, *On Television***
Matt Groening, *The Simpsons*

GENERATING CLASS DISCUSSION AND IN-CLASS WRITING

Pinsky's poem charts the narrator's changing view of television, which is personified throughout the poem. You might ask students to trace the steps in this change. Initially the narrator has only negative associations with television, viewing it as a "little thief, escort / Of the dying and comfort of the sick." He remembers his father and sister spending hours "Snuggled in one chair watching" television while his mother was ill. In some ways, their closeness reflected "In a blue glow" from the television set drove him away, and he "scorned" the television. Now, older, the narrator finds his own comfort in television, calling it "brilliant / And reassuring." He gives thanks to television for all it has offered him in its fleeting images.

Students might discuss how the narrator describes television. They might list the descriptive phrases. For example, television is a "Terrarium of dreams and wonders." In this phrase Pinsky offers the sealed image of the miniature greenhouse that is a terrarium and suggests that television grows not ferns but "dreams and wonders"—providing a positive gloss on the medium. Likewise, referring to older incarnations of the TV set, the narrator speaks of the "Cotillion of phosphors / Or liquid crystal." Students might discuss why Pinsky chose the word *cotillion* rather than *dance* or *ball*. How does word choice throughout the poem (e.g., *terrarium, coffer, ordained, cotillion, acquiescence*) elevate the status of television? This process might be seen to culminate in the link between television and Hermes, the messenger-god.

The narrator recounts what he remembers from television, and his examples may be alien to many students today. You might ask them to list images they remember from television. Why are these particular images special and memorable? Do your students share the narrator's sense that these messages are "Fleeter than light"?

Most students are probably familiar with *The Simpsons* as a television show, but they may never have looked at it critically. (Although it does not occur until later in this chapter, you might want to assign the Talking Pictures exercise about *The Simpsons* in conjunction with this image.) To guide them in this direction, you might ask them to think about the very basics of the image: the colors and shapes. The colors are bright and highly unnatural, reinforcing the comic book feel of the show. The shapes are simple—rounded or squared. Again, the simplistic scheme underscores the cartoon quality and is repeated in the sparse decoration within the Simpsons' living room. Little distracts the viewer from the family; only a few additional objects call attention to themselves and their significance and to their own simple lines. In fact, the carefully conceived world inside the Simpsons' home contrasts with the out-of-control world outside it—as exemplified by the sinking ship in the picture above the sofa or the barred circular window on the door. You might ask students to list the objects within this living room and contrast it with their own—chances are their own spaces are crowded with things piled on every surface. The Simpsons' space is carefully drawn and colored by scores of animators to direct viewer attention at all times.

You might ask students to consider the family relationship depicted in the cartoon: Homer, Marge, Lisa, and Maggie together—and Bart apart. Although the entire family directs its attention to the TV set, only Homer and Marge seem especially pleased by what they see. Students might discuss how the control of the TV by Homer sets the tone for the family. Do your students watch the same shows their parents do? Why or why not? Students might also discuss how television can bring family members together yet still keep them isolated from each other.

Groening's composition of the frame intentionally foregrounds the television in a way that emphasizes its importance to the family. Students might note the exaggerated distance between the sofa and the television. Even though the box is across the room, it pulls in the family. The TV actually emits a glow. The family and the room are oriented around it. In one way the portrait of the Simpsons expresses the ultimate in television dependence: A TV family cannot tear itself away from TV. You might ask students to think about the arrangement of their own living spaces. How many of them have placed a TV set as the focal point of their living rooms, bedrooms, or kitchens? How does the spatial design of their home reflect the importance of television?

ADDITIONAL WRITING TOPICS

1. Ask students to reread Pinsky's poem, paying close attention to the descriptive terms he uses for the television. Then, direct them to write their own "Ode to a TV," carefully choosing descriptions to convey a specific attitude about television.

2. In *The Simpsons*, "the jokes also address current social issues, and the writing often conceals sophisticated social commentary" (p. 388). Direct students to write an essay that indicates how this image of the family addresses a current social issue.

3. Pinsky writes of television, "In a blue glow my father and little sister sat / Snuggled in one chair watching you." The same familial proximity is depicted in the cartoon of the Simpsons. However, the tone projected by Groening's piece seems less cozy than that offered by Pinsky's poem. Ask students to explain how each artist views the relationship between television and family.

CONNECTIONS WITH OTHER TEXTS

1. In the next selection, Pinsky writes about television and the Simpsons in an essay. Ask students to read a few paragraphs of Pinsky's essay. How is Pinsky the poet similar to and different from Pinsky the essayist?

2. Pinsky's poem could be described as an ode to television, to a lifelong relationship with the set and its images. Ask students to compare Pinsky's descriptive strategies with those used by Larry Woiwode in "Ode to an Orange" (Chapter 1, p. 48). How does each object symbolize family and comfort?

SUGGESTIONS FOR FURTHER READING, THINKING, AND WRITING

print

Cusac, Anne Marie. "U.S. Poet Laureate" (Interview). *The Progressive,* May 1999: 35.

Groening, Matt. *Cartooning with the Simpsons.* New York: Harperperennial, 1993. Groening explains how he invented and then perfected the characters known as the Simpsons.

———. *Homer's Guide to Being a Man.* New York: Harperperennial, 2000.

Pinsky, Robert. *History of My Heart.* New York: Moonday Press, 1997.

———. "Robert Pinsky on The Simpsons (My Favorite Show)." *New York Times Magazine,* 20 September 1998: 55.

(www) web

www.favoritepoem.org   This project, created by Pinsky in his capacity as poet laureate, features the favorite poems of a wide array of Americans. Everyone is invited to add their own selection as well.

www.poets.org   When you type Pinsky's name into this site's search engine, it provides links to a number of excellent Pinsky resources.

www.snpp.com   A large site devoted to the Simpsons.

Links for the selections in this chapter can be found at www.seeingandwriting.com.

Robert Pinsky, *Creating the "Real" in Bright Yellow and Blue*

GENERATING CLASS DISCUSSION AND IN-CLASS WRITING

In his essay on *The Simpsons,* Pinsky discusses television as an art form. In his discussion he praises *The Simpsons* for its clever bridging of reality and unreality. A guiding question for his essay is "how might television, and a witty fiction like 'The Simpsons,' be related to an art like poetry, or to mass media like the movies and radio?" (para. 2). He briefly touches upon film (para. 7) and radio (para. 8), but the comparisons do not extend throughout the essay. Pinsky begins with poetry because it is the subject he knows best. As he observes, poetry "is the opposite of a mass medium; one person is the medium. That scale is part of poetry's power as well as its limitation" (para. 3). He recognizes the power of poetry in an age of mass media but notes that poetry is not always deserving of its elevated status: "there have been many stupid, trivial poems. And television has produced brilliant works amid its great mountain ranges of dross" (para. 4).

An important similarity between poetry and television is that each depends upon the nature of its medium and its past: "Great poems achieve a new understanding of their vocal, intimate medium while respecting its nature—they vault beyond repetition of past formulas by understanding the art's history, in order to warp, adapt or defy the old conventions in new ways" (para. 5). Outstanding television, Pinsky claims, works in the same way. It recognizes the nature of the medium and twists conventions to make something new. Television has a literal quality lacking in other mediums. Movies are larger than life, and radio depends on imagination. "Television's great moments have had to do with presence, immediacy, unpredictability: Oswald wincing at Ruby's bullet; Carlton Fisk dancing his home run onto the right side of the Fenway foul pole" (para. 9).

Citing *I Love Lucy* and *Seinfeld,* Pinsky notes that the finest sitcoms "have played with television's literal quality" (para. 10). In *Seinfeld*—often described as a show about "nothing"—Jerry Seinfeld plays a character of the same name "who is pitching a show about 'nothing'" (para. 10). *The Simpsons* also plays with the conventions of television, often parodying its drama, comedy, news, and stars (para. 15). Pinsky also notes that certain shows, including *The Simpsons,* have excelled because they are shows made not by stars, but by artists or writers: "The relative absence of stars allows an astonishing kind of imaginative freedom even within the restraints of a rigid, mass-medium format" (para. 18).

Television has had success with shows based on reality, such as *Hill Street Blues* and *St. Elsewhere*, and shows that are unreal, such as cartoons and *Sesame Street*. Sitcoms play with this real/unreal divide on television by featuring cartoonish characters. As examples, he notes Ted Baxter from *The Mary Tyler Moore Show* and Kramer and Newman from *Seinfeld*. As Pinsky notes, "The medium's best work in comedy has sometimes attained that level [of art] by exploring in a self-reflecting way television's peculiar relationship between the literal and the fake" (para. 17). *The Simpsons* does this as well: "Balloonlike yet also human, they convey the complex play between the literal and the imagined, the fake and the genuine, that is a central vibration in life, and in television" (para. 20).

ADDITIONAL WRITING TOPICS

1. Ask students to freewrite about how they view different mediums—film, television, print (poetry and prose), radio—as art forms.

2. Pinsky argues that poetry is glorified unnecessarily and that television deserves more respect (para. 4), a fairly uncommon view. In the academy, television and film are generally viewed as "popular culture" and, therefore, less deserving of study than poetry and prose. Ask students to write an essay that argues whether television should be studied in college.

3. Have students write a persuasive essay on another medium that deserves more respect. You might suggest that they compare and contrast the medium with other mediums for a sense of perspective, as Pinsky does. Some possible subjects: film, photography, drama, comic books, Internet sites.

CONNECTIONS WITH OTHER TEXTS

1. In his essay, Pinsky praises the Simpsons and the powers of television. Ask students to read Pinsky's poem "On Television" and compare it to his essay. What does Pinsky do in his poem that he cannot in his essay (and vice versa)? Which surprises students more—an essay about television, or a poem about television?

2. In his essay "Killing Monsters" (p. 582), Gerard Jones argues the possible benefits of violent media. Criticisms have been leveled at the Simpsons as a popular television family due to the often selfish and crude behavior of Bart and Homer. Ask students to consider ways in which the portrayal of the Simpsons as a family is good for viewers.

www. Links for the selections in this chapter can be found at www.seeingandwriting.com.

PORTFOLIO: **David Graham**

GENERATING CLASS DISCUSSION AND IN-CLASS WRITING

Before engaging students in discussion of the Seeing questions, you might ask them to examine the photographs for similarities and differences. Students will probably find the *Mike Memphis Lepore as Elvis* photo similar to *Miss Bucks County* in that a dressed-up figure is centered in each one. They will probably note that the subject of *Frankie Nardiello* is also centered, but his whole body is not shown. If you ask students where their eyes are drawn in this picture, most will probably refer to Nardiello's hair and the shark on the wall. Ask students to consider why this photograph is framed differently from *Mike Memphis Lepore* and *Miss Bucks County*. Perhaps Nardiello's hair and wall art reveal more about him. Some of these details would certainly be lost if the focus were Nardiello's body. Students might see the *Army Navy Game* photograph as the most exotic photo here. Have them note how the photograph directs the viewer's eye. The soldiers begin at the center of the photograph but gradually move to the right, bringing the viewer's eye with them. Drawing the viewer's attention in this way accentuates the exotic nature of the scene. If Graham had presented only one soldier from a different angle, he would be seen as an anomaly by the viewer, who would then examine the rest of the details in the photograph (the football players, the stadium, etc.). If students have difficulty discussing the first Seeing question, ask them to write a brief response to it, which you would then discuss as a class.

ADDITIONAL WRITING TOPICS

1. Ask students to write a short essay that explains why a particular Graham photo most appeals to them. They should address the photograph's subject, perspective, and tone.

2. Divide students into groups, asking each group to do a close reading of one of the photos. In the close reading, students should note every detail in the picture. Once the groups are done, they should report their findings to the class.

CONNECTIONS WITH OTHER TEXTS

1. Instruct students to write an essay that compares and contrasts Graham's photographs with those of another Portfolio photographer in the book. What is the style of each photographer, and how does each achieve this style?

2. Ask students to find more of Graham's photos on the web and to write a description of at least five pictures. The students should then report back to the class: Do the photos in this collection match the style of those found on the Internet?

SUGGESTIONS FOR FURTHER READING, THINKING, AND WRITING

print

Graham, David. *American Beauty.* New York: Aperture, 1987.

———. *Land of the Free: What Makes Americans Different.* New York: Aperture, 1999.

———. *Only in America.* New York: Knopf, 1991.

 web

Links for the selections in this chapter can be found at www.seeingandwriting.com.

Andrew Sullivan, *The Pursuit of Happiness: Four Revolutionary Words*

GENERATING CLASS DISCUSSION AND IN-CLASS WRITING

Sullivan's essay celebrates the Declaration of Independence's inclusion of the phrase "the pursuit of happiness" alongside "life" and "liberty," and it explains how this inclusion is one reason why "the United States still elicits such extreme hatred in some parts of the world" (para. 1). As Sullivan notes, the phrase now seems prosaic, but when it was first put forth, it "was perhaps the most radical political statement ever delivered" (para. 1). The essay contains references to Islamic fundamentalism and was written in response to the events of September 11. You might begin discussion by reading the opening of the Declaration of Independence to your students. Do they find the words powerful or familiar?

In the second paragraph, Sullivan explains how the word *pursuit* makes the American government different: "It's about the process of seeking something. It's about incompletion, dissatisfaction, striving, imperfection" (para. 2). Sullivan cites imperfection as a major reason for human suffering at the hands of the government: "In the Europe of the preceding centuries, armies had gone to war, human beings had been burned at stakes, monarchs had been dethroned, and countries torn apart because imperfection wasn't enough" (para. 2). Because it allows and even strives for imperfection, the United States invites dissent and does not feel the need to enforce holiness or virtue. Sullivan notes that such imperfection does not suit the mindset of modern Islamic fundamentalists: "For them, the spiritual and intellectual life is not about pursuit; it's about submission" (para. 3). Point out to students how Sullivan repeats the structure of the previous sentence in the next: "It's not about inquiry into the unknown. It's about struggle for the will of Allah" (para. 3). Note how Sullivan uses repetition of key words—*doubt* and *struggle*—to create smooth transitions and a graceful rhythm for the rest of the paragraph.

Sullivan states that the American founders encountered similar religious fundamentalism from European Christians, which caused the founders to create a government that would not concern itself with how citizens chose to live: "No political authority would be able to lay down for all citizens what was necessary for salvation, or even for a good life" (para. 4). He observes that the United States of America has differed from other governments and philosophers by viewing happiness as an end in itself. Happiness, he notes, had been previously subjected to moral evaluation. Although American citizens might disagree about the way to achieve happiness, the important issue for Sullivan "is that the government of the United States take no profound interest in how any of these people define their own happiness" (para. 6).

Students might note that Sullivan fails to mention certain exceptions—marijuana use, same-sex marriage, and so on. You might mention that he has written about the contradictions of American freedom regarding marijuana and marriage laws. This might be a good point to discuss audience awareness. Why might he have not written about such contradictions in this essay? Who is this essay's audience? Would he have possibly offended his audience by coming out in favor of marijuana legalization and same-sex marriages?

Sullivan briefly mentions some of the "many reasons why America evokes hostility across the globe" (para. 7). He notes American wealth, power, foreign policy, and history. However, he focuses upon the spread of American ideals and products. Foreigners can either integrate by moving forward or resist by going backward. He notes that Islamic fundamentalists have chosen the latter: "Far, far back is where some in the Middle East now want to go. The roots of Islamic fundamentalism go back centuries and bypass many more recent, and more open, strains of Islam" (para. 9). They have chosen to resist because of how their society and religion would change under American influences.

ADDITIONAL WRITING TOPICS

1. Ask students to research what the phrase "pursuit of happiness" meant to Jefferson and his contemporaries. If the phrase was in dispute during Jefferson's time, have students write an essay that explains how the current meaning won. If the meaning has changed, students could write an expository essay on the phrase's transformation over time.

2. Direct students to consider how some pursuits are limited; consider same-sex marriage, drug use, legal drinking age, seatbelt laws, and so on. Encourage students to freewrite about why certain pursuits might be limited—what is the basis of our laws? Then have them write a paper that argues for or against a certain law currently under dispute.

CONNECTIONS WITH OTHER TEXTS

1. Ask students to type the phrase "the pursuit of happiness" into an Internet search engine. How is the phrase currently being used? Do students find that it is largely being used by advertisers? Ask students to write an essay that explores how the phrase is being used in popular culture.

2. According to Sullivan, the American pursuit of happiness is a significant reason for anti-American feelings, particularly those manifested by the actions of terrorists on September 11. He observes that Islamic fundamentalists want to go "far, far back" to escape American notions of happiness (para. 9). Students might recall that Don DeLillo also noted the terrorists' desire to bring back the past (p. 279). Although DeLillo and Sullivan might make valid points, they show no evidence for their statements. Their focus allows little room for improvement or changes on the part of the United States. Ask students to investigate other possible reasons for anti-American feelings.

SUGGESTIONS FOR FURTHER READING, THINKING, AND WRITING

print

Jayne, Allen. *Jefferson's Declaration of Independence: Origins, Philosophy and Theology*. Lexington: University Press of Kentucky, 1998.

Sullivan, Andrew. *Love Undetectable: Notes on Friendship, Sex, and Survival*. New York: Vintage, 1999.

———. *Virtually Normal: An Argument about Homosexuality*. New York: Vintage, 1996.

www. *web*

www.andrewsullivan.com/ Andrew Sullivan's homepage. Many of his essays appear here, including several that support same-sex marriage.

www.indegayforum.org/articles/sullivan12.html An essay by Sullivan called "Enemies of Pleasure, Enemies of Health," which addresses how the U.S. government's view of marijuana is antithetical to its promise of "the pursuit of happiness."

www.pbs.org/jefferson/ PBS page on Ken Burns's film about Thomas Jefferson. The site contains documents written by Jefferson, including several drafts of the Declaration of Independence. It also includes a gallery of pictures that try to illustrate contemporary meanings of "the pursuit of happiness."

Links for the selections in this chapter can be found at www.seeingandwriting.com.

audio/visual

Save Our History: Declaration of Independence. 50 min. 2001. VHS videocassette. Distributed by A&E Television Networks. Relates the history of the document and explains its social and political influence throughout the world.

Diesel, *Freedom Is Now Sponsored by Diesel*

GENERATING CLASS DISCUSSION AND IN-CLASS WRITING

This ad is unconventional, bold, and fun—much like the clothing it presents. It features three people in a field. The man's dark clothing and the woman's light clothing create a sense of balance for the picture, and make them stand out against the reds, greens, and yellows of the field. The brand of clothing is presented as unconventional and fun. She's wearing a tie as though it were a necklace. He wears necklaces and an open shirt.

The squat, round character in the middle wears a suit of red and has a white head—colors matching those in the "Freedom is now sponsored by Diesel" tagline in the ad's upper left corner and in the text box in the lower right corner. Beyond the figures the field stretches into the distance, and a sense of depth is created as the details become less distinct and mix into patches of green and yellow. This wide-open field under a blue sky represents the land of opportunity, of freedom.

You might begin discussion by asking students to describe their favorite ads or commercials. Do the ads discussed share any similarities? Have the class consider what makes these ads and commercials so effective. You might point out that a key aim of advertising is to be memorable. The ad can be humorous or annoying, sexy or repulsive, clever or dumb, but it has to be memorable. The Diesel ad will prompt a wide range of responses among students, but most will probably agree that it is memorable.

ADDITIONAL WRITING TOPICS

1. Have students write a short paragraph that records their response to the ad. Who is the ad's main figure? Ask students to consider the possible ways in which Daniel, the Diesel mascot, operates in this ad.

2. Instruct students to write an essay that compares and contrasts this Diesel ad with ads by other clothing manufacturers. How does each company sell its product? What methods are used? Tell students to apply the directions in Seeing question 2 to the ads they describe. They should write under the assumption that their readers will never see the ads, but they should cut out or photocopy the ads for you. In this way, students will strengthen their descriptive writing abilities, and you will be able to assist them since you will be able to examine the ads they describe.

3. Ask students to watch commercials for one night and record the commercials and the television shows in a journal. Can they categorize the commercials by method? How much do the commercials represent the product being advertised? Students could also do this with magazine ads. Have them report their findings to the class.

CONNECTIONS WITH OTHER TEXTS

1. Ask students to compare and contrast this ad with Coca Cola's *America* ad (p. 127), particularly in regard to the use of color. Also ask students whether the Diesel ad could function as an ad for the *America* campaign.

2. You might point out that the 1998 Murray bicycle ad (p. 69) also uses the American value of freedom to sell its product, but not as playfully as Diesel does. Ask students to investigate ads from other countries to see how cultural values play into their ads.

SUGGESTIONS FOR FURTHER READING, THINKING, AND WRITING

[www.] *web*

www.diesel.com/   Diesel's homepage.

Links for the selections in this chapter can be found at www.seeingandwriting.com.

VISUALIZING COMPOSITION: **Audience**

GENERATING CLASS DISCUSSION AND IN-CLASS WRITING

Audience awareness is a vital part of writing, yet it is often neglected by beginning writers. Students often assume the audience to be either the instructor or anyone in general. When you give writing assignments—from freewriting exercises to research essays—stress the issue of audience. Freewriting often has the writer as its sole audience; so when you intend for students to share their freewriting with the class, you should either tell them beforehand to write with that in mind, or tell the students after the writing has been done not to judge the quality of the shared results. For formal assignments, you might alternate between prompts that have built-in audiences and prompts that allow students to choose their audience. By alternating such assignments, students get practice in writing for particular audiences and in finding audiences on their own.

You might ask students to consider the different possible audiences of an essay about binge drinking on campus. They will probably list parents, students, teachers, and university administrators. Put students into groups, and ask each group to list the characteristics of a particular audience. How would such an essay be important to each audience? How would examples and tone differ for the audiences? When the groups are done, ask them to share their lists with the class. Or you might ask students to individually draft a letter to each audience about the issue. From these exercises, students might see how tone, word choice, and supporting details will differ for each audience.

Regarding the ad, most students will realize that the ad is aimed at a young audience and will point to the young man as evidence. However, students might have a harder time articulating how the ad's message is conveyed. You could ask them to imagine how the ad would be different without the guitar. How would the young man appear then? Without the guitar, he might appear lazy, sleeping his life away when he could be out using his Visa card. The guitar shows how he has spent his money and suggests that he is sleeping the day away because his night life has improved.

ADDITIONAL WRITING TOPICS

1. Ask students to imagine that their favorite high school teacher has asked them to write an essay about their high school experience. Their audience is first-year high school students. Essentially, the essay should advise teens on how to approach the challenges of high school. Your students should consider educational and social challenges in the essay. You can provide other audiences for such an assignment. Students could direct their advice to parents, advising them how best to help their children through high school. The essay could also be aimed at high school administrators, helping them understand how the high school could better prepare students for college.

2. To prepare for the first writing prompt, you could have students write a letter to a first-year high school student about how to face the challenges of high school. Ask students to read their letters out loud. As classmates listen, they should determine whether each letter displays the appropriate word choice, tone, and examples.

3. Some students might not remember the feelings they had during their first year of high school. In effect, their essays might regurgitate the clichés they ignored from their parents when they were in high school. In order to get a better feel for the audience, ask students to write a brief essay that reflects on the feelings they had during their first week of high school.

CONNECTIONS WITH OTHER TEXTS

1. Ask students to examine the Diesel ad. Who is its audience? What details suggest this? How is its audience similar to and different from the Visa ad's (p. 406) audience?

2. Tell students to choose an essay from the text and analyze its audience. In their analysis, they should explain how each author anticipates the audience's expectations and responses. They should also consider how the essay would change for a different audience.

(www) Links for the selections in this chapter can be found at www.seeingandwriting.com.

Joel Sternfeld, *A Young Man Gathering Shopping Carts*

GENERATING CLASS DISCUSSION AND IN-CLASS WRITING

Sternfeld's picture is well described in the headnote. This picture is interesting in how it presents contradictions. The man's striking looks make him stand out in the parking lot of a generic grocery store, Foodtown. His shirt and tie suggest professionalism, yet the shirt is open, the sleeves are rolled up, and the tie is loose. We make the connection that he is a cart-gatherer not only through the title but also through the way the picture is tied together by the similar colors of the carts, the Foodtown sign, and the shirt hanging from the man's pants. His expression seems to be one of indifference, yet one of his hands almost looks like a clenched fist.

You could start discussion by asking students to examine the photograph and note the order in which they see things. Students will probably look at the man first, and then their focus will shift to the cart next to him, and follow the rest of the carts to the Foodtown sign. Ask students how Sternfeld made their eyes follow a certain path. Why does the young man have the button-down shirt and tie as well as the shirt hanging from his pants? Since the orange shirt recalls the color of the Foodtown sign, is it possible that the shirt and tie do not belong to the man, that they were used just for the picture?

ADDITIONAL WRITING TOPICS

1. Imagine this photo as an ad. What product would be advertised? What would be the ad's tagline?

2. Ask students to freewrite about the tone of the photograph. How does Sternfeld create a sense of tone here?

3. This picture comes from Sternfeld's *Stranger Passing*. Ask students to examine other photos from this collection (some can be found on the Internet) and write an essay that explains what his intentions seem to be and how he meets them in his pictures.

CONNECTIONS WITH OTHER TEXTS

1. You might direct students to examine Sternfeld's photo along with other images from this chapter: Gursky's *99 Cent* and Diesel's *Freedom* ad. Ask students to write a paper that compares and contrasts these images in terms of their use of color.

2. Students might recall Sternfeld's *Taylor Hall Parking Lot* from Chapter 2 (pp. 186–87). They might note how the images look nothing alike, despite their being taken by the same person. You could discuss how authorship seems hard to distinguish in certain art forms. For example, a writer's pseudonym is often uncovered by fans who recognize stylistic and thematic similarities. People attuned to Sternfeld's work might not have any difficulty in recognizing each of these pictures as Sternfeld's.

SUGGESTIONS FOR FURTHER READING, THINKING, AND WRITING

print

Sternfeld, Joel, Ian Frazier, and Douglas R. Nickel. *Stranger Passing*. Boston: Bulfinch Press, 2001.

www. web

www.hainesgallery.com/JSTERN.statement.html
Haines Gallery web page contains images from and a statement on Sternfeld's work. Links for the selections in this chapter can be found at www.seeingandwriting.com.

James B. Twitchell, *In Praise of Consumerism*

GENERATING CLASS DISCUSSION AND IN-CLASS WRITING

As the title suggests, Twitchell not only defends consumerism—he praises it. He notes that in recent years the consumer has been viewed as less of a participant and more of a victim in the material world. You might begin discussion by asking students to generate a list of the things they've bought in the last week and why they bought each item. Have students share their lists with the class. Do they feel in control of their purchases, or can they not explain why they buy certain items?

The central question of Twitchell's essay is "How and why did the consumer get dumbed down and phased out so quickly?" (para. 6). Twitchell blames academics for the current perception of consumerism: "the academy has casually passed off as 'hegemonic brainwashing' what seems to me, at least, a self-evident truth about human nature: We like having stuff" (para. 7). He notes that the main message of cultural studies courses is that consumers are being oppressed and manipulated: "In macrocosmic form, the oppression is economic—the 'free' market. In microcosmic form, oppression is media—your 'free' TV" (para. 9). And when consumers view advertising, packaging, and fashion in an innocent way, this "only proves their power over [us]" (para. 10).

Twitchell observes that people desire things that exceed our natural needs: "Once fed and sheltered, our needs have always been cultural, not natural" (para. 12). Students might note that Twitchell does not back up this statement with any evidence.

You might also point out to students that Twitchell's use of the word *always* should alert them to question the validity of the statement. Can students refute or defend Twitchell's statement?

He does admit that consumerism has its problems: "Consumerism is wasteful, it is devoid of otherworldly concerns, it lives for today and celebrates the body" (para. 14). He even notes personal struggles he has with consumer culture (para. 15). However, he wants his readers to realize that we are not being forced into this lifestyle. Even though we may not like it, "it is far closer to what most people want most of the time than at any other period of modern history" (para. 18). Again, students might note that examples or evidence for this statement would be helpful in determining its validity. Students will probably find Twitchell's comparison of a Trollope novel to a Steve Martin film (paras. 19–25) to be unhelpful. This might be a good opportunity to discuss different kinds of evidence.

Twitchell notes that consumerism will not fix poverty, racism, and other social ills (para. 26), but he does think that it results in a more democratic, egalitarian world (para. 25). You might ask students to consider how our capitalistic society allows for more democracy and equality than noncapitalistic cultures.

ADDITIONAL WRITING TOPICS

1. Ask students to freewrite about how their experiences in school have shaped their views of consumerism.

2. Have students write an argument essay that supports or refutes Twitchell's thesis. Students should analyze his points, add their own, and supply examples.

3. Twitchell's harsh characterization of academics makes it clear that this essay does not have them in mind as an audience. Put students in groups, and have each group generate a list of how this essay would be different if it were aimed at academics.

CONNECTIONS WITH OTHER TEXTS

1. Twitchell's essay opens with Helen Landon Cass's statement to advertisers: "Sell [consumers] their dreams. Sell them what they longed for and hoped for and almost despaired of having" (para. 1). Ask students to choose two or three ads from the text that apply Case's advice. How would they classify the "dreams" being represented in the ads?

2. Twitchell has a problem with Channel One TV in the classroom (para. 15). Ask students to research Channel One and write a paper that argues for or against its being in the classroom.

SUGGESTIONS FOR FURTHER READING, THINKING, AND WRITING

print

Cross, Gary S. *An All-Consuming Century: Why Commercialism Won in Modern America.* New York: Columbia University Press, 2000.

Ewen, Stuart. *Captains of Consciousness: Advertising and the Social Roots of the Consumer Culture.* New York: Basic Books, 2001.

Frank, Thomas. *The Conquest of Cool: Business Culture, Counterculture, and the Rise of Hip Consumerism.* Chicago: University of Chicago Press, 1997.

Schor, Juliet B. *The Overspent American: Why We Want What We Don't Need.* New York: HarperCollins, 1999.

Twitchell, James. *Adcult USA: The Triumph of Advertising in America.* New York: Columbia University Press, 1997.

——. *Lead Us into Temptation: The Triumph of American Materialism.* New York: Columbia University Press, 1999.

——. *Living It Up: Our Love Affair with Luxury.* New York: Columbia University Press, 2002.

——. *20 Ads That Shook the World: The Century's Most Ground-Breaking Advertising and How It Changed Us.* New York: Crown Publishers, 2000.

[www.] web

www.look-look.com   Homepage of the youth-culture research group.

www.pbs.org/wgbh/pages/frontline/shows/cool/ Web page for the *Frontline* documentary *The Merchants of Cool.* A great resource that deals with many of the issues raised in this section.

www.phatfarmstore.com/   Phat Farm's official homepage.

Links for the selections in this chapter can be found at www.seeingandwriting.com.

audio/visual

Frontline: The Merchants of Cool. 60 min. 2001. VHS videocassette. Distributed by PBS. This film focuses on the main aspect of this section: the marketing of "cool" to teens.

VISUALIZING CONTEXT: **A Culture of Consumption**

GENERATING CLASS DISCUSSION AND IN-CLASS WRITING

The text notes that "advertisements frequently repeat certain themes and concerns. As such, they offer a remarkably sensitive portrait of the collective hopes and aspirations, fears and anxieties of any—and every—generation of Americans." You might ask students to think of ads that repeat similar themes. Students might recall that in the wake of September 11 automobile ads asked consumers to "help keep America rolling." This was an appeal to support America not only patriotically but financially as well.

You might direct students to the Palmolive Soap ad from 1942 that asks women to do their part in the war effort by guarding their beauty for the men in the armed forces. A striking blonde is in the ad's forefront, pledging to guard her beauty, while numerous women do the same in the background. Although the woman seems to be looking at the three uniformed men at the top of the ad, the suggestion is that she is looking up at the American flag. You might direct students to the text of the ad. What does the word *Pledge* suggest? Some students might note that the typeface of the pledge is similar to that used in the Declaration of Independence. They should also note the bandwagon appeal not only in the overall premise of the ad but in its text as well: "Turn now, as so many charming women are doing, to Palmolive for your beauty care." You might also point students to the last two lines of the ad and ask whether they read any other meanings behind the ad's message: "Keep your pledge of beauty with Palmolive. Guard your loveliness . . . 'til he comes marching home!" Do any students read *loveliness* as *chastity?*

ADDITIONAL WRITING TOPICS

1. Invite students to research the images of women in ads during World War II. Based on this research, students can write an essay that explains how and why women were presented in certain roles.

2. The text notes that "advertisements frequently repeat certain themes and concerns" (para. 3). Ask students to research ads that have been deemed most popular or most effective. Do they repeat certain themes or concerns? How do they appeal to American culture? Have students write an expository essay on the basis of the research. In the essay, they should describe the use of language and image in the ads.

CONNECTIONS WITH OTHER TEXTS

1. Students are likely to note how much women's roles have changed since this ad first appeared. Ask them to examine how gender roles are portrayed in the bicycle ads from Chapter 1. How do they change over time?

2. Direct students to examine current advertisements for themes that relate to America's war on terrorism (e.g., car ads that declare "Let's Keep America Rolling"). Ask students to bring the advertisements to class to discuss their methods and effectiveness. How are men and women portrayed in these ads?

[www] Links for the selections in this chapter can be found at www.seeingandwriting.com.

Guillermo Gómez-Peña, *Authentic Cuban Santeria*

GENERATING CLASS DISCUSSION AND IN-CLASS WRITING

The photograph makes a strong statement about public conceptions. Notice how objects like the headdress, taco pizza, clothing, sunglasses, and Coca-Cola bottle are presented as ludicrous representations of Santeria as a religion. The photograph points out a lack of knowledge and understanding. By focusing on misconceptions and Hispanic stereotypes, Gómez-Peña forces the viewer to acknowledge the dangers of making general assumptions about race and culture. You might ask students to give their initial reaction to the photo. Then ask them to write about the artist's intent. What do they consider to be the purpose of this photograph? How do their reactions change?

Also ask students how the image reflects a change in the concept of double consciousness over time. What details of the image, medium, or style suggest the period in which it was created?

 For an interactive visual exercise for this selection, go to www.seeingandwriting.com.

ADDITIONAL WRITING TOPICS

1. Ask students to write an essay that describes Gómez-Peña's picture. As they describe the figures, the clothing, the props, and the background, they should comment on the statements made by each of the photographer's choices.

2. Invite students to find other works by Gómez-Peña. Have them write an essay that explains what two or three of his images reveal about the style and subject matter of his work.

CONNECTIONS WITH OTHER TEXTS

1. Gómez-Peña's photograph depicts how products and people are packaged and sold under a guise of authenticity. You might ask students to bring to class current ads that show how stereotypes are being "sold" along with products.

2. Ask students to consider how this picture ties in with the chapter's theme. How does it relate to other texts in the chapter? What does it say about America?

www. Links for the selections in this chapter can be found at www.seeingandwriting.com.

Before beginning this assignment, students may want to look at a web community that is not identified with any specific ethnic group in order to get a sense of the standard conventions of such communities. For example, they might look at iVillage (a women's online community) or even a generic Internet gateway, such as AltaVista or Netscape Home. In this way, students will have a better sense of what elements appeal to an ethnic audience when they visit either the web sites suggested by the text or other sites.

As an alternative assignment, students might use the web to find a museum devoted to the art and culture of a specific ethnic group. Two excellent examples that re-late to the Retrospect in this chapter are www.eiteljorg .org and www.heard.org, both of which showcase Native American culture. You might direct students to write an essay that addresses the construction and focus of the site. What messages is the site sending about the culture it features? Does the site assume that the visitor holds any preconceptions about this culture? How does it incor-porate into the site the imagery and design associated with the culture? Students might offer their classmates a tour of the sites they discuss in their essays.

Students can complete the Re: Searching the Web exercises online at www.seeingandwriting.com. Addi-tional tips and links for each exercise are also available.

Shane Young, *Carol Gardner and Bumper Sticker Wisdom, 1995*

GENERATING CLASS DISCUSSION AND IN-CLASS WRITING

In Young's photograph, Gardner presents her book—*Bumper Sticker Wisdom*—as she re-clines on the top of her car, which is covered with bumper stickers. Her pose on the car is reminiscent of that used by scantily clad, busty models in car magazines. Be-cause Gardner and her car do not resemble the models and cars in those images, Young creates a clever contrast. As viewers examine her posture, they look at her from left to right—exactly the way they read the bumper stickers. Since the picture is framed vertically with the focus being on the car and Gardner, viewers look up and down at first, associating the bumper stickers with Gardner.

Although it's difficult to glean a person's personality from bumper stickers, it seems safe to say that Gardner is open-minded and liberal (or at least anti-gun), which can be seen in the "CELEBRATE DIVERSITY" and "ARMS ARE FOR HUGGING" stickers. She also seems to have a good sense of humor because she chose "I'm Pink, Therefore I'm Spam," "If Elvis was still alive, He'd be DEAD by now," and "Paranoid people aren't al-ways wrong." And she possibly sees herself as a lifelong learner: "STUDENT DRIVER."

ADDITIONAL WRITING TOPICS

1. Ask each student to write a bumper slogan that is personally representative. Tell them to consider color, size, and typeface. Then they should write a paragraph that explains why the bumper sticker is so fitting.

2. The second writing prompt in Seeing and Writing asks students to compare and contrast the statements on shirts with those on bumper stickers. You could also ask students to focus only upon the messages on shirts. As they examine shirts sold in malls and department stores, they might notice differences between the messages on men's shirts and women's. Have your students write a paper that examines how these messages are different and why women's shirts have a wider range of messages than men's. For example, shirts for men express the same suggestive message in different ways: "Tell your mom I said 'Thanks'"; "Porn Star." Women's shirts express a range of messages: from "Princess" and "Angel" to "Hottie" and "I Like Your Boyfriend."

CONNECTIONS WITH OTHER TEXTS

1. In Chapter 4, Moyra Davey's photo *The City* (p. 363) invites viewers to infer personality traits from the desktop's items and their arrangement. Young's picture of Gardner's car makes a similar invitation. To carry the inference exercise outside of the text, you might let some trash build up in your office trash can—perhaps even fellow colleagues' trash cans—and bring the garbage to your class (throw away food, though, since students would understandably be disgusted with searching through that). As students look through the trash, they can make inferences about the owner or owners.

2. Ask students to study a car on campus that has multiple bumper stickers. Based on the car and its bumper stickers, the students should write a brief description of the car's owner.

SUGGESTIONS FOR FURTHER READING, THINKING, AND WRITING

print

Gardner, Carol. *Bumper Sticker Wisdom: America's Pulpit above the Tailpipe*. Hillsboro: Beyond Words Publishing, 1995.

web

www.internetbumperstickers.com/ A web site that provides Internet bumper stickers for e-mail messages and web sites.

Links for the selections in this chapter can be found at www.seeingandwriting.com.

Charles M. Young, *Losing: An American Tradition*

GENERATING CLASS DISCUSSION AND IN-CLASS WRITING

In his essay "Losing: An American Tradition," Charles Young probes the word *loser* to discover why it is the worst insult to Americans. Young synthesizes a variety of sources as he examines this issue, referencing personal examples, interviews, books, and films (to name but a few). He examines why losing seems to be more of an issue for men, and he also questions the value of competition. Before you have students read the essay, ask them to write down their own definitions of *winning, losing, winner,* and *loser*. Collect the definitions, read them aloud, and pass them back when you discuss the essay in class. At that time you might ask students to reread their definitions and discuss how Young's essay supported or challenged their definitions.

In the opening paragraphs Young describes the Prairie View Panthers, a college football team, as it struggles with a record losing streak, losing 77 games and winning none (paras. 1–3); the controversy over how Shannon Sharpe called Dan Marino a "loser" and later apologized (paras. 3–6); and how losers are portrayed by films and magazines (paras. 7–12). Referring back to the Sharpe–Marino incident, he then summarizes how all of these examples show that Sharpe "implied that Dan Marino was: unworthy of sex or love or friendship or progeny, socially clueless, stupid, parasitical, pathetic, poverty-stricken, cowardly, violent, felonious, . . . hated by himself, hated by all good Americans, hated by God" (para. 16). And Young finds this confusing because "Dan Marino is one of the best quarterbacks ever to play football" (para. 16).

Young focuses on how winning and losing are important concerns for men. Losing, it seems, is an emasculating experience. Young asks a former player for the Panthers about how to play during a losing streak. The player responds, "'You got to have a nut check. Either I'm going to get whipped like a girl, or I'm going to come out like a man and get on with it'" (para. 27). Reflecting on this, Young notes, "When I was losing football games in college, it seemed like the worst thing you could call somebody was a pussy" (para. 28). The coach of the Panthers seems to agree: "'Football is a test of manhood, a test of who has the biggest *cojones*'" (para. 19).

As Young observes, winning does not seem as important to women because they "are simply born to womanhood," whereas men must "supposedly win" manhood (para. 37). An anecdote told by motivational speaker Ray Pelletier seems to support this view. After he gave a speech to a women's basketball team about how the team deserved to win, one of the players asked, "'Haven't the girls in the other locker room worked really hard, too? Don't they deserve to win, too?'" (para. 51). More support is found from Dr. Donald Nathanson, a psychologist, who states, "I don't think anyone gets over the shame we have of not being adequately identified by the right gender. . . . Men are concerned that they'll be called not just female, but female genitalia" (para. 68).

Young wonders whether there is any value in competition. Nathanson sees nothing wrong with it until it moves beyond people playing a game: "'When parents and schools and bureaucracies start getting involved and demanding wins, then it gets pathological'" (para. 74). Young also consults educational philosopher Alfie Kohn, who, as Young puts it, has seen "a way out" from the destructiveness of competition (para. 83). Kohn's book "cites study after study demonstrating that competition hinders work, play, learning, and creativity in people of all ages" (para. 83). Ask students how they reacted to the ending, in which Young asks readers to admit that they're losers: "You, you're probably holding on to some putrefying little shred of self-esteem, denying that you're a loser in a country inhabited by Bill Gates and 260 million losers" (para. 85).

ADDITIONAL WRITING TOPICS

1. Ask students to write an essay that similarly analyzes how a word or phrase operates in our culture. You might encourage students to think beyond "An American Tradition," suggesting "A College Tradition," "A Male Tradition," "A Female Tradition," and the like.

2. In his essay, Young touches on how losing and winning seem to be regarded differently by the sexes. His focus, however, is on how losing is emasculating to men. Ask students to expand on this notion in an essay that explores how women regard winning and losing.

CONNECTIONS WITH OTHER TEXTS

1. In his essay "Inside Every Superhero Lurks a Nerd," Neal Gabler notes how Peter Parker is regarded as a nerd—that is, a loser—before he gains his superpowers. Students familiar with comic book heroes will notice the trend—powers are usually bestowed upon outcasts. According to Gabler, the Spider-Man film was a success because viewers could identify with the character's underdog status. Yet, don't we only root for Parker because we know he will rise above his loser sta-

tus? Young notes how we should all admit to being losers (para. 85). But what kind of loser does he mean? Ask students to look back through Young's list of loser qualities (para. 16). Why are some qualities more acceptable than others?

2. Young notes that men must "supposedly win" manhood (para. 37). Ask students to examine the portrayals of men in the Chapter 4 Retrospect. How do these images portray manhood as an achievement, as something won?

print

Byrne, David. *Your Action World: Winners Are Losers with a New Attitude.* San Francisco: Chronicle Books, 1999. Using text and images, Byrne parodies motivational books and ads.

Evans, Gail. *Play Like a Man, Win Like a Woman: What Men Know about Success That Women Need to Learn.* New York: Broadway Books, 2000.

James, Oliver. *Juvenile Violence in a Winner-Loser Culture: Socio-Economic and Familial Origins of the Rise of Violence against the Person.* London: Free Association Books, 1995. James examines how America's "winner-loser" culture has increased the level of violence against the individual.

Jones, Charlie. *What Makes Winners Win: Thoughts and Reflections from Successful Athletes.* New York: Broadway Books, 1998.

 web

Links for the selections in this chapter can be found at www.seeingandwriting.com.

RETROSPECT: **Projecting Family Values**

GENERATING CLASS DISCUSSION AND IN-CLASS WRITING

This Retrospect presents images of television families from 1957 to 2000. Before students examine the pictures, you might ask them to list the most memorable television families. Even if students have never seen the shows, most will probably name the families from *Leave It to Beaver* and *The Brady Bunch*. If this is the case, ask why these families still remain as American touchstones. Students will probably reply that each family represents a simpler, better time in American history. Will any current television families be among the ranks of the Cleavers and the Bradys in twenty, thirty years?

You might separate students into groups, giving each group a different image to examine. Have them consider how the pose of the family might support what the family is supposed to represent. How does each family fit into its historical period? If students have a difficult time examining the picture, ask them to write a list of words evoked by each family. When the groups are finished studying the pictures, they must then report their analyses to the class.

Students might note that the 1957 picture of the Cleavers presents a strong family unit. The family is dressed respectably and drawn closely together for the pose. The black and white picture suggests simplicity, innocence. At the picture's center, Ward

Cleaver is clearly presented as the head of the family. Some students might feel that the crossed arms of the mother and the youngest son make the family seem closed off to outsiders.

The 1970 picture of the Bradys shows the family on the stairs, youngest at the top, oldest at the bottom. Colors abound in the clothing and the set, reflecting the show's lighthearted attitude. Even though the Bradys seem unconventional compared to the Cleavers since the Brady children came from previous marriages, it should be noted that each parent was widowed, not divorced. You might ask students to describe the kinds of problems faced by these families. Some students have undoubtedly watched reruns or have seen various spoofs based on the shows (two films parodied the Brady series). What problems were real families facing in those times?

The 1993 image from *The Cosby Show* shows only three members of the family. Cliff Huxtable looks disgruntled as Theo makes some kind of plea. Cliff's wife, Claire, seems amused by the encounter. Students might observe that this picture presents a more realistic family than the previous two pictures because it is unposed. With the family's father and mother being a doctor and a lawyer, respectively, *The Cosby Show* was one of the first shows to present African Americans in an upper-middle class family. However, the show never dealt with the issue of race. Bill Cosby's goal was to present the Huxtable family as just another television family.

Students might note that the Sopranos and the Cleavers are presented in a similar way. The family is well dressed, tightly knit, and centered around the father. The similarities, however, end there. Unlike Ward Cleaver, Tony Soprano is in charge of the most powerful criminal organization in New Jersey, and he is unfaithful to his wife. Due to the stress of the job and the problems in his marriage, he turns to a psychiatrist. Although his wife, Carmela, primarily raises the children, she has also used her position as a mob boss's wife to influence others. Tony and Carmela worry about their daughter's choice in boyfriends and their son's problems at school—problems faced by other television families.

ADDITIONAL WRITING TOPICS

1. Ask students to freewrite about which family they identify with the most.

2. Encourage students to research other television families that fill in the gaps of the years presented in this Retrospect. They should write an essay that compares and contrasts the families and explains how each family is a product of its time. For example, you might suggest that students research *Father Knows Best*; *All in the Family*; *Family Ties*; *Party of Five*; and *Gilmore Girls*.

3. Ask students to write a personal essay about the television families they watched in their childhood and early teen years. Why were they drawn to these families? How did these television families affect their view of what a real family should be?

CONNECTIONS WITH OTHER TEXTS

1. If you have more than five groups for the group activity, you might add the image of the Simpsons found earlier in the chapter.

2. In preparation for the next chapter, you might ask students to discuss these families as American icons. What does each family represent? How do these families support and refute certain views of America?

SUGGESTIONS FOR FURTHER READING, THINKING, AND WRITING

print

Leibman, Nina. *Living Room Lectures: The Fifties Family in Film and Television.* Austin: University of Texas Press, 1995.

Pungente, John, and Martin O'Malley. *More Than Meets the Eye: Watching Television Watching Us.* Toronto: McClelland and Stewart, 1999.

 web

www.bradyworld.com/   *Brady Bunch* fan site includes history, episode guide, and photo gallery.

www.hbo.com/sopranos/   Official web site of *The Sopranos.*

www.tvland.com/nickatnite/cosby_show/   Nick at Nite's web page on *The Cosby Show.*

www.tvland.com/shows/litbeaver/   TVLand's *Leave It to Beaver* page includes pictures, sounds, and episode guide.

Links for the selections in this chapter can be found at www.seeingandwriting.com.

Neal Gabler, *Inside Every Superhero Lurks a Nerd*

GENERATING CLASS DISCUSSION AND IN-CLASS WRITING

Gabler's essay attempts to explain why *Spider-Man* was such a phenomenal box-office hit. Gabler looks beyond the film's hype and timing, and he observes that one possible reason for the film's success is that it "exists at the nexus and confluence of two fundamental American rites: adolescence and moviegoing" (para. 2). Although much of Gabler's essay focuses on teenage alienation, it also touches upon responsibility and how this value resonates with America and adolescents. You might begin discussion by asking students whether they saw *Spider-Man*, and if so, why they did or did not enjoy it.

As Gabler notes, Spider-Man is different from other superheroes. The creators of the Spider-Man character "revised the standard superhero mythology" by making the superhero an adolescent instead of someone "from another planet, like Superman" or a "rich, handsome do-gooder, like Batman" (para 3). Most teens easily identify with Peter Parker before he becomes Spider-Man. He is shy around the girl he adores and weak around the guys who pick on him. When he becomes Spider-Man, however, "he achieves the ultimate adolescent dream. He is transformed from an outcast into the toughest kid in the school. No wonder teenagers respond" (para. 4). You might note that teenage alienation and adolescent change are also major themes of two successful television shows, *Buffy the Vampire Slayer* and *Smallville*.

Students might have some problems with the brief section on Columbine. Gabler observes that the idea of turning the tables on bullies "offers an awful reminder of Columbine, Colo., where two alienated teenage outcasts took revenge on their more popular classmates in a bloody high school rampage" (para. 5). Gabler states that the film "takes the sense of powerlessness in its audience and displaces it onto the screen, providing catharsis" (para. 6). Gabler uses Columbine as an example of extreme teenage alienation. Some students might read Gabler as stating that the film is intentionally trying to relieve teens' fears about school shootings. His statements could be interpreted as implying that events similar to the Columbine shootings have made teens even more responsive to the film. You might ask students whether they thought of school shootings when they saw *Spider-Man*.

Although Gabler credits some of the film's success to Toby Maguire's performance that allows the audience to see itself in Spider-Man, he admits that most popular movies offer "wish fulfillment" and involve stars "with whom viewers can identify and through whom they can transcend themselves" (para. 7). *Spider-Man*, he notes, is also successful because it addresses an issue crucial to both Americans and adolescents: responsibility. Gabler notes that America has always tried to find a balance between rugged individualism and communal responsibility. Adolescents, too, must balance individual desire with responsibility.

Gabler observes that many movies address this issue. Even though Hollywood movies "celebrate individualism," they also present heroes who act for the greater good. As he notes, heroes are not heroic for standing on their own: "Villains after all, often stand alone" (para. 12). A film hero "deploys his individualism for the larger good, which is how the movies reconcile the American problem of self and society" (para.12). Spider-Man realizes that his powers entail responsibility. In this way, the film "gives teenage viewers the high of public service" (para. 13).

ADDITIONAL WRITING TOPICS

1. Ask students to freewrite about the appeal of superheroes, especially to adolescents.

2. Direct students to write an expository essay about a television show or film that has also met with success because of the way in which it resonates with American ideals.

3. Superman, Batman, and Wonder Woman are arguably the three most popular superheroes. They have been presented in television shows, cartoons, and films (a Wonder Woman film is in the works). Have students write an essay that compares and contrasts these three figures and explains why they have found such popularity in American culture.

CONNECTIONS WITH OTHER TEXTS

1. Gabler focuses on how teens can identify with Parker's transformation. Ask students to examine other popular films that feature transformations. Students might look at films that involve transformations of beauty (*She's All That; Miss Congeniality*), gender (*Tootsie; Mrs. Doubtfire; The Crying Game*), or age (*Big; 18 Again*) as just a few possibilities. Direct students to write a paper that explores why these films strike such a chord with audiences.

2. Audiences pay a lot of attention to the physical changes (e.g., costumes, makeup) actors and actresses undergo for their roles, but pay less attention to the transformations of scenery. However, audiences have become more aware of such changes with news coverage of shots of the World Trade Center being removed from recent films (a teaser ad for *Spider-Man* that involved them was pulled). You might show students the changes to a Toronto house for the film *My Big Fat Greek Wedding*, which Naomi Harris captured on film (pp. 442–43). Ask them to write about why a change in environment can have such a strong effect on people.

SUGGESTIONS FOR FURTHER READING, THINKING, AND WRITING

print

Gabler, Neil. *Life the Movie: How Entertainment Conquered Reality*. New York: Knopf, 1998.

[www] *web*

www.spiderman.sonypictures.com/   The film's official web site.

Links for the selections in this chapter can be found at www.seeingandwriting.com.

Links for the selections in this chapter can be found at www.seeingandwriting.com.

audio/visual

Spider-Man. Directed by Sam Raimi. 121 min. 2002. Distributed by Columbia Pictures.

Starring Tobey Maguire, Kirsten Dunst, and Willem Dafoe. You might play the scene in which Peter Parker defends himself against Flash Thompson, the high school bully.

Naomi Harris, *The Makeover*

GENERATING CLASS DISCUSSION AND IN-CLASS WRITING

Harris's pictures present the changes made to a Toronto home for the exterior shots of the film *My Big Fat Greek Wedding*. The main goal behind the changes was to make the house look bigger. To achieve this goal the film crew expanded the lawn, removed a power line, and created a driveway, a fake garage, and a façade of a second floor. As the title suggests, the film is a comedy so exaggeration is expected.

After students have examined the pictures, you might play a scene from the movie that features the house. Students might be surprised at how little the house is in the film for all the work that was involved. Ask students to consider why the film-makers felt the need to make the house "more Greek."

ADDITIONAL WRITING TOPICS

1. In the headnote, Harris is noted for presenting a lighter side to old age and a darker side to spring break. Ask students to find a topic that is usually seen in a certain way and write an essay that persuades readers to consider it in a different way. For example, a fairly persuasive paper could argue against the common view that nothing good comes from war by showing how wars can stimulate the economy, bring about social change, overthrow violent dictators, and so on.

2. You could turn the first topic into a group project by putting students into pairs and asking each pair to pick a subject for each member to present in opposite ways. After the initial essays have been written (and turned in for a grade), the pair could then combine them into one essay, collaborating on the introduction and conclusion (for a separate grade).

3. The act of making the house "more Greek" shows the need to play on a stereotype for audiences. Ask students to consider how ethnic groups are portrayed in films or television shows. Direct students to write about the portrayal of an ethnic group in a film or television show, arguing whether the portrayal helps or hinders the way the group is perceived.

CONNECTIONS WITH OTHER TEXTS

1. You could expand the second Writing question by asking students to analyze television shows about makeovers, such as *Trading Spaces; While You Were Out; A Makeover Story* on The Learning Channel.

2. Have students find a television show or movie that features an apartment or house that has been exaggerated in some way. They could write a two-page essay explaining the exaggerations and the reasons for them, or they could tape a few minutes of the show or movie and present the exaggerations to the class.

SUGGESTIONS FOR FURTHER READING, THINKING, AND WRITING

 web

www.tlc.discovery.com/fansites/tradingspaces/tradingspaces.html   This is The Learning Channel's web page for *Trading Spaces*, a popular show that films two sets of neighbors redecorating a room in each other's home with the help of the show's carpenter and decorators. The web page features photo galleries, including a before-and-after gallery.

Links for the selections in this chapter can be found at www.seeingandwriting.com.

audio/visual

My Big Fat Greek Wedding. Directed by Joel Zwick. 96 min. 2002. Distributed by IFC Films. Stars Nia Vardalos and John Corbett.

Talking Pictures

A recently popularized cultural group that transcends racial stereotypes is based on age; it is reflected in television programming that features teenage angst. In shows such as the earlier *90210* and *Melrose Place* and the more current *Dawson's Creek* and *Safe Harbor*, the dramas and dilemmas of late adolescence and early adulthood are portrayed. Ask your students to gather data from shows like these and to write an essay describing the characteristics of teenage culture in the United States today.

Looking Closer:
Marketing Cool

GENERATING CLASS DISCUSSION AND IN-CLASS WRITING

The images in this section provide different takes on "cool," and the readings discuss how it is discovered and commodified. You might begin discussion by asking students to discuss how they determine what is cool. Many students will probably respond that they are not concerned with what is seen as cool. Others might note that their choices are naturally limited by what is available at stores. If possible, you could show *Frontline's* documentary *The Merchants of Cool,* which addresses the concerns raised in the following texts.

Donnell Alexander, *Cool Like Me*

This essay takes the reader across the slippery slope of cool as a style and an attitude. Donnell Alexander opens his piece with a rap-like list of the ways he is cool, but his introduction ends with the caveat that we should "Know this while understanding that I am in essence a humble guy" (para. 10). (Evidently, modesty is cool.) Alexander maintains that "[t]he question of whether black people are cooler than white people is a dumb one, and one that I imagine a lot of people will find offensive" (para. 14). Nonetheless, he asserts, "But, cool? That's a black thang [sic], baby" (para. 15). The origins of cool, according to Alexander, are in black slavery. He says that the impulse to make "massa's garbage, hog maws and chitlins—taste good enough to eat" (para. 16) gave rise to cool:

> That inclination to make something out of nothing and then to make that something special articulated itself first in the work chants that slaves sang in the field and then in the hymns that rose out of their churches. It would later reveal itself in the music made from cast-off Civil War marching-band instruments (jazz); physical exercise turned to public spectacle (sports); and street life styling." (para. 16)

As Alexander catalogues the essence of what's cool and what's not, he acknowledges that "[w]hite folks began to try to make the primary point of cool—recognition of the need to go with the flow—a part of their lives" (para. 19) and asserts that Elvis brought cool to the white majority. Alexander warns, however, that there are strains of cool and that big business has sensed that cool is a marketable commodity. He wants us to beware of tainted cool such as this: "an evil ersatz cool . . . that fights real cool at every turn" (para. 23). This is the cool of "[a]dvertising agencies, record-company artist-development departments, and over-art-directed bars" (para. 23).

In the end, he wants even the black originators of cool to be careful of the business of cool. He says, "blacks remain woefully wedded to the bowed head and blinders. Instead of bowing to massa, they slavishly bow to trend and marketplace" (para. 29). He warns us not to be taken in by "clone cool" but to recognize that "the real secret weapon of cool is that it's about synthesis" (para. 29).

Lauren Greenfield, *Scott 16, Beverly Hills*

Greenfield's photo is taken from the set of a high school rap band's video. The main figure, Scott, is only 16 years old, a sophomore in high school. You might ask students to react to the fact that someone so young is making a video. Also direct students to point out the elements of "cool" within the photo.

Dee Dee Gordon and Sharon Lee, *Look-Look*

In this interview, Gordon and Lee explain how their company, Look-Look, provides information on youth culture. They send correspondents to find and hire trend-setting kids to report on the interests and activities of their peers. By posting this information on the Internet, they are able to keep up with the constantly changing youth culture.

Phat Farm, *Classic American Flava*

The clothing line featured here is called "Classic American Flava." You might ask students to consider how the line's interesting name applies to the picture of two men in a front yard with a dog. What aspect of this picture represent "Classic American"? What aspects represent "Flava"?

Naomi Klein, *No Logo: Taking Aim at the Brand Bullies*

Klein would probably take issue with the kind of "cool hunting" endorsed by Gordon and Lee. At one point she refers to "cool hunting" as "youth stalking" (para. 12). Her main issue with the "brand bullies" is how they play upon the country's race relations. Just as Donnell Alexander claims that cool is a "black thang" (para. 15), Klein argues that "cool hunting simply means black-culture hunting" (para. 3). She explains how Nike, Adidas, and Tommy Hilfiger have worked to make their brands seem cool to black youth. Klein notes how Hilfiger transformed itself from being "white-preppy wear" to urban wear (para. 9). Hilfiger noticed how inner-city youths saw activities such as skiing, golfing, and boating as signs of status, and Hilfiger not only associated the clothing with those sports but also redesigned it for "hip-hop aesthetic" (para. 9). No longer preppy, the ghetto Tommy now appealed to the larger market of middle-class whites and Asians. As Klein states, "Like so much of cool hunting, Hilfiger's marketing journey feeds off the alienation at the heart of America's race relations: selling white youth on their fetishization of black style, and black youth on their fetishization of white wealth" (para. 10).

Adbusters, *Follow the Flock*

This ad is a spoof of Tommy Hilfiger ads. Above the message "Follow the flock," sheep stand before a large American flag (the flag is standard in Tommy ads). Adbusters is playing on the way in which people buy Tommy products because of their popularity and coolness. Students should note the contradiction stressed by the "Follow the flock" line. The Tommy logo bears the red, white, and blue of the American flag. In regular Tommy ads, the flag and the logo seem to represent a unity of cultures and American pride. Adbusters, however, seems to present the American flag as a cheap form of bandwagon appeal. It presents the follow-the-flock mentality of Tommy buyers as contradicting the rugged individualism of America.

ADDITIONAL WRITING TOPICS

1. Ask students to generate lists of things they consider "cool" and "uncool." Then ask them to generate lists for what high school students might consider "cool" and "uncool." Discuss the differences among all the lists. Are your students' mechanisms for choosing *cool* any different from those used by high school students?

2. Naomi Klein is horrified by the notion of a "corporate-fueled youth culture stalking itself," but she does not explain why this horrifies her or why it should concern her readers. Ask students to write an argument essay that supports or refutes Klein's essay. Can students see the harm in the "cool hunting" Klein describes? Or can they see benefits to it?

3. Ask students to gather other examples of slang words that are currently used in their peer groups, such as *tight*, and to write a definition essay for their own peer group by using the language of that group.

CONNECTIONS WITH OTHER TEXTS

1. According to Klein, Tommy Hilfiger, Adidas, and Nike are trying to sell a version of "cool." Put students into groups, and ask each group to choose two ads from the book. In one word, what is each ad trying to sell?

SUGGESTIONS FOR FURTHER READING, THINKING, AND WRITING

print

Klein, Naomi. *No Logo: Taking Aim at the Brand Bullies.* New York: St. Martin's Press, 1999.

Lasn, Kalle. *Culture Jam: The Uncooling of America.* New York: Eagle Brook/William Morrow, 1999.

Majors, Richard. *Cool Pose: The Dilemmas of Black Manhood in America.* New York: Lexington Books, 1992.

Turow, Joseph. *Breaking Up America: Advertisers and the New Media World.* Chicago: University of Chicago Press, 1998.

[www.] web

www.adbusters.org Homepage of Adbusters featuring spoof ads, commercials, and campaigns that criticize corporations and the media.

www.look-look.com Homepage of the youth-culture research group.

www.phatfarmstore.com/ Phat Farm's official home page.

Links for the selections in this chapter can be found at www.seeingandwriting.com.

audio/visual

Frontline: The Merchants of Cool. 60 min. VHS videocassette. Distributed by PBS. This film focuses on the main aspect of this section: the marketing of "cool" to teens.

Chapter 6

Reading Icons

Introduction

GENERATING CLASS DISCUSSION AND IN-CLASS WRITING

The chapter opens by describing how words and images are engaged in a "competition" or "battle" for the public's attention. An icon might be a "representation of a sacred figure," "an illustration of a plant or animal," or simply a symbol of "the secular and the mundane" (p. 465). It is significant that all the definitions rely on the notion of images that "communicate specific meanings" (p. 466) and that attract cultural attention. You might ask students to list current cultural icons and explain what these icons represent for them. Direct students to consider both people and things that may convey the same ideas: For example, Pamela Anderson Lee and the Barbie Doll are both cultural touchstones for notions of plastic sexuality, male fantasy, and the dumb blonde.

You might also ask students to consider how America's cultural icons have come to represent us—not always in a positive way—to the world. In America the McDonald's arches may convey convenience and ingenuity, but in other cultures they may signify an oppressive American presence that is crushing local culture. Even within our borders, certain commercial icons of success—such as Wal-Mart or Walt Disney—have been criticized for representing a move away from American individualism toward conformism. Other icons—such as Elvis Presley and Marilyn Monroe, who are featured in this chapter—have come to symbolize both the American dream and the American nightmare. You might ask students to identify contemporary icons that play a paradoxical role within our culture. In this way, students could begin to answer the question that ends the introduction: "How do these multiple perspectives differ from, alter, or contribute to [their] understanding of—and experience with—icons in contemporary American culture?" (p. 466).

For additional resources for the selections in this chapter (including exercises and annotated links), go to www.seeingandwriting.com.

Mercedes-Benz, *What Makes a Symbol Endure?*

GENERATING CLASS DISCUSSION AND IN-CLASS WRITING

Most students will immediately recognize the Mercedes icon and know that it stands for wealth and prestige. Indeed, during the 1980s many Mercedes owners in large urban areas lost their hood ornaments to thieves who began wearing them as status-symbol necklaces. Fewer students may take the time to relate the symbol to the others in the ad. You might ask students to relate the circular Mercedes icon to the other circular images: the smiley face, the yin and yang, the traffic light, even the atomic symbol of progress. All these lend a positive association to the Mercedes image while making it appear less stuffy. You might direct a discussion on how each of the other icons lends authority and audience appeal to the Mercedes icon.

Students might also consider how the layout of the ad plays the icons off each other. The viewer's eye is drawn through the matrix by color associations (the repeated green, yellow, red-orange, and purple-blue) that contrast with the simple background. Also, the missing cell seems designed for the Mercedes-Benz icon that has been broken out and carried across the ad, directly along the bottom edge of the matrix. You could ask students to think about the construction of this ad as a composition with a clear thesis that connects all the evidence shown in the design. What would that thesis be? It might be that a Mercedes is a sound purchase because it is enduring like the icons shown. Or it might be that a Mercedes fits perfectly into one's life, completing all these cultural connections just as its icon would complete this matrix.

ADDITIONAL WRITING TOPICS

1. Ask students to look back through the images presented in Chapter 5. How many icons do they find? What do these icons say about America?

2. Later in this chapter, David Butow's photo of a storefront window captures a number of icons—Betty Boop, James Dean, the Three Stooges, and the Statue of Liberty (to name but a few). Ask students to imagine the ad and the photo swapping each other's contents, with the ad's icons being displayed in a window as trinkets and the photo's items being pictured in this ad. How does that affect the students' view of the icons?

CONNECTIONS WITH OTHER TEXTS

1. In Jane Yolen's poem, "Grant Wood: American Gothic," the narrator states "We are not what we own/We own what we would be" (p. 473). Ask students to analyze the Mercedes logo using Yolen's poem as a framework.

2. The array of icons in the Mercedes ad may remind some people of Jesse Gordon's Op-Art in the same chapter (pp. 524–25). Ask students to imagine the people in Gordon's photos as icons. What connections among the people do they see when viewing them through this lens?

SUGGESTIONS FOR FURTHER READING, THINKING, AND WRITING

print

Kimes, Beverly Rae. *The Star and the Laurel: The Centennial History of Daimler, Mercedes and Benz, 1886–1986.* Montvale: Mercedes-Benz of North America, 1986.

Margolin, Victor. *The Promise and the Product: 200 Years of American Advertising Posters.* New York: Macmillan, 1979. A large book with many illustrations.

(www.) *web*

www.mbusa.com/brand/container.jsp/heritage
A short pictorial history of the evolution of trademarks as symbols from 1902 to 1989.

www.mercedes-benz.com/e/mbclassic This page shows the development of the car throughout the company's history.

Links for the selections in this chapter can be found at www.seeingandwriting.com.

PAIR: Grant Wood, *American Gothic*
Guy Davenport, **excerpt from *The Geography of the Imagination***
with Jane Yolen, ***Grant Wood: American Gothic***

GENERATING CLASS DISCUSSION AND IN-CLASS WRITING

Wood's painting should be familiar to most students. Even if they've never seen the original, they will probably recognize it from the numerous parodies that have been created for—among other things—cartoon characters and film posters. You might begin discussion by asking students why this 1930 painting has endured as an American icon. Some students might note that the stoic farmer represents the hardworking individual, the backbone of America. Other students might feel that the painting is outdated and no longer represents America. You could also ask students to freewrite about the lives of the figures in the painting. Ask students how they see the people in the painting. How do they read their expressions? What is the relationship between the man and the woman? Why is the woman looking away?

You might have students read the essay after they have discussed or written about the painting. Davenport states that Wood's sister and dentist posed for the painting in 1929, and that the dentist had held a rake and not a pitchfork (para. 2). The rest of the essay examines elements of the painting—from the architecture of the house to the clothing of the figures—and supplies the historical and cultural derivation for each, providing readers with a different way to look at "this painting to which we are blinded by familiarity and parody" (para. 3). In the fifth paragraph, for example, Davenport notes that the bamboo sunscreen is from China and the sash-windows from Europe, while the screen door is "distinctly American." He provides a brief look at the lineage of the wife's cameo brooch: "an heirloom passed down the generations, an eighteenth-century or Victorian copy of a design that goes back to the sixth century B.C." (para. 6). Yet it's the pose that pre-dates everything: "The pose is rather that of the Egyptian prince Rahotep, holding the flail of Osiris, beside his wife Nufrit—strict with pious rectitude, poised in absolute dignity, mediators between heaven and earth, givers of grain, obedient to the gods" (para. 11).

Davenport does discuss the painting's formal organization, but only briefly in regard to the pitchfork "whose triune shape is repeated throughout the painting, in the bib of the overalls, the windows, the faces, the siding of the house, to give it a formal organization of impeccable harmony" (para. 21). Davenport acknowledges the possibility of the painting being "a statement about Protestant diligence on the American frontier," but he observes another theme: "a tension between the growing and the ungrowing, between vegetable and mineral, organic and inorganic, wheat and iron" (para. 22).

 For an interactive visual exercise for this selection, go to www.seeingandwriting.com.

ADDITIONAL WRITING TOPICS

1. Ask students to freewrite about their reaction to the painting. Are they able to see it from a fresh perspective, or have they been "blinded by familiarity and parody" (para. 3)?

2. If the freewriting exercise proves Davenport's statement regarding the painting being too familiar, you could discuss how his purpose—to present the familiar in a different way—should be a guide for the students' own essays. You might also suggest that they research a famous piece of artwork from another culture and write an essay that offers a fresh perspective on it.

(This might be a good alternative to the second Writing prompt in the text if students have difficulty approaching familiar art from new perspectives.)

3. At first, art critics were offended by the possibility that Wood was mocking rural Americans. Ask students to research this painting's critical background. How did the painting become an American icon? Based upon this research, ask students to argue whether they feel this painting should remain an American icon.

CONNECTIONS WITH OTHER TEXTS

1. Students could research Raghubir Singh's (p. 198) status as an artist in his country and write a paper that explains how his art reflects his culture's values.

2. Ask students to take another look at Joe Rosenthal's picture of the flag raising on Iwo Jima (p. 226). Rosenthal and Wood have created two of the

most popular American images. Ask students to write a paper that compares and contrasts the American values represented in each.

 Links for the selections in this chapter can be found at www.seeingandwriting.com.

GENERATING CLASS DISCUSSION AND IN-CLASS WRITING

Gordon Parks's photograph *American Gothic* plays upon Grant Wood's famous painting of the same name. Taken in 1942 (twelve years after Wood's painting), the photograph features a black cleaning woman holding a broom and standing next to a mop in front of the American flag. You might begin discussion by asking students to examine the photograph and freewrite about the feelings it evokes. Then ask students to compare the photograph to Wood's painting. If they wrote about their reaction to Wood's painting, ask them to compare their reactions to each. Do they find that Wood's painting celebrates America, whereas Parks's photograph indicts it? Do they see stoicism in the farmer's face and in the cleaning woman's? Do they see Parks's photograph as a mere parody of Wood's work? If students are in disagreement over these issues, ask them to back up their statements. If you are in a computer classroom, you could have students search the Internet for other takes on Wood's painting, many of which are clearly parodies; if you are not in a computer classroom, you could print out a few parodies and bring them to class.

Next you might direct students to examine the compositional elements in each work. Students will quickly note that the woman's presentation matches the farmer's: the stare, the glasses, the broom (replacing the pitchfork). The pitchfork is the center of Wood's painting and ties it together. Parks placed the cleaning woman between a broom and a mop—what does this suggest about her status? Just as Wood included pitchfork shapes in his painting to give it unity, Parks repeats certain images to tie his work together. Students might observe that the white dots on the woman's uniform resemble the blurred stars in the flag. Less obvious is the repetition of the flag's vertical stripes in the vertical ridges of the broom. You might also ask students about the position of the flag. Would they react differently to this picture if the flag were horizontal instead of vertical? Do they see oppression in the way the stripes fall on the woman?

ADDITIONAL WRITING TOPICS

1. You might suggest that students reread Jane Yolen's poem on Wood's painting. Ask them to follow the form of Yolen's poem as they write their own poem about Parks's photograph. If stu-

dents have a difficult time comparing the photo-graph and the painting in class discussion, this might provide another way.

2. Poverty and racism are often the subjects of Parks's photography. Ask students to research Parks's work as well as the status of African Americans in the 1940s. Then have them write an essay that explores how this information affects their reading of his photograph and its use of Wood's painting.

CONNECTIONS WITH OTHER TEXTS

1. In the chapter's Looking Closer section, the mural in Sunnyside, Queens re-creates the famous image of the flag raising at Iwo Jima. In this image, though, firefighters and police officers replace the soldiers. How do the artists use Rosenthal's image in this painting? How do they want it to be perceived?

2. If students express interest in the parodies of *American Gothic*, they could search the Internet for parodies and write an expository essay about how the parodies tap into our understandings of the original to create new meanings. On the surface, many parodies will merely seem to be selling something, not creating new cultural meanings; urge students to examine how the goals of the parodies are meanings in themselves. For variety, you could also suggest that students research Leonardo da Vinci's *Mona Lisa*, Edvard Munch's *Scream*, James McNeill Whistler's *Whistler's Mother*, and Michelangelo's *Creation of Adam*.

[www.] Links for the selections in this chapter can be found at www.seeingandwriting.com.

Adbusters, *Ten Steps to the Creation of a Modern Media Icon*

GENERATING CLASS DISCUSSION AND IN-CLASS WRITING

In this essay, Kingwell satirizes the media by presenting the predictability with which it turns people into icons. In the previous class session, you might ask students to bring pictures of media icons (preferably dead ones because death occurs in King-well's fourth step) to class for discussion of this essay; if you are in a computer class-room, you could have students search for images on the Internet. You could use the pictures as points of reference as you discuss Kingwell's ten steps. Or you might begin discussion by asking students to each write a list of five media icons. As you discuss the essay, you can ask the students how the icons they listed fit into Kingwell's steps.

The first step defines "icon" as "'image,' which is everything" (para. 1). According to Kingwell, the public loves what cameras love: "So create an image—one the cameras, and therefore we, will love" (para. 1). The second step states that the image's aesthetic appeal must be at one extreme or the other: "The image must be drastically beautiful or compellingly ugly" (para. 2). Kingwell is at his most specific in the second step, naming actual icons, which he does not do in other steps. He states that the female icon must have a "smooth face" and "impeccably 'tasteful' clothing" (para. 2). Students might note that female celebrities attending award ceremonies are often the focus of the "Best and Worst Dressed" analyses in magazines and television shows. The best-dressed women are complimented by the media; the worst-dressed are ridiculed. Kingwell also observes that the female icon is "a flat surface of emotional projection, the real-world equivalent of a keyboard emoticon" (para. 2). He then gives examples, providing the equivalent icon for each: "Icon frowning bravely at diseased child or crippled former soldier in hospital bed: :-(" (para. 2). What is Kingwell's tone here? How do students read the examples? Is Kingwell targeting the women for being fake? Or is he implicating the media in choosing women whose expressions fit this criteria? He later lists "Jackie, Di, [and] Barbra" as examples of women with "faux-intimate" names. Do they fit the female icon criteria?

The male icon, on the other hand, needs to appear "so overwhelmingly tawdry and collapsed, preferably from some high-cheekbone peak of youthful beauty, that it acquires a can't-look-away magnetism, the sick pull of a human car wreck" (para. 2). Students should note how Kingwell creates a definite tone in this sentence by equating the icon's magnetism with "the sick pull of a human car wreck." Do students agree that the attention given to icons is "sick"? Signs of "hard living" are also crucial. Kingwell lists musicians—Johnny Cash, Mick Jagger, Kurt Cobain, to name a few—whose faces are "leathery" and "pitted," showing "evidence of drug use and chain-smoking" (para. 2).

The remaining steps involve the separation of the person from the icon. The third step states that "[t]here must be a narrative structure that bathes the icon in the pure light of the fairy tale or morality play" (para. 3). The nature of the narrative largely depends upon the icon's death since, as Kingwell states, "iconography is very much a postmortem affair" (para. 4). The completion of the icon's life "is the business of storytellers and their audience, the cameras and their lights" (para. 4). The story becomes more effective if the death is "violent, messy, and a bit mysterious" (para. 4). Specific names are noticeably absent here. You might ask students to consider why Kingwell does not provide obvious examples: Elvis, Marilyn Monroe, Kurt Cobain, Princess Di. By not supplying such a list, he makes the readers fill in the blanks; this only helps him by not having to attempt an exhaustive list but also proves the essay's point: The media's narrative is so predictable that he does not *need* to provide specific names. Can students think of an icon's death that does not match Kingwell's criteria? You might point out that Princess Di's death was followed a few days later by Mother Theresa's. Yet Mother Theresa's death was overshadowed by Di's in the media. Was it because the cameras loved Di more? Ask students to apply Mother Theresa and Princess Di to each of Kingwell's steps, particularly steps 5 to 8, which seem to obliquely refer to Di.

Following the death is "an outbreak of hysterical mourning, baseless and all the more intense for being so. (Nobody feels so strongly about someone they actually know)" (para. 5). Some students might be offended by this statement. The media showed the enormous loss felt by some fans on the passing of Kurt Cobain, George Harrison, and Aaliyah. Do some students identify with this sense of loss, or do they agree with Kingwell's assertion that it is "baseless"? Kingwell mentions "panel discussions" and funeral broadcasts, which will probably remind students of the media coverage given to the deaths of George Harrison and Princess Di. As an example of the media's predictable "narrative structure," some students might even recall that Elton John's song "English Rose" for Princess Di was a lyrical reworking of "Candle in the Wind," his song for Marilyn Monroe.

If the fifth step involved the public's bringing on the icon, the purging comes in the sixth step. This step involves the public noting the icon's "real faults and shortcomings" (para. 6). By now, the icon has become so disengaged from the person that faults become "evidence that the icon was 'after all' human—a suggestion, that, in its very making, implies the opposite" (para. 6). Kingwell notes that the reaction to this development—by the media and the public—is characterized by thoughtlessness. The media tells the icon-is-human story "because individual producers and anchors will be unable to imagine doing otherwise" (para. 6). Then the public mindlessly accepts the media's story: "Most people will accept this because to do otherwise would hurt their brains" (para. 6). Are students offended by Kingwell's tone in this sentence? You might remind them to consider Kingwell's original audience—readers of *Adbusters*, people accustomed to criticism of the media and the public.

In steps 7 to 9, the icon begins "its final divorce from the person depicted" (para. 7). It appears everywhere: "The face (or rather, The Face) looms outward from glossy paper, T-shirts, fridge magnets, posters, Halloween masks and coffee mugs" (para. 7). Step

8 involves academic studies, sightings, and conspiracy theories. Step 9 occurs years later and fully separates the icon from the person: "the icon now becomes pure zero-degree image, a depicted lifestyle without a life, a face without a person, a spiritual movement without context or meaning" (para. 9). In the final line of the ninth step, Kingwell provocatively states that this focus upon a media icon prevents us from engaging in real interactions. It is "the everything (and nothing) we sought all along: communion without community" (para. 9). Ask students to consider why we might desire such an outcome. Is it safer to feel close to an icon rather than to one's neighbor?

Although the ten-part structure helps to maintain the theme of how predictably icons are manufactured by the media, it also limits Kingwell's areas of discussion. Students might wonder about ideas that Kingwell does not address. How has the media fallen into this lock-step pattern? How much of a part do celebrities play in their own iconography? What are the broader implications here? Kingwell implies that the public's focus on media icons prevents them from doing important things: "[It] keeps them happy and ensures that no larger form of public participation—say, protesting a tax hike or program cut, resisting a corporate takeover—will ever cross their minds as possible, let alone desirable" (para. 5). However, Kingwell does not elaborate upon this idea. The ten-part structure permits little deviation to consider such ideas.

ADDITIONAL WRITING TOPICS

1. Ask students to freewrite about the celebrity they find the most fascinating or meaningful.

2. Have students research several icons to see how well Kingwell's steps apply to them. Based upon this research, students can write a paper that either builds upon Kingwell's ideas or refutes them.

3. Kingwell hints at broader implications of the public's fascination with media icons. Direct students to develop one of these ideas in an essay of their own.

CONNECTIONS WITH OTHER TEXTS

1. In "Show and Tell" (p. 637), Scott McCloud considers the importance of both the verbal and the visual in texts. Skim through the opening pages of McCloud's piece, and then ask students to consider how Kingwell could have included the visual in his essay. Did they "see" images of people or events as they read his essay? Would Kingwell have benefited from inserting pictures in his essay?

2. Kingwell notes how female icons must wear "impeccably 'tasteful' clothing" (para. 2). In Tom Perrotta's essay, he notes how much of Britney

Spears's popularity is dependent upon her sexuality, much of which came from her midriff-baring outfits. You might ask students to consider the popularity of such clothing throughout the music industry and society. Students will probably note how other teen pop-singers—Christina Aguilera, Jessica Simpson, Mandy Moore—quickly fell in line with similar outfits. During this discussion, the subject of the influence of media icons upon society might arise. If students show interest in the subject, you might ask them to write an essay that explores how media icons and society influence each other.

SUGGESTIONS FOR FURTHER READING, THINKING, AND WRITING

print

Kingwell, Mark. *Better Living: In Pursuit of Happiness from Pluto to Prozac.* New York: Crown Publishing, 2000.

———. *Marginalia: A Cultural Reader.* Toronto: Penguin, 1999.

———. *The World We Want: Virtue, Vice and the Good Citizen.* Toronto: Viking, 2000.

🌐 web

www.adbusters.org/home/   Homepage of Adbusters, featuring spoof ads, commercials, and campaigns that criticize corporations and the media.

Links for the selections in this chapter can be found at www.seeingandwriting.com.

audio/visual

Simone. Directed by Andrew Niccol. 2002. Distributed by New Line Cinema. Starring Al Pacino and Catherine Keener. Pacino plays a film producer who fools the public with a digitally created actress.

Andy Warhol *Large Triple Elvis, 1963; The Twenty Marilyns, 1962*

GENERATING CLASS DISCUSSION AND IN-CLASS WRITING

Each of Warhol's paintings involves repetition of an iconic image. You might ask students to comment on this repetition and the way in which it is achieved. For example, Elvis Presley is presented in full form but seems to be fading away, as if disappearing from the viewer's sight. In fact, this image is fairly representative of Elvis's cultural status at the time the painting was done. In contrast, Marilyn Monroe is shown only in a head shot, so that she almost seems disembodied. Also, each image varies slightly from the others—more smudged, more blonde, and so on. Students might read this as a representation of the different fantasies and dreams projected onto Monroe. Or they might discuss how the repeated images stress Monroe as a commodity rather than a person, "transform[ing] her face into a series of brightly colored semi-abstract icons" (p. 479).

ADDITIONAL WRITING TOPICS

1. Ask students to freewrite about how a more modern icon might be presented by Warhol today.
2. Direct students to compare Warhol's paintings of Elvis and Marilyn. In well-written essays they should account for all elements of the works: coloration, size of the icons, number of repetitions, and so on. How is the message about each icon similar to the other? How do the icons differ?

3. The headnote alludes to Warhol's "fascination with all things glamorous" (p. 479). Ask students to identify a glamorous celebrity they might select for a Warhol-style portrait. What image of this celebrity would they begin with? Why? What message would they want their painting to send about the chosen cultural icon?

CONNECTIONS WITH OTHER TEXTS

1. Ask students to compare the repeated images of Marilyn Monroe with those of Madonna later in this chapter (pp. 508–09). In the early images Madonna was playing on Marilyn Monroe's image, yet her life has clearly turned out differently from Monroe's. How are the destinies of these icons reflected in their portraits?
2. Have students find additional Warhol paintings, such as *Campbell's Soup Cans* and *Coke Bottles,* on the Internet. Warhol's paintings of everyday things may remind students of Alfred Leslie's *Television Moon* (p. 88). Ask students to compare these works and their approaches to commonplace objects. Do students sense that Warhol and Leslie have different attitudes toward their subjects?

SUGGESTIONS FOR FURTHER READING, THINKING, AND WRITING

print

Warhol, Andy. *Andy Warhol: A Retrospective.* New York: Museum of Modern Art, Bulfinch Press, 1989.

www. *web*

www.artchive.com/ftp_site.htm   An excerpt on Warhol from a Robert Hughes piece, an image gallery, articles, and links to the many Warhol sites online.

www.warhol.org   The web site of the Andy
    Warhol Museum in Pittsburgh, Pennsylvania.
Links for the selections in this chapter can be
    found at www.seeingandwriting.com.

audio/visual

Superstar: The Life and Times of Andy Warhol. Directed by Chuck Workman. 91 min. 1990. VHS videocassette, NR. Distributed by Vestron Video. Includes commentary from many people who were prominent in the entertainment industry during the 1960s and 1970s.

Sharon Olds, *The Death of Marilyn Monroe*

GENERATING CLASS DISCUSSION AND IN-CLASS WRITING

Olds's poem offers readers an image of the dead Marilyn Monroe, fallen far from her status as a screen goddess. You might ask students to consider the images in the poem: "cold body," "heavy as iron," "flattened by gravity." All convey an impression of Monroe's mortality and physicality; all deconstruct her luminous sexuality. In the end, Marilyn Monroe the icon was simply a human being who may not have been able to live under the weighty burden of serving as a living fantasy. Have students analyze the poem in terms of how the men treat Monroe's body, attempting to "close" her off from this world, and how their encounter with the mortal Monroe forever changes their relationship with each other. You might ask students if they have ever had a chance encounter with an icon and how this meeting changed their impression of the person.

Olds also addresses the contrast between the ideal and the real for the ambulance drivers. Students might discuss why the men's lives change. For example, why did one have nightmares, another become disenchanted with his family, and the last pause to listen to breathing? The men are impacted by Monroe's death, by her passing from the screen to the stretcher, from mortality to immortality. You might ask students to think about how a star becomes an icon. Is dying while still young and beautiful a requirement? They might think about other icons, such as James Dean or even Tupac Shakur. Contemporaries of stars like these who grew older and less idealized, such as Kim Novak (for Monroe) or Dr. Dre (for Shakur), have lost their status as icons and now seem to be mere celebrities, even almost has-beens.

ADDITIONAL WRITING TOPICS

1. Ask students to write a short response to Olds's poem. How would they describe its tone? What feelings does it evoke? Ask them to point to specific words and phrases.

2. Instruct students to find an image of Marilyn Monroe and to write a short essay that contrasts the vitality of the icon in the image with the gravity and weight of the dead woman in the poem.

3. Marilyn Monroe's status as an icon of female sexuality has grown over the years. Ask students to find two or three images of Monroe. They should write an essay that analyzes the qualities within the images that consistently establish an iconic portrait of Monroe. What stays the same throughout all the images? What is symbolized by these qualities?

CONNECTIONS WITH OTHER TEXTS

1. Ask students to turn back to Andy Warhol's presentation of Marilyn Monroe. How do Olds and Warhol comment on her role as an icon? Do they seem to make larger statements about the role of the icon in American culture?

2. The poem presents a contrast to Monroe's iconic sexuality. You might bring in some popular pictures of Monroe for students to examine as you discuss the poem.

SUGGESTIONS FOR FURTHER READING, THINKING, AND WRITING

print

Baty, S. Paige. *American Monroe: The Making of a Body Politic.* Berkeley: University of California Press, 1995. This book's focus is on Marilyn Monroe as America sees her now: "a surface that mirrors everything it touches, a site upon which to explore the character of the postmodern condition."

Monroe, Marilyn. *My Story.* New York: Stein and Day, 1974.

Olds, Sharon. *Blood, Tin, Straw.* New York: Alfred A. Knopf, 1999.

Rudnick, Paul. "The Blond: Marilyn Monroe." *Time*, 14 June 1999: 128ff. This article talks about Monroe as a "pop confection"; it also con-

tains a "Death as a Career Move" section highlighting other celebrities whose popularity seems to have increased after they died.

[www] web

www.ellensplace.net/marilyn.html   An extensive Marilyn Monroe fan site.

www.members.aol.com/PjaySin/marilyn.htm   A monthly e-zine about Monroe, with plenty of photographs and links as well.

www.salon.com/weekly/interview960701.html   A transcript of an interview with Sharon Olds.

www.wilmington.org/poets/olds.html   A sound recording of Olds reading her poem *The Un-*

justly Accused Child, and a link to an article that contains two more poems.

Links for the selections in this chapter can be found at www.seeingandwriting.com.

audio/visual

Bromwich, David, and Alicia Ostriker, with John Ashberry and Sharon Olds. 1991. Recording. Poets in Person Series. Distributed by the Modern Poetry Association.

Marilyn Monroe: Life after Death. Directed by Gordon L. Freedman. 2 cassettes (100 min.). 1995. Videocassettes, NR. Distributed by United Artists Theatre Circuit. Performers include Hugh Hefner, Liz Smith, and Susan Stasberg.

The Seven Year Itch. Directed by Billy Wilder. 105 min. 1955. VHS videocassette, NR. Distributed by CBS/Fox Video. Performers include Tom Ewell and Marilyn Monroe.

Holly Brubach, *Heroine Worship: The Age of the Female Icon*

GENERATING CLASS DISCUSSION AND IN-CLASS WRITING

Brubach argues that women have a very different relationship to their icons than do men. She points out that female icons "prompt a fit of introspection" and "self-recrimination" in women (para. 6). In part, Brubach feels this is the result of the way in which we choose icons and how they are "made famous, packaged as commodities and marketed to a public eager for novelty" (para. 3). You might ask students to comment on Brubach's argument that men and women respond differently to celebrity icons. Students could list current icons and explain what they represent to women and to men. Do the male students agree with Brubach that men do "not so much . . . desire to be [a male icon] as . . . desire to be accepted by him" (para. 6)? Do the female students agree that women look at female icons and feel "that they need to remake themselves" (para. 8)?

Brubach also addresses the relationship between the proliferation of images of women and the effect of icons on women. In the past, "[t]here were no magazines, no photographs," so "[m]ost likely a girl would have modeled herself on a female relative, or on a woman in her community" (para. 10). Now, Brubach believes, women are overly influenced by the visual icons that surround them. Because of these icons and the iconic role of women in culture, women feel "the need to assess [their] own potential to be found beautiful" (para. 14) rather than the need to achieve. In discussing these assertions, you might ask students to think about the people on whom they have modeled themselves. If they do not mention a relative or someone close, you might direct them to explain their choices. Have the female students followed Brubach's suggestion that "[i]n the spirit of post-modernism, we piece ourselves together, assembling the examples of several women in a single personality" (para. 16)? Have the male students followed a similar path? Or do they fall into the icon-trap that Brubach describes?

Students might also discuss Brubach's rhetoric. She clearly wants to isolate women and their relationships to iconic figures. She makes several very broad generalizations about men's relationship to icons—with little support—and then dismisses them. You might ask the class to find examples that refute Brubach's argument about men—or about women. Overall, the essay does little to link her assertions to specifics. It may even offer some misleading evidence. For example, Brubach's entire "pantheon" of nineteenth-century female icons consists of three women: Sarah Bernhardt, George Sand, and Florence Nightingale. Her choices reflect her desire to argue that these women were noted for their accomplishments. However, one could easily compile another pantheon of nineteenth-century women—real and created—who were noted only for their looks, such as Lillie Langtry and even the Gibson Girl. You might ask students to consider how writers use evidence and examples to sway readers.

ADDITIONAL WRITING TOPICS

1. Ask students to respond to Brubach's point that "a man's idiosyncrasies enhance his looks; a woman's detract from hers" (para. 15). Do they agree with Brubach?

2. Throughout the essay, Brubach's definition of *icon* seems to shift—to expand and contract. Have students write an essay in which they isolate and analyze Brubach's definition.

3. Brubach writes, "the images of women confronting a girl growing up in our culture are far more diverse, though not all of them can be interpreted as signs of progress" (para. 12). Instruct students to find several images of women they believe function as contemporary icons. Do these images represent progress for women?

CONNECTIONS WITH OTHER TEXTS

1. Brubach asserts, "Women have been the immemorial repository of male fantasies—a lonesome

role that many are nonetheless loath to relinquish, given the power it confers and the oblique satisfaction it brings" (para. 14). Ask students to analyze the 1998 photo of Cindy Jackson (p. 370) using Brubach's statement as a framework. How does this image support or refute her statement?

2. Direct students to interpret the images of Madonna in this chapter's Retrospect as evidence that either supports or refutes Brubach's argument.

SUGGESTIONS FOR FURTHER READING, THINKING, AND WRITING

print

Goodrich, Norma Lorre. *Heroines: Demigoddess, Prima Donna, Movie Star.* New York: Harper-Collins, 1993.

 web

www.salon.com/people/feature/1999/11/11/brubach/index.html   An interview with Holly Brubach.

Links for the selections in this chapter can be found at www.seeingandwriting.com.

VISUALIZING COMPOSITION: Metaphor

GENERATING CLASS DISCUSSION AND IN-CLASS WRITING

As the text notes, metaphor can be utilized during any stage of the writing process (para. 1). Most textbooks, however, only teach students how to differentiate metaphor from simile, and they feature exercises that help students to not mix metaphors. There is no easy way to show students how metaphor can help generate ideas. As with any invention technique, metaphors can fail to spark ideas as often as they succeed. To begin, though, you could engage students in a general discussion of how often we use metaphors. Many students will probably find humor in the school-as-prison metaphors presented in the text. Ask students how school is and is not like prison. For more examples, you could note how many of our social ills are discussed in violent terms:

1. We "fight battles" against poverty and homelessness. What is the benefit of discussing these issues in this way? Fighting involves opposing sides, enemies. Who is the enemy in the battle against poverty? Since there is no clear enemy, might this directionless aggression sometimes fall upon the poor and the homeless?

2. We wage a "war" against drugs. What is involved in warfare? How are war tactics applied against drugs? Isn't the "war" against drug growers, pushers, and users? How does this metaphor affect our treatment of drug users? How might our thinking be different if instead of waging a "war" on drugs we sought to "cure" a drug "epidemic"? By discussing these examples, you can show students how thinking about metaphor can provide a new way of looking at a subject.

For practice, you might ask students to think of other metaphors to use in the Volkswagen ad. For the metaphor to be completely effective, it must also be applied to the last sentence: "We pluck the lemons; you get the plums." In the previous chapter's Visualizing Composition section, students examined a Visa ad that used the tagline "It's your life. How do you want to spend it?" Ask students to discuss how life can be "spent." Students might note that we spend time, which is what measures life. Since it is a credit card ad, the line also suggests "It's your money. How do you want to spend it?" How are money and time similar? How are they different?

The text also notes that metaphor can help writers "create a structure for that prose" (para. 2). As an example, you could note how John Gray has structured many books around the metaphor that "men are from Mars" and "women are from Venus." Similarly, a student writing about the horror of high school could structure an essay around the metaphor that he or she was Dante and that the high school contained the nine circles of Hell.

ADDITIONAL WRITING TOPICS

1. Ask students to create a metaphor to describe writing and to develop a paragraph around that metaphor. You can expand on this activity by asking students to list five activities and to create metaphors for those. (There are a number of metaphorical quotes by writers on writing that you could find and bring to class as examples.)

2. Ask students to write a brief essay that explores a commonly used phrase that depends upon metaphor.

3. Students could bring to class an essay written earlier in the semester. Have them exchange essays every five minutes as they read for possible ways in which to use metaphor.

4. Have students list the subjects they have written on or might yet write on during the semester. Ask them to spend five to ten minutes exploring ways in which to use metaphors for those subjects. You could then have students pass the lists around to suggest more ideas or help develop the metaphors.

CONNECTIONS WITH OTHER TEXTS

1. Ask students to turn back to Charles M. Young's essay "Losing: An American Tradition" (p. 423). In it, he notes how sports imagery and war imagery are used interchangeably (para. 7). Direct students to come up with examples of war imagery used in sports and to discuss the effects such imagery might have.

2. Have students examine Chapter 7's Visualizing Context section, which features the classic anti-drug ad that equates an egg in a frying pan with a brain on drugs. Why do we need a metaphor to tell us how drugs affect the brain? Ask students to attempt to explain how drugs affect the brain without using metaphors or similes. Students will probably unknowingly use metaphors.

SUGGESTIONS FOR FURTHER READING, THINKING, AND WRITING

print

Gray, John. *Men Are From Mars, Women Are From Venus*. New York: Harper Collins, 1992.

Lakoff, George, and Mark Johnson. *Metaphors We Live By*. Chicago: University of Chicago Press, 1980.

[www.] *web*

Links for the selections in this chapter can be found at www.seeingandwriting.com.

PORTFOLIO: **Tibor Kalman**

GENERATING CLASS DISCUSSION AND IN-CLASS WRITING

Kalman's photos are recolorings, literally, of celebrity portraits. The headnote indicates that his "often humorous design vocabulary . . . critiques the dishonesty and superficiality of most corporate public relations and advertising" (p. 493). The same vocabulary is operating here, as Kalman critiques our fascination with both celebrity and race. Viewers' reactions to the photos show that what some may claim is a "superficial" quality—race—is actually often a determining factor in their attitudes toward others.

The Michael Jackson portrait plays with what many cultural critics have already identified as Jackson's apparent desire to be white. He has resculpted and recolored his appearance so that little trace remains of the Michael who first gained fame as a member of the Jackson 5. Kalman's photo simply finishes the job by adding blue eyes and blond hair. You might ask students to consider how the message of this portrait might be different from that of the photo of Spike Lee. Unlike Jackson, Lee has put himself forward as a leader in the African American cultural community and has been quite outspoken about his belief that white Hollywood has actively tried to undermine African American success. Students might address the impact of the Malcolm X hat in the recolored Lee photo. On a black Spike Lee the association would be somewhat appropriate, but on the recolored white Lee the hat seems at best incongruous and at worst ridiculous.

The portraits of Arnold Schwarzenegger and Queen Elizabeth have been recolored and retouched to resemble black persons. Schwarzenegger was a leading action star of the 1980s and 1990s, a period that saw few inroads for African Americans in Hollywood. You might ask students to consider what his chances for success would have been if he were African American. For example, would his career have been like Danny Glover's—as the "buddy" but not the star? Would it have been like Eddie Murphy's—as the "comedian" but never the action hero? The portrait of the Queen is complicated by the historical fact that for hundreds of years the English monarchy held slaves of many ethnic backgrounds in colonies around the globe. Direct students to analyze the image in that context. Most students probably think of England as a predominantly white society, which is still largely true outside of London and a few other major cities. You might ask students if a black woman ever could be Queen of England. Because the crown passes through generations within the same family, the answer is almost certainly no; and for the most part, the upper echelon of Britain's Parliament is white as well. Students might discuss the ways in which a monarchy sends a different message to ethnic populations than a democracy does. Does a black woman stand a chance of becoming a senator? a cabinet member? the president?

ADDITIONAL WRITING TOPICS

1. Ask students to write a short reaction to the recoloring of any one of these portraits. How has the recoloring process changed their thinking about the celebrity depicted?

2. Kalman says of our economic system that it "'tries to make everything look right'" (p. 493). Instruct students to choose one of the images and analyze it as a commentary on how everything is not "right" with our current system. For example,

they might explore why Michael Jackson would want to be white. What would he gain in our economic system? What would Spike Lee gain?

3. Have students do a quick survey of their friends and family by making two requests: Name at least three white individuals in political office in the United States or any other major country; and name at least three black individuals in political office in the United States or any other major country. Then, use the results to comment on the image of Queen Elizabeth. How many respondents could name black individuals in public office?

CONNECTIONS WITH OTHER TEXTS

1. Ask students to compare Kalman's photos with that by Guillermo Gómez-Peña (*Authentic Cuban Santeria,* p. 418). All the photos use humor to comment on the significance of race and ethnicity in our culture. Have students write a short essay in which they explain how effective humor may or may not be in dealing with such a serious subject, using the photos as evidence.

2. In this chapter's Visualizing Context section, Gordon Parks's photograph plays on Grant Wood's painting in a number of ways, perhaps the most prominent being in the race of the person pictured. Ask students to write an essay that compares the strategies used by Kalman and Parks and that explains the effects of those strategies.

SUGGESTIONS FOR FURTHER READING, THINKING, AND WRITING

print

Kalman, Tibor. *Perverse Optimist.* New York: Princeton Architectural Press, 1998. Published on the occasion of the San Francisco Museum of Modern Art's exhibit of Kalman's works.

www *web*

www.sfmoma.org/exhibitions/exhib_detail/99 _exhib_tibor_kalman.html   An exhibit by the San Francisco Museum of Modern Art called "Tibor City." Includes a brief summary of Kalman's career.

Links for the selections in this chapter can be found at www.seeingandwriting.com.

audio/visual

Do the Right Thing. Directed by Spike Lee. 120 min. 1989. VHS videocassette, rated R. Distributed by MCA Home Video. A race riot breaks out after a dispute between an Italian pizzeria owner and an African American customer. Performers include Danny Aiello, Ossie Davis, Ruby Dee, Richard Edson, Giancarlo Esposito, Spike Lee, Bill Nunn, and John Turturro.

Tom Perrotta, *The Cosmic Significance of Britney Spears*

GENERATING CLASS DISCUSSION AND IN-CLASS WRITING

To find out whether Britney Spears matters in regard to popular culture, Perrotta compares Britney to Elvis, Madonna, and Kurt Cobain. It might be a good idea to begin discussion by getting students' opinions of Britney out of the way. You should ask what they think of Britney as a singer, a performer, and an icon. Most will probably speak negatively of Britney, although others might sheepishly admit that they like her. A few students might even take a positive stance regarding the pop singer. If you think that students might repeatedly interrupt discussion with rounds of Britney-bashing, this might be a way to avoid such a problem. Then you could take the students through the essay, examining Perrotta's claims and his methods of comparing and contrasting the artists. You might also begin discussion by asking students to read from their reading-response journals (see Additional Writing Topic 1).

Perrotta opens the essay by writing about the difficulty he had working after the September 11 attacks, especially since his essay's subject matter seemed insignificant in comparison. His tone seems embarrassed, almost apologetic: "In my case, this fairly common emotional response was exacerbated by the fact that I happened to be writing an essay about Britney Spears" (para. 2). Then he admits that he even had problems taking his subject seriously before the tragedy. Do students think that Perrotta is trying to avoid criticism by beating the critics to the punch? Or do they read genuine discomfort in his statements? You might remind students that this essay was published in December 2001, only a few months after the tragedy.

In the fourth paragraph, Perrotta asks the question that prompts the essay: "Does the fact that she's currently one of the biggest pop stars in the universe . . . make her by definition a figure of sociological influence?" He notes that we could easily "write her off as just another teen idol" (para. 5), but, as he points out, we have been surprised by other pop stars who became significant cultural figures. As an example, he points to Michael Jackson, "whose ghoulishly altered face tells a mythic and terrible story about race and celebrity in America" (para. 6). To see how she stands with other iconic artists, Perrotta breaks the essay into three sections in which he compares Britney to Elvis, Madonna, and Kurt Cobain.

Perrotta notes that Britney is similar to Elvis in the way she presents herself: "As Elvis did before her, Britney presents herself to the world as a divided personality—

shy and self-effacing in private, shockingly bold in public" (para. 8). Britney and Elvis also share southern roots and strong ties with their mothers. However, Elvis's sound clearly bears the musically rich heritage of the South; Britney's, on the other hand, shows no such signs and is "the musical equivalent of a big-budget Hollywood action movie" (para. 11). Elvis took the separate sounds of blues and country and combined them, creating a new musical style. Elvis made a new product, whereas Britney was made into a product: "Elvis created himself out of the materials at hand; Britney had a musical identity imposed on her that she gratefully accepted" (para. 13).

Regarding Britney and Madonna, Perrotta at first observes a major difference: Madonna has a challenging persona; Britney does not. Referring to Madonna's film *Truth or Dare*, Perrotta notes that she "portrays herself as an unapologetic celebrity monster—vain, self-obsessed, willing to mock and humiliate anyone who crosses her path" (para. 15). Britney, on the other hand, in her *MTV Diary*, "emerges as the anti-Madonna, the celebrity without an ego" (para. 16). Next, Perrotta observes that they are both spiritual and sexual figures, but in different ways: "Britney may be more conventionally devout in her personal life, but Madonna is far and away the more religiously engaged artist of the pair" (para. 18). Even though Madonna has spoken about her Catholic background, listeners of her music would be aware of that background if she had never spoken of it. Britney's music does not show her religious side, which can only be gathered from what she tells the public. Some of her songs might seem sexually suggestive, but her videos and musical performances are undeniably sexual; however, sexual themes infuse nearly every aspect of the media for Madonna. In a way, Madonna and Elvis have a genuine quality that Britney does not for Perrotta: "All I really know is that Madonna always seems deadly serious about what she's doing or saying, whereas Britney always seems as if she's kidding around" (para. 22).

Perrotta links Britney and Cobain by the circumstance of time and presents them as "the opposing bookends of the 1990s, poster children for a schizoid decade" (para. 25). Cobain's dark side represents "a gloomy time of war and recession"; Britney is the "chipper emblem of a fat, happy country bubbling over with irrational exuberance" (para. 25). Cobain was uncomfortable with fame; Britney welcomes fame with open arms: "she was raised for success, in the same way that Cobain seems to have been raised for unhappiness" (para. 28).

Both ancillary pieces—a defaced poster of Britney (in a costume that recalls Elvis's Vegas years) and an interview with a former college admissions dean—present negative views of Britney. The defaced poster is obviously negative, spoofing a Mastercard commercial as it lists prices for Britney's nose, lips, and breasts. The interview is less caustic, but far from glowing. In it, the dean recommends a course in "'The Art of Superficiality'" for Britney.

ADDITIONAL WRITING TOPICS

1. Before you assign this reading, you might ask students to keep a journal of their reactions as they read the essay. Have them make notes on how the essay surprises them and on how Perrotta structures it. Students should write about the expectations created by the essay's title, and they should also consider why Perrotta mentions September 11 in the essay's opening.

2. Ask students to freewrite about how musicians influence culture. Then, they can free-write about how musicians become icons. This freewriting can prepare them for the next prompt.

3. Direct students to write an essay in which they argue in support of a musical artist who they think is or will become an important cultural figure. You might recommend that, as Perrotta does in this essay, they compare and contrast this artist with musicians who have become important cultural figures.

CONNECTIONS WITH OTHER TEXTS

1. In "Heroine Worship" (p. 486) Holly Brubach observes that female icons "prompt a fit of introspection" and "self-recrimination" in women (para. 6). Do your female students feel this way regarding Britney Spears? How do the male students view Britney? Does any introspection take place when they consider her?

2. During discussion, some students might state that Britney Spears is not that attractive—it's her fame, lifestyle, and unattainable status that make her so appealing. You might remind students that in Bruce Bower's essay "Average Attractions" (p. 332) psychologist Ellen Berscheid makes a similar claim regarding celebrities, "whose appeal sometimes lies largely in perceptions indirectly linked to facial beauty, such as glamour and fame" (para. 17). How do students view Britney after reading this statement? Could they ever imagine her as an "ordinary" student in their class?

SUGGESTIONS FOR FURTHER READING, THINKING, AND WRITING

print

Cross, Charles. *Heavier Than Heaven: A Biography of Kurt Cobain*. New York: Hyperion Press, 2001.

Guralnick, Peter. *Careless Love: The Unmaking of Elvis Presley*. Boston: Little, Brown, 1998.

———. *Last Train to Memphis: The Rise of Elvis Presley*. Boston: Little, Brown, 1995.

Kelly, Karen, and Evelyn McDonnell, eds. *Stars Don't Stand Still in the Sky: Music and Myth*. New York: New York University Press, 1998.

Perrotta, Tom. *Election: A Novel*. New York: Putnam Publishing, 1997.

———. *Joe College*. New York: St. Martin's Press, 2000.

———. *The Wishbones*. New York: Penguin Putnam, 1998.

Robb, Jackie. *Britney Spears: The Unauthorized Biography*. New York: HarperCollins, 1999.

Spears, Britney, and Lynne Spears. *Britney Spears' Heart to Heart*. New York: Crown Publishing, 2000.

Taraborrelli, J. Randy. *Madonna: An Intimate Biography*. New York: Simon and Schuster, 2001.

[www] *web*

Links on the selections in this chapter can be found at www.seeingandwriting.com.

audio/visual

Madonna. *The Immaculate Collection*. 1990. Compact disc. Distributed by Warner Brothers.

You might play "Like a Virgin" and "Justify My Love" and ask students to compare them to songs by Britney Spears.

Nirvana. *In Utero*. 1993. Compact disc. Distributed by Geffen Records. Since most students are probably too familiar with Nirvana's "Smells Like Teen Spirit," you might play "Heart Shaped Box" or "All Apologies," songs that capture Cobain's bleak despair noted by Perrotta.

Presley, Elvis. *Elvis '56*. 1996. Compact disc. Distributed by RCA. You might play "Hound Dog" to give students an idea of the new sound to which Perrotta refers.

Spears, Britney. *Britney*. 2001. Compact disc. Distributed by Jive. You might play "I'm a Slave 4 You," Britney's most suggestive song to date, and ask students to compare it to Madonna's songs.

RETROSPECT: *Madonna, 1982–2002*

GENERATING CLASS DISCUSSION AND IN-CLASS WRITING

This series of photographs shows the various ways in which Madonna transformed her image over twenty years. According to the chapter introduction, one of the uses of the word *icon* is "to identify certain individuals who are the objects of attention and devotion, people who have taken on the status of an idol" (p. 466). These photos of Madonna demonstrate some of the strategies she has used to re-create her public persona. It is notable that she has never presented herself as a static image but instead as a continually shifting one. Thus, viewers are invited to experience a world of process with this "idol."

You might ask students which images of Madonna they can identify with a particular period, controversy, or work of hers. Which images are the most familiar? Why?

ADDITIONAL WRITING TOPICS

1. Ask students to choose one photograph from this group and to use their skills of observation and analysis to write an explication of the Madonna icon they see represented.

2. Direct students to examine the first and the last of the images. Then, have them draft a comparison/contrast essay analyzing the similarities and differences between the two images. What conclusions can they draw about Madonna's life as an icon from observation alone?

3. Invite students to do a ten-minute in-class freewrite about the connotations of the word *Madonna*. "Perhaps the oldest association of the word [icon] is with the religious representation of a sacred figure" (p. 465). In what ways do Madonna as an image and Madonna as a word invite religious comparisons? Ask several students to share their writing with the class.

4. Have students write an essay in which they analyze the lyrics of a song that Madonna has written. Ask them to address the way in which the words do or do not support her image as an icon.

CONNECTIONS WITH OTHER TEXTS

1. Ask students to imagine these pictures recolored by Tibor Kalman. How would the black Madonna's career have been different throughout the years pictured here?

2. Have students look at Susan Bordo's essay "Never Just Pictures" in Chapter 7 (p. 557). Then, ask them to imagine Bordo's analysis of these photos of Madonna.

SUGGESTIONS FOR FURTHER READING, THINKING, AND WRITING

[www.] *web*

Links for the selections in this chapter can be found at www.seeingandwriting.com.

audio/visual

Truth or Dare. Directed by Alex Keshishian. 120 min. 1991. VHS videocassette, rated R. Distributed by Artisan Entertainment. A behind-the-scenes documentary of a Madonna world tour. Performers include Madonna et al.

Talking Pictures

This Talking Pictures assignment has students analyze a logo according to Rand's list of seven qualities of effectiveness. Students sometimes have difficulty distinguishing between summary and analysis, so you might remind them that they have to provide concrete details in support of each quality mentioned by Rand. Some qualities may seem closely related—for example, durability and timelessness. You might ask students to define the terms as a group in class before undertaking the assignment.

As an alternate assignment you might instruct students to compare and contrast two or three network logos according to several of Rand's criteria. It might be particularly interesting for students to contrast the logo of an older network (e.g., ABC, CBS, or NBC) with that of a newer network (e.g., Fox, UPN, or WB) or with that of a cable network (e.g., HBO, Comedy Central, or Lifetime). How do the newer logos differ from the older ones? Does each logo target a particular viewing audience (young or old; male or female)?

Touré, *Kurt Is My Co-Pilot*

GENERATING CLASS DISCUSSION AND IN-CLASS WRITING

Touré's essay on Dale Earnhardt Jr. touches on many subjects: race cars, the history of racecar driving, Earnhardt Jr.'s place in the sport, and Junior's relationship with his father. The main point of interest in this essay is how Touré makes Earnhardt Jr. accessible to his *Rolling Stone* readers by writing about the racecar driver's love of music.

You should point out how the title is aimed at *Rolling Stone* readers: Only the most casual reader would not connect Nirvana's Kurt Cobain as the Kurt in the title. The opening paragraphs relate how Earnhardt Jr.'s life changed once he heard Nirvana's song "Smells Like Teen Spirit" (paras. 1–7). Nirvana exposed him to other music, which further exposed him to ideas he had never considered before: "'I never really was rebellious against my parents. I never really thought the government was fucked up. I never really paid much attention to the schools suckin'" (para. 7). As the class examines the essay, you should ask students to note how Touré manages to unify his many subjects by referring to music and, therefore, supporting his main idea that when Earnhardt Jr. heard Nirvana, he was "pulled from the good-ol'-boy path and rebaptized by rock & roll" (para. 3).

After noting Earnhardt Jr.'s love of music, Touré connects it with his place in stock-car racing: "Junior followed Dad into big-time stock-car racing, and now, in a sport filled with good ol' boys, he's known as the rock & roll driver" (para. 8). He observes how the wealthy racecar driver is similar to the "MTV generation" readers of *Rolling Stone:* "A kid like you, maybe, who on Monday, Tuesday, and Wednesday does little or nothing—fixes up the house, plays paint ball and Sega NFL2K with the guys" (para. 8). In paragraphs 10 to 13, Touré writes about Earnhardt Jr.'s cars, often giving details one would expect to read in a car magazine: "He added a new transmission, a new aluminum-head Corvette engine, and a 2,500-rpm stall converter" (para. 11). Touré keeps music involved, though, by including Earnhardt Jr.'s thoughts on Dr. Dre and by describing how "the malevolent funk of Dr. Dre booms out the [car's] window" (paras. 12–13).

A similar pattern can be seen throughout the rest of the essay. Paragraphs 14 to 26 show Junior on the racetrack but do not neglect music (para. 18). You might note how these paragraphs do not assume that the audience is familiar with racecar driving in the way that it is with Nirvana and Dr. Dre. For instance, readers of *Car & Driver* would not need the interior of a racecar described to them: "There is only one seat (roll bars are where the passenger seat would be), and that seat is form-fitted to Junior's body like shrink-to-fit jeans" (para. 19). Touré describes Earnhardt Jr. interacting with his father—a legendary racecar driver—in paragraphs 27 to 37; these paragraphs set up the next section, which provides a brief history of stock-car racing and notes how Earnhardt Jr. is different from his father (paras. 38–45). As Touré notes, he is part of a new breed of drivers, representing "a titanic shift in the cultural direction of NASCAR" (para. 43). Touré quotes Junior on how NASCAR has changed its image: "'Just look at the TV coverage. Ten years ago, when they'd go to break, it'd be some fiddle banjo-pickin' music. And now it's this jammin' rock music'" (para. 44).

In the rest of the essay Touré continues to incorporate music, but he does so less and less. You might ask students to consider why he might have done this. Is it because he has already made *Rolling Stone* readers interested in Earnhardt Jr. the racecar driver and does not need to present Earnhardt Jr. the music lover?

ADDITIONAL WRITING TOPICS

1. Put students in pairs, and ask each member to interview the other. Each student should come up with interview questions that aim to reveal different sides of the interviewee's personality. You might discuss some possible questions as a class. Based upon the interview material, students should write two short essays on the interviewee, each for a distinct audience.

2. Ask students to write an expository essay about how music has changed their lives. They should describe themselves before and after the change.

3. Direct students to record the different subjects found in Touré's essay and to write a brief explanation as to how each could have been the main focus in another magazine for a different audience. For instance, the section about Earnhardt Jr. and his friends arguing about racing movies would have been an integral part of an article in *Premiere* magazine about how people see their professions being portrayed in film.

CONNECTIONS WITH OTHER TEXTS

1. Touré inserts the subject of music into his essay on Earnhardt Jr. to meet the interests of *Rolling Stone* readers. You might ask students to turn back to Perrotta's *GQ* essay on Britney Spears. How does Perrotta meet the needs of his predominantly male audience?

2. Ask students to research an unfamiliar icon, past or present. You might suggest some icons or ask students to consider some they've heard of but know very little about. Students could then write an essay or prepare a presentation that would introduce this icon to their classmates.

3. Assign students to research magazines for an essay similar to Touré's in how it presents an unfamiliar figure to its audience. The students can write a short essay that analyzes how the author presents certain aspects of the figure to meet the needs of the magazine's audience.

SUGGESTIONS FOR FURTHER READING, THINKING, AND WRITING

print

Persinger, Kathy. *Dale Earnhardt Jr.: Born to Race.* Champaign: Sports Publishing LLC, 2001.

Touré. *The Portable Promised Land.* Boston: Little, Brown, 2002.

 web

www.dalejr.com/ Earnhardt Jr.'s official site with news, story archive, fan club, and merchandise.

Links for the selections in this chapter can be found at www.seeingandwriting.com.

David Butow, *Hollywood Walk of Fame, Los Angeles, September 30, 2001*

GENERATING CLASS DISCUSSION AND IN-CLASS WRITING

Butow's photograph shows a window display that features American objects and figures. Most of the objects are novelties—Elvis, Betty Boop, James Dean, the Three Stooges, a Route 66 sign, a tiny Statue of Liberty, a large golf ball. All of these objects surround the American flag at the center of the display. According to the sign above the display, the store offers passport photos. The items are small and offer a slice of Americana—ideal for a traveler about to go abroad.

You might begin discussion by asking students to form groups to examine the picture. Ask each group to note details about the display and to form inferences based upon the details. If the groups have difficulty with this exercise, you might have them look at the Seeing questions for more direction. When the groups finish examining the picture, they should report their findings to the class. As a class you can point out missed details or expand upon certain observations.

ADDITIONAL WRITING TOPICS

1. Ask students to write a description of a personal window display for themselves, filling the display with objects from their room. As each student writes the description, he or she should consider the following questions: Which objects would go in the display? Why would certain objects be left out? How would the items be arranged? What would the display say about the person? Students should write a four-digit code on the paper for anonymity (you might suggest the last digits of phone numbers).

2. After students have completed the first writing prompt, collect the descriptions and redistribute them. Ask each student to write a brief response—a paragraph or two—that infers personality traits from the personal window display. Collect the essays, again, read the codes, and return the essays to their owners. Then ask the students to discuss the inferences made about their window displays. If you joined the class in writing your own window display, you could read yours first.

1. The readings in the chapter's Looking Closer section involve the uses and meanings of the American flag. Ask students to skim through the images of the flag at the end of the chapter. How is the flag being used in Butow's picture?

2. Ask students to look back at Camilo José Vergara's photographs that cover twenty-one years of the same Harlem storefronts (p. 150). If Butow had taken his photo twenty years earlier and twenty years later, how might it be different?

[www.] Links for the selections in this chapter can be found at www.seeingandwriting.com.

 Re: Searching the Web

Icons are prevalent in many areas of American life. Sites such as The Museum of Advertising Icons enable students to explore a variety of icons—in this case, many related to toys (see www.toymuseum.com/main.html). The Collector's Corner offers a section, for example, on "What Makes an Advertising Icon a Collectible?" and archives of icons ranging from the Jolly Green Giant to Big Boy and Tele-Tubbies (see www.toymuseum.com/info.html).

Ask students to explore the history of advertising icons at this web site. Direct them to examine the style of particular icons that they choose from different periods and to comment on the marketing strategies they observe in these examples. Students might want to determine which icons at present have the most value to collectors.

Students can complete the Re: Searching the Web exercises online at www.seeingandwriting.com. Additional tips and links are also available.

Looking Closer:
The Stars and Stripes

GENERATING CLASS DISCUSSION AND IN-CLASS WRITING

This section of images and texts focuses exclusively on the American flag—its representation and the laws that govern its treatment. The flag is the legal symbol of our nation. As such, it has the potential to evoke strong patriotic (or unpatriotic) emotions. It is a more abstract and arbitrary type of icon than an image of Madonna or the sign for a restroom, though. In the latter cases there is a concrete referent that resembles the icon. In the case of the flag, however, the connection rests almost exclusively on a convention, or agreement, about what the stars and stripes represent.

You might begin discussion by asking students to freewrite about America and the American flag. After some students share their writing, ask them to examine the comments about America in Jesse Gordon's piece. As students read the following selections, have them consider how each is a product of its time.

Jesse Gordon, *What Is America?*

In each of the twenty-four pictures, a person holds a small American flag and answers the question "What is America?" The answers vary from "freedom" and "possibility" to "hot dogs" and "sex." You might ask students to consider how the respondents' answers might be influenced by their place of origin.

David Foster Wallace, *Wednesday*

This selection was written in reaction to the proliferation of American flags after the events of September 11. Wallace notes that more of a statement is made by not waving a flag. What might this statement be?

Justice William J. Brennan Jr., *Majority Opinion of the U.S. Supreme Court in* Texas v. Johnson *(1989)*

Justice Brennan asserts that on the basis of protection under the First Amendment—freedom of speech—Gregory Lee Johnson should not be convicted of desecrating a flag. A few of the main points of Brennan's argument are that (1) no one was hurt or injured, (2) there is no law protecting the flag specifically, and (3) the decision to overturn the ruling against Johnson is in fact "a reaffirmation of the principles of freedom and inclusiveness that the flag best reflects, and of the conviction that our toleration of criticism such as Johnson's is a sign and source of our strength" (para. 21).

Plateau Indian Bag

This representation of the American flag is a Native American one. On one side of the bag there is an image of a frontiersman; on the other is an Indian. Each figure is approximately the same size and is in the same position. Above each figure, resting on a shield of stars and stripes, are two identical crossed American flags. The symmetry of the flags suggests an equal balance between the frontiersman and the Indian.

Chief Justice William H. Rehnquist, *Dissenting Opinion in* Texas v. Johnson *(1989)*

In contrast to Justice Brennan, Chief Justice William H. Rehnquist asserts that the power of the symbol of the American flag constitutes a special case and that therefore "a governmental prohibition against flag burning in the way respondent John-son did here" (para. 1) is justified. He disagrees with Justice Brennan's claim that the flag's value is strengthened by permitting its desecration in the name of free speech. Rehnquist argues, "in my considered judgment, sanctioning the public des-ecration of the flag will tarnish its value—both for those who cherish the ideas for which it waves and for those who desire to don the robes of martyrdom by burning it" (para. 14).

Matt Groening, *Pledging the Flag*

Groening's cartoon calls attention to the pledge to the flag rather than to the flag it-self. In this case, the cartoon figure rises for the morning salute to the flag (from a desk, apparently in school) and repeats malapropism after malapropism that vaguely and comically approximate words of the pledge. When the cartoon student is reprimanded by the teacher, he retorts with another well-known American say-ing, "It's a free country." These words, however, are not a malapropism. In this way, Groening demonstrates how the formal discourse of the Supreme Court is echoed in popular culture as well as in the conflict many communities face about the appro-priateness of requiring students to repeat the Pledge of Allegiance.

Norman Rockwell, *Rosie the Riveter*

You might have to provide students with some background on Rosie the Riveter. Dur-ing World War II, traditionally male occupations had to be filled by women. Rosie the Riveter embodies the working woman of World War II—strong, confident, and patri-otic. You might ask students to describe the pose of Rosie in Rockwell's image. Have them consider why women might have needed such a symbol during the war. You might point out a particularly telling part students might overlook—Hitler's *Mein Kampf* crushed under Rosie's foot.

Several Artists, *Section of Sunnyside, Queens*

This mural seems to have been made in response to the tragedy of September 11. The ruins of the World Trade Center can be seen in the background. However, the image of the flag raising at Iwo Jima is the focus. How does the famous image work here? Ask students to compare the images. Both depict a time of war, but the soldiers in this scene are firefighters and police officers. How do these artists envision the Iwo Jima image? Students might note that the mural offers an image of resilience by reminding us that America has been hurt before yet managed to prevail.

ADDITIONAL WRITING TOPICS

1. Rosie the Riveter was a symbol of the patriotic working woman. She is still used today to bolster the image of women in jobs typically regarded as masculine. Ask students to research how Rosie has evolved over time. How did the men and women of the World War II period perceive her?

CONNECTIONS WITH OTHER TEXTS

1. Rockwell's *Rosie the Riveter* painting was produced around the same time as the Palmolive Soap ad in Chapter 5's Visualizing Context: A Culture of Consumption. Each portrays women in a different supporting role: In the Palmolive ad, she is preserving her beauty—and possibly her chastity—for her man fighting overseas; as Rosie the Riveter, she is preserving the economy by entering the workforce. Ask students to consider whether these images were aimed at different women. Why doesn't Rosie look more like the Palmolive woman? Students should also know that women were portrayed in various ways during the war—as the spoils of war, as objects to be protected from the enemy, as hopeless gossips, and so on. You might even suggest students look into the subject for a research paper.

SUGGESTIONS FOR FURTHER READING, THINKING, AND WRITING

print

Gluck, Sherna. *Rosie the Riveter Revisited: Women, the War and Social Change.* Boston: Twayne, 1987.

Honey, Maureen. *Creating Rosie the Riveter: Class, Gender, and Propaganda during WWII.* Amherst: University of Massachusetts Press, 1984.

Wallace, David Foster. *Infinite Jest.* Boston: Little, Brown, 1996.

———. *A Supposedly Fun Thing I'll Never Do Again: Essays and Arguments.* Boston: Little, Brown, 1997.

www web

www.davidfosterwallace.com/ This unofficial David Foster Wallace web site run by fans contains news, a brief biography, and links to interviews.

www.rosietheriveter.us/ Provides Rosie the Riveter pictures, history, and merchandise.

www.rosietheriveter.org/ Rosie the Riveter Trust homepage. Contains indispensable information regarding Rosie.

Links for the exercises in this chapter can be found at www.seeingandwriting.com.

audio/visual

The Life and Times of Rosie the Riveter. Directed by Connie Field. 65 min. Videocassette. Distributed by Direct Cinema Limited. Five women talk about their working experiences during World War II.

Chapter 7

Challenging Images

Introduction

GENERATING CLASS DISCUSSION AND IN-CLASS WRITING

The chapter opens by describing "[the] battle . . . between words and images" (p. 542). You might ask students to trace the rhetoric used to discuss the interplay of words and images in this introduction. Why is it presented as a battle? The metaphor of warfare sets the stage for the discussion of images: They are "winning" and "dominate" (p. 542); digital images are "rapidly advancing" (p. 542); image has "'driven out the natural'" (p. 543). Because many works within the chapter oppose text to image and regard text as superior, it may be worth some time in class to have students discuss the dichotomy of "text versus image." Are the two mutually exclusive? Must one win out over the other? Because this chapter comes at the end of the textbook, students should be ready to engage in such a discussion.

Students are also asked to consider a new literacy, "visual literacy" (p. 543), that is increasingly important in a society in which most information is conveyed via visual media such as television and the Internet. Several issues are intertwined with the notion of visual literacy. For example, how does a consumer of information determine what is "real" and what is "image"? How does an information consumer process all the data that are available today? How does an information producer create material that is appealing to a consumer raised on images? You might ask students to research one of the questions raised in the introduction and develop the topic in an essay. None of these questions has an easy answer. And although the critics mentioned in the introduction (notably Neil Postman and Neal Gabler) may have negative views about the ways in which images shape and inform our culture, students could just as easily find critics who celebrate the multiplication of images and meanings that a media culture produces.

Visual and digital information is becoming available at an ever increasing pace. You might ask students to list the ways in which they currently send and receive information (e.g., by traditional telephones, cell or digital phones, pagers, computers, television, DVD players, VCRs). Then, direct them to consider how many of these modes of information delivery were available ten years ago or twenty years ago. How have these new avenues of information dissemination changed the ways in which students understand and expect to receive information? For example, a DVD player allows a viewer to (virtually) change the camera angle in a film, to essentially re-edit the picture—something that a VCR could never do. Has this changed the way in which students view films or the way in which they expect to be able to interact with them? Do these technologies create more active or more passive information consumers?

 For additional resources for the selections in this chapter (including exercises and annotated links), go to www.seeingandwriting.com.

Barbara Kruger, *Untitled*

GENERATING CLASS DISCUSSION AND IN-CLASS WRITING

You might first ask students to break down this image into its component parts: a film editing machine, a length of film, a pair of hands holding a scissors that is about to cut the film, a face of an editor. A caption overlays the image: "A picture is worth more than a thousand words." From this point, students may want to rebuild the image and attempt to construct meaning from these elements. During the process of editing, a filmmaker creates meaning from many mags of film that have been shot. The process enables him to shape the audience's reading of an image. Thus, the scissors in Kruger's piece might represent the editing process: They break the real flow of time and begin to create "film time." Students might want to engage some of the terms from the chapter introduction in discussing this work. How is a film "inauthentic" or "fake"? Students might refer to the headnote on Kruger that stresses her "insider's view of how the media can manipulate the public" (p. 545).

The text in the image can be read in several ways. For example, students might consider it a simple variant of the traditional maxim, "A picture is worth a thousand words." Or they might discuss the issue of "worth"; what does it mean here? The image suggests that a great deal is invested in creating the exact picture desired. Thus, students might read "worth" in economic terms. Money is spent in order to direct an information consumer in a certain way, in order to generate the right "more than a thousand words." Students might discuss how pictures—in films, television, magazines, newspapers, and so on—are created. They could research this process; it undoubtedly involves many more people and much more money than they ever thought.

Students might also discuss the composition of Kruger's image. The red and white text stands out against the black and white background, drawing the viewer's eye. It also runs on a diagonal that is almost, but not quite, parallel to the diagonal formed by the length of film stock. Students might draw out the line of sight from the editor's eye to the film; they will find that it completes the diagonal running almost corner to corner of the image, dividing the work in half. The text fills the upper half, the scissors the lower half—implying a relationship between the two. In fact, the scissors create the picture—and the large font of "picture" as compared to the smaller font used for "is worth more than a thousand words" reinforces the power of the image. Finally, students might want to consider how shadow and light within the image add an ominous tone and a sense of secrecy to the process of film editing.

ADDITIONAL WRITING TOPICS

1. Ask students to write a short personal reflection on Kruger's work. How does *Untitled* make them feel? Do they sense that the artist wants to leave a positive or a negative impression about the subject presented? How and why do they come to this conclusion?

2. Neal Gabler writes, "Everywhere the fabricated, the inauthentic and the theatrical have gradually driven out the natural, the genuine and the spontaneous" (p. 543). Ask students to discuss how Kruger's work comments on the act of fabricating a picture and how the artist might be expressing a point of view similar to Gabler's.

3. Direct students to attempt to trace the source of the maxim, "A picture is worth a thousand words." How does Kruger's version, "A picture is worth more than a thousand words," change its meaning? Why might her version better fit our culture?

1. Ask students to examine the next selection, Francisco Goya's etchings of war and Susan Sontag's essay on Goya. Sontag seems to suggest that words fail to capture the horror depicted by Goya. How does Sontag's essay relate to Kruger's contention that "A picture is worth more than a thousand words"?

2. Have students review the icons displayed in the Mercedes-Benz ad (Chapter 6, p. 464) in light of Kruger's commentary on the way images are crafted in order to be "worth more than a thousand words." Students might choose one of the icons displayed in the ad and list all the words it conjures.

[www] Links for the selections in this chapter can be found at www.seeingandwriting.com.

PAIR: Francisco Goya, *The Disasters of War*
Susan Sontag, *Looking at the Unbearable*

GENERATING CLASS DISCUSSION AND IN-CLASS WRITING

If you have students examine the etchings first, it might be a good idea to give them some background. Otherwise, you might find some students will react with laughter to the first etching. Or you could pursue this possibility and ask why they have a hard time taking these etchings seriously. Students will be more likely to see the etchings in a serious light, though, if they read Sontag's essay first.

The two etchings are from a series by Goya called "The Disasters of War." Sontag's essay is a response that struggles with how to respond to the depiction of such atrocities. The first is a brutal, gruesome etching that depicts men in the act of torturing another man: Two men splay his legs as another strikes at the man's groin with a sword. The caption seems to imply that the man has already been brutalized enough and that this act is overkill: "What more can be done?" It also suggests that the unimaginable brutality of this act begs the question of what other inhumanities could be committed. The second etching is a scene of desolation and death: Against a nondescript background a man holds hand to head as he stands among at least three dead or dying people.

Sontag seems drawn to the etchings because of their timelessness. She seems disturbed by them not only for the heinous acts they depict from Goya's time, but also for the sense of despair they cause by reminding us that such acts still occur: "For it is not simply that this happened: Zaragoza, Chinchón, Madrid (1808–13). It is happening: Vucovar, Mostar, Srebrenica, Stupni Do, Sarajevo (1991–)" (para. 7). While Sontag states that the images are "relentless, unforgiving," she focuses on them because of how they comment upon the present: "The images tell us we have no right not to pay attention to the crimes of this order which are taking place right now" (para. 9).

She uses Emerson's language to approach the "unbearable" nature of Goya's work: "Emerson wrote 'He has seen but half the universe who has never been shown the house of pain.' It seems optimistic now to think that the house of pain describes no more than half the universe" (para. 8). You might ask students whether they agree—is the world becoming increasingly cruel?

Direct students to consider who is speaking in the captions. According to Sontag, the captions combine the "voices of the murderers" and the "lamenting artist-witness" (para. 9). Have students look at the etchings and imagine the captions from each perspective. How do the different readings of the captions affect the readings of the images?

ADDITIONAL WRITING TOPICS

1. Ask students to write a brief essay called "Looking at the Unbearable" that deals with photographs or video from the events of September 11. They do not have to follow Sontag's format, but they should see the essay's purpose as being more exploratory than informative or argumentative. You might even encourage them to attach captions to the images they consider for the essay.

2. Ask students to freewrite about the most disturbing images of war they have seen. Were they from documentaries, photographs, films?

3. If the freewriting exercise elicits a number of responses regarding films, you could ask students to analyze a war film. How does it present the "unbearable" to its audience? Does it moralize? Does it tone down the violence?

CONNECTIONS WITH OTHER TEXTS

1. In his essay "Killing Monsters" (p. 582), Gerard Jones argues that violent entertainment can help children learn to deal with rage and to overcome feelings of powerlessness. How are Goya's images good for people?

2. Ask students to consider the following line in relation to the photographs of September 11 from Chapter 3: "The images are relentless, unforgiving. That is, they do not forgive us—who are merely being shown, but do not live in the house of pain" (para. 9). Reading the line in this different context might enable students to get a sharper sense of what Sontag means.

SUGGESTIONS FOR FURTHER READING, THINKING, AND WRITING

print

Buchholz, Elke Linda. *Goya*. New York: Barnes and Noble Books, 2000.

Hirsch, Edward, ed. *Transforming Visions: Writers on Art*. Boston: Little, Brown, 1994.

 web

www.artcyclopedia.com/artists/goya_francisco _de.html   Artcyclopedia's page on Francisco Goya.

Links for the selections in this chapter can be found at www.seeingandwriting.com.

Nick Hornby, *Richard Billingham*

GENERATING CLASS DISCUSSION AND IN-CLASS WRITING

Before students read Hornby's essay, they should examine Billingham's photographs and record their reactions. After they read the essay, you might take them through the text's Seeing questions. Or you might ask similar questions as you read the essay with the class and come across Hornby's statements on the pictures.

Hornby wants to make readers aware of the thought-provoking, complicated nature of Billingham's photographs. In the essay's opening, he mentions other works of art that cause only momentary distractions. Billingham's photographs are different, however, because they "detain" viewers: "Wandering off is simply not an option, not if you have any curiosity at all: there is too much to think about, too much going on, too much narrative" (para. 2). Later, he describes the photographs as "rich and strange" (para. 6).

Students might see sadness or disgust—perhaps even the invasion of privacy—in the photograph of Richard's father, Raymond, sitting next to the toilet. Regarding this picture, Hornby is impressed with how Billingham is empathetic without being sentimental: "It was never going to be a pretty picture, but Billingham's pitiless, neutral gaze doesn't overweigh it, and consequently it is allowed to take its place in the ongoing narrative of his parents' life together" (para. 4). Whereas students might feel sorry for Billingham, Hornby applauds the photographer's "impeccable judgement" in not allowing the pictures to "become self-pitying" (para. 5).

Part of how he achieves this, Hornby notes, is by giving each parent the same consideration and by taking "pains to show that this marriage has its moments of calm domesticity and evidently peaceable companionship" (para. 6). One of Hornby's examples of this "calm domesticity" is the picture of Elizabeth doing a jigsaw puzzle, which he describes as "a brilliantly realized shot, this, with the jigsaw pieces, Elizabeth's floral print dress, and her tattoos coming together in an orchestrated riot of synthetic color" (para. 6). The picture of Raymond throwing the cat through the air will probably elicit laughter from students. Hornby sees it as "a strangely matter-of-fact, life-goes-on moment" (para. 6).

Students will probably be surprised by the picture of Elizabeth striking Raymond because it is not the typical portrayal of domestic violence. Hornby's reaction is somewhat similar: "There is an inherent and perverse fascination, of course, in seeing grown people knock lumps off each other, and the fascination in this case is intensified by Elizabeth's obviously immense physical power" (para. 8). Even though the photographs depict violence as a daily occurrence in the marriage, Hornby points out how Billingham does not simplify his family's situation: Billingham's exhibition ends with a picture of Raymond and Elizabeth cuddling. In this way, Billingham shows how "the truth is a lot more complicated" (para. 9).

ADDITIONAL WRITING TOPICS

1. Ask students to write a personal narrative about a relationship that others simplified or misunderstood. The relationship could have been one they were involved in—with a sibling, friend, significant other, parent—or one that they understood well (e.g., as Billingham understands the complexity of his parents' relationship).

2. Billingham records many uncomfortable moments in his photographs. Ask students to freewrite about an uncomfortable moment they witnessed between their parents. They don't have to share their freewriting, but do ask them to comment on how honestly their freewriting captured the moment. Is their writing as honest as Billingham's photographs?

3. Regarding Billingham, Hornby states, "the immediacy of his medium seems to expose people in a way that writing never can" (para. 3). Ask students to refute or support Hornby's claim about photography's advantage over writing by referring to essays and photographs within the *Seeing & Writing* text.

CONNECTIONS WITH OTHER TEXTS

1. In the previous essay, Susan Sontag struggled with how to view Goya's "unbearable" depictions of war. Hornby is also offering a way to view Billingham's difficult photographs. Ask students whether they had a harder time viewing Goya's work or Billingham's. Does the immediacy of and familiarity with photography have anything to do with their response?

2. Direct students to research what others have said about Billingham's work. How common are Hornby's views?

SUGGESTIONS FOR FURTHER READING, THINKING, AND WRITING

print

Billingham, Richard. *Ray's a Laugh*. New York: Scalo Publishing, 2001.

Hornby, Nick. *About a Boy*. New York: Riverhead Books, 1998.

———. *High Fidelity*. New York: Riverhead Books, 1995.

———. *How to Be Good*. New York: Riverhead Books, 2001.

Hughes, Robert, ed. *Writers on Artists*. New York: DK Publishing, 2001.

[www.] *web*

www.bbc.co.uk/arts/news_comment/artistsinprofile/billingham.shtml   BBC's profile on Richard Billingham. Includes a few pictures by Billingham.

www.penguin.co.uk/static/packages/uk/articles/hornby/   Penguin's page on Nick Hornby.

Links for the selections in this chapter can be found at www.seeingandwriting.com.

Susan Bordo, *Never Just Pictures*

GENERATING CLASS DISCUSSION AND IN-CLASS WRITING

One way to begin discussion of this essay is to ask students to consider the possible significance of the title. This might be a good time to restate the case for the predominance of images in American cultural life and the importance of training ourselves to read these images with critical awareness—after all, as Bordo states, they are "Never Just Pictures."

In this essay, though, Bordo primarily addresses cultural images of the body—both male and female—and the destructive effect that media images have on our self-images and psychological health. The subheading Bodies and Fantasies alerts us to her viewpoint.

Bordo asserts, "Our idolatry of the trim, tight body shows no signs of relinquishing its grip on our conceptions of beauty and normality"; she calls it an obsession that "seems to have gathered momentum, like a spreading mass hysteria" (para. 1). Her tone is one of alarm. She is warning us of what she sees as a dangerous trend—"pummeling and purging our bodies, attempting to make them into something other than flesh" (para. 1). Moreover, this cultural malaise is not limited to adults. Bordo states, "Children in this culture grow up knowing that you can never be thin enough and that being fat is one of the worst things one can be" (para. 1).

Bordo traces the beginning of this obsession to the end of World War II. She demonstrates the shift in preferred body type with an advertisement for CitraLean, a diet product. The ad pictures a woman of the 1940s or 1950s in an old-fashioned bathing suit and an old-fashioned body style—the caption reads, "All our mothers needed to diet" (p. 557). We can see, then, that although people in the 1940s and 1950s might have been more relaxed about body image, this is no longer the case. Children today may even prefer to be disfigured rather than fat, Bordo suggests (para. 1). She further traces the trend toward skinniness when she says, "Movie stars, who often used to embody a more voluptuous ideal, are now modeling themselves after the models . . ." who feature ". . . a blatant glamorization of the cadaverous, starved look" (para. 2).

As if the emaciated look were not enough, Bordo's analysis of the most current advertisements indicates that now it is fashionable to "appear dislocated and withdrawn, with chipped black nail polish and greasy hair, staring out at the viewer in a deathlike trance" (para. 7). She questions, "Why has death become glamorous?" (para. 8). Bordo wants us to realize that these advertising images are not merely superficial but a "complex, multilayered cultural 'symptom'" (para. 5) generated by a sophisticated industry fueled by a very strong motive—profit. The images "reflect the designers' cultural savvy, their ability to sense and give form to flutters and quakes in the cultural psyche. . . . They want their images and the products associated with them to sell" (para. 10).

In conclusion, Bordo notes that the latest strategy seems to involve the unadorned face, perhaps the irregular face—but always paired with a flawless, rail-thin body. Although on the surface these more individual faces might signal a welcome variety in body types, in fact they do not. They merely communicate the insidious message that "fixing up their faces rather than buying clothes is not in their [the fashion industry's] best interests" (para. 12). The clothing manufacturers "are reasserting the importance of body over face as the 'site' of our fantasies" (para. 12).

ADDITIONAL WRITING TOPICS

1. Refer students to Mario Testino's pictures of models Shalom and Linda (p. 307). Ask students to analyze those body images on the basis of Bordo's criteria. Do students consider them to be "healthy" images?

2. Have students examine the photographs of Madonna from the Retrospect in Chapter 6 (pp. 508–09). Ask them to analyze the differences between the context of the typical fashion shot Bordo describes and the contexts in which Madonna is pictured. Discuss the bodies and expressions presented in the different contexts.

CONNECTIONS WITH OTHER TEXTS

1. Ask students to find photographs of famous athletes on the Internet and to analyze those body images on the basis of Susan Bordo's criteria. Do your students consider them to be "healthy" images? (You might refer them to Bordo's discussion of the Olympics on p. 558).

2. Guide students to the Madonna photographs in Chapter 6 (pp. 508–09). Ask them to analyze the difference between the context of the typical fashion shot Bordo describes and the context of the publicity photos for which Madonna posed. Discuss the bodies and expressions of the women in each.

SUGGESTIONS FOR FURTHER READING, THINKING, AND WRITING

print

Bordo, Susan. *The Male Body: A New Look at Men in Public and in Private.* New York: Farrar, Straus and Giroux, 1999.

Shute, Jenefer. *Life-size.* Boston: Houghton Mifflin, 1992. The novel follows the battle of the narrator, Josie, as she struggles with anorexia. The writing is darkly humorous and terribly poignant; the book ties in well with Susan Bordo's essay.

[www] *web*

www.cddc.vt.edu/feminism/Brodo.html   This site includes biographical information and lists books and articles by Susan Bordo.

Links for the selections in this chapter can be found at www.seeingandwriting.com.

W. E. B. DuBois, *Double Consciousness*

GENERATING CLASS DISCUSSION AND IN-CLASS WRITING

The concept of "double consciousness" may be difficult for students to grasp. You might start a discussion to help define the phrase more clearly, pointing out how DuBois describes African Americans as having both a view of themselves, as well as a view of how other's see them. Have them re-read the line "One never sees his two-ness,—an American, a Negro; two souls, two thoughts, two unreconciled strivings; two warring ideals in one dark body, whose dogged strength alone keeps it from being torn asunder." Students will probably have different ideas on what DuBois means.

The opening sentence is one that has been used often since DuBois wrote it: "The problem of the twentieth century is the problem of the colorline." Do students agree with that statement? Why or why not? Try to tease out the notion of double consciousness; if students have a hard time talking about race, you might apply the same concept to gender, class, or sexuality. As we enter the twenty-first century, demographics are shifting; there may be a time in the near future when whites will be a clear minority (this may already be the case in your student population). How do students see the colorline shifting with the census count? Will double consciousness still rule? Where do the unifying ideals that DuBois talks about, the "greater ideals of the American Republic" (para. 4), come from? Do they still exist?

ADDITIONAL WRITING TOPICS

1. Ask students to freewrite about their own sense of racial identity, separating out as much as possible the strands of how they think about the complicated concept. What does double consciousness mean to them personally?

2. Instruct students to write a brief essay that describes how an image from this text displays double consciousness.

CONNECTIONS WITH OTHER TEXTS

1. You might ask students to consider how the notion of double consciousness is complicated by Tibor Kalman's recolorings of famous whites into blacks and blacks into whites (pp. 494–97).

2. In Chapter 2's Looking Closer section (p. 202), Marita Golden echoes some of Dubois's thoughts. Ask students to reread Golden's piece and to note the year in which each was written. Do students get a sense of progress from Golden?

www. Links for the selections in this chapter can be found at www.seeingandwriting.com.

Cream of Wheat, *Giddap, Uncle*

GENERATING CLASS DISCUSSION AND IN-CLASS WRITING

Students will probably start a discussion of this image by expressing surprise or shock that such a racist image could ever have been used in an advertisement. You might want to bring in an example of a contemporary Cream of Wheat product and show them that even today the packaging features an image of a black waiter. Encourage students to talk about what this ad might have conveyed in 1921 and what it conveys today; then have students identify what has survived from this image as reflected in contemporary ads for Cream of Wheat.

ADDITIONAL WRITING TOPICS

1. Ask students to refer back to Guillermo Gómez-Peña's photograph *Authentic Cuban Santeria* (p. 418). How would they describe the purpose and tone of each? How are the works similar? How are they different?

2. Have students consider how this ad is evidence of DuBois's statement about an African American having the "sense of always looking at one's self through the eyes of others."

www. Links for the selections in this chapter can be found at www.seeingandwriting.com.

RETROSPECT: *Reel Native Americans*

GENERATING CLASS DISCUSSION AND IN-CLASS WRITING

These four images—two movie posters and two movie stills—convey some of the stereotypes of Native Americans in our movie culture. The Buffalo Bill poster shows explicitly the relationship between the native population and the newly hegemonous European white culture. Ask students to consider the vertical axis of the image—the white man rides a white horse, has blond hair and light skin, and occupies the entire upper half of the poster. Furthermore, he is named; he has an identity as an individual—he is Buffalo Bill and his life story is worth three reels of film. In the lower half of the poster the "others," in this case the Native Americans, are grouped. They are huddled around the rock pedestal on which the white man astride his horse towers dramatically. They are unnamed, they have no horses, they sit in submissive postures below the white man. The vertical axis clearly identifies the man on the horse as the most powerful figure in the image. In contrast, you might ask students to discuss their observations about the grouping of the Native Americans along the horizontal lower third of the frame.

The movie poster entitled "Redskin" presents a different image. Here the Native American is the main focus of the poster, as there are no other clear images of people in the frame. At the bottom, a dark skinned man leads a foot race, while a white man struggles to keep up. There is also a city in the background, which suggests a struggle between Native American tradition and the modern world. Students may notice these visual cues and understand that the movie focuses on a Native American, rather than the more common white American point of view.

The image from the animated Disney movie *Pocahontas* is unlike the posters from 1910 and 1926, whose painted images suggest black and white film technology; the *Pocahontas* still is in color and represents a seventy-year leap forward in cinema. Not only has the film stock moved from black and white to color, but the relationship between the two races has changed as well. The man and the woman are situated in the center of the horizontal and vertical axes and are embracing, holding each other tenderly instead of dominating or harming each other. This is not a picture of warriors and soldiers; it is of a romantic duo. The story of Pocahontas and Captain John Smith is portrayed as an idealized version of the relationship between the two races. This reproduction from the animated film depicts a contemporary version of first contact.

He is the square-jawed, white-skinned man who falls in love with the native woman of color. Ultimately, they save each other.

The image from the movie *Smoke Signals,* directed by Chris Eyre and based on a book by Sherman Alexie, shows a laughing individual in the center of the frame and a serious individual in the background. The movie places these young men in a narrative context that is not about war, romance, or a particular historical incident; rather, it is about friendship, father-son relationships, community, and these two friends' journey into adulthood.

Thomas, the reservation "nerd," is always telling stories that people don't want to listen to; nonetheless he is a cheerful and optimistic narrator, as is evident from his smiling face. His friend, Victor, who is pictured with a serious expression, is dealing with the death of his absentee father. The friends travel together to bring back the body of Victor's father for burial. The two young men are participants in a narrative that could take place in the context of many ethnic groups. Both the photo and the movie are more about individuals than about races.

ADDITIONAL WRITING TOPICS

1. You might direct students to the web to search for other posters from movies that portray the colonization of the western United States. Then, have students analyze the posters in terms of their depiction of Native Americans.

2. Ask students to write a research paper about the legend of Pocahontas by looking up the story in history textbooks from different decades. If they find any images of Pocahontas or John Smith, ask them to compare and contrast those images with the one in the Retrospect.

3. You might invite students to read Sherman Alexie's book, *Smoke Signals,* and to see Chris Eyre's movie, *Smoke Signals,* and then to write about the differences in the cinematic and literary versions of the story. Students might begin with the stereotype suggested by the words *smoke signals* and then explore the complex kinds of communication that the movie and the book address.

CONNECTIONS WITH OTHER TEXTS

1. Ask students to consider how the historical image of the Native American changes from the first image in the Retrospect to the last. In what ways has the visual image shifted?

2. Have students compare this series of images of Native Americans with the images of women in the Chapter 7 Retrospect (pp. 566–67) in terms of the portrayal of gender and race.

SUGGESTIONS FOR FURTHER READING, THINKING, AND WRITING

print

Alexie, Sherman. *The Lone Ranger and Tonto Fistfight in Heaven.* New York: Atlantic Monthly Press, 1993.

Custer, George Armstrong. *My Life on the Plains— Or, Personal Experiences with Indians.* Norman: University of Oklahoma Press, 1962.

Erdrich, Louise. *The Antelope Wife.* HarperCollins, 1999. This short novel covers a century of myth and loss of Native American culture. The tale is told through the visions of a contemporary woman interwoven with the story of her family history.

Heard, Norman J. *White into Red: A Study of the Assimilation of White Persons Captured by Indians.* Metuchen: Scarecrow Press, 1973.

Hilger, Michael. *From Savage to Nobleman: Images of Native Americans in Film.* Metuchen: Scarecrow Press, 1995.

Rothenberg, Randall. "A Native-American Ad Agency Bids to Change Tired Images." *Advertising Age* (August 2, 1999): 24.

[www.] web

www.eiteljorg.org   The Eiteljorg Museum site, devoted to Native American art.

www.heard.org   The Heard Museum of Native American Art (in Phoenix).

www.uiowa.edu/~commstud/resources/ GenderMedia/asian.html   A site from the University of Iowa that provides links from Asian-American to Indigenous.

Links for the selections in this chapter can be found at www.seeingandwriting.com.

audio/visual

American Indians: Yesterday and Today. Directed by Don B. Klugman. 20 min. 1993. VHS videocassette. Distributed by Film Fair Communications. People from three tribes in different areas of the country (California, Montana, and New York) talk about past and present lifestyles.

The Indian Fighter. Directed by Andre DeToth. 88 min. 1995. Videocassette. Distributed by United Artists. This 1955 movie demonstrates many classic stereotypes of the Western genre; in the story a wagon train scout becomes involved with a Native American chief's daughter. Performers include Kirk Douglas, Lon Chaney, Walter Matthau, Elsa Martinelli, and Diana Douglas.

Sherman Alexie. 21 September 1993. Recording. Distributed by WHYY, Philadelphia. Terry Gross, host of NPR's *Fresh Air,* interviews Alexie. He was 23 years old at the time of this recording.

Smoke Signals. Directed by Chris Eyre. 89 min. 1998. VHS videocassette, rated PG-13. Distributed by Miramax. Written by Sherman Alexie. Performers include Adam Beach, Evan Adams, and Irene Bedard.

Kenneth Cole, *Think You Have No Privacy? You're Not Alone*

GENERATING CLASS DISCUSSION AND IN-CLASS WRITING

In this ad for Kenneth Cole clothing, the clothing is downplayed for a message regarding privacy. In a foggy mirror, a man's form can be made out along with the message "Think you have no privacy? You're not alone. —Kenneth Cole." Kenneth Cole is not the only company to raise the issue of privacy in its ads, and privacy is not the only issue raised in its ads. After you go through the Seeing prompts in the text with the students, you might ask them to consider how raising such an issue could help or hinder sales. Is it important to know where any company stands on a social issue? Do social messages make ads—and, therefore, the products—more memorable? Do they make companies seem more altruistic?

ADDITIONAL WRITING TOPICS

1. Kenneth Cole has come under fire for some of its social messages, most notably in the ad that compared the number of people dead from terrorist attacks on September 11 to those killed every day by AIDS. Ask students to research the messages displayed in Kenneth Cole ads. They should choose the most affecting ads and write an essay that analyzes how the ads work in terms of image, text, message, and audience. As they analyze, they should also persuade the reader to see the ads as they do.

2. During discussion, students might have recalled how other companies use social issues in their ads. You could ask students to imagine that they are in charge of the next Kenneth Cole ad. In an essay, they should describe the ad and how it will present its social message. They should explain what its central message is and why that message is important.

CONNECTIONS WITH OTHER TEXTS

1. The Mercedes ad (p. 464) does not feature a car, relying instead on the images of different icons to represent the company's slogan "What makes a symbol endure?" Of course, Mercedes is a well-known car manufacturer. People may not be as familiar with Kenneth Cole, so is Cole taking a chance by focusing on a social message in its ads? Or does the message make the ad more memorable than other clothing ads?

2. You might recall that the Diesel ad (p. 404) declared in a tongue-in-cheek fashion that the company "now sponsors freedom." Its message seems to parody message-heavy ads. You might ask students what they recall about the Diesel ad. Do they remember the clothing? the mascot? the slogan? What are they likely to remember about the Kenneth Cole ad?

SUGGESTIONS FOR FURTHER READING, THINKING, AND WRITING

print

Etzioni, Amitai. *The Limits of Privacy*. New York: Basic Books, 2000.

Rosen, Jeffrey. *The Unwanted Gaze: The Destruction of Privacy in America*. New York: Knopf, 2001.

[www.] *web*

www.kennethcole.com   Kenneth Cole's web site. Links for the selections in this chapter can be found at www.seeingandwriting.com.

Katharine Mieszkowski, *Nowhere Left to Hide*

GENERATING CLASS DISCUSSION AND IN-CLASS WRITING

In this essay, Mieszkowski writes about the invasion of privacy of inmates and considers how citizens will be next. After you assign the essay, you might ask students to write a few paragraphs in response to the essay to bring to class for discussion. The piece begins with a description of an Internet broadcast of a shakedown at a women's jail cell. By using such words as *sick* and *freak show*, Mieszkowski makes her viewpoint on this situation clear: "Getting arrested in Maricopa County can make you a star—a star in a sick webcam drama that turns the inside of a local jail into a worldwide freak show for any voyeur with a Web connection" (para. 6).

Although she is certainly against what is going on in this prison, she is more concerned with what it could mean for civilians: "What rights do any of us have to our own images these days? Is your image property you own or something you give up by venturing out in public?" (para. 10). Students should be aware of the vague sources to which the author refers: "one estimate suggests that we're each taped an average of 30 times a day" (para. 11). Although the number seems alarming, students should wonder about the source of the single estimate. The source seems to be the CEO of a company that provides face-recognition technology (para. 25). You might ask students to consider the reliability of this source. When Mieszkowski raises a concern over "Big Brother-style tracking" of citizens, she cites unnamed "privacy experts" who "predict that it won't be long before security cameras are net-worked" (para. 12).

Mieszkowski considers how face-recognition technology could be used for crime prevention as well as for privacy invasion. She notes how this technology matched the faces of nineteen people at a Super Bowl game to images of wanted criminals (para. 24). Mieszkowski does not directly state her opinion on this technology, instead offering statements by supporters and opponents of it (paras. 25–30). However, she seems to lean toward the side of the opposition, particularly when she notes how we have as little control over our images as inmates do (para. 32). The essay's final sentence is also telling as it considers the possibility of networked security cameras: "And if there used to be no easy way for the images from the cameras in the Madison Street Jail to make it into your living room, now there's an easy way for your own image to go places that you can't even picture" (para. 32).

The ancillary image is a cartoon that depicts a police officer reading an altered version of the Miranda rights to a handcuffed man. How does this image capture the anxiety expressed in Mieszkowski's essay?

ADDITIONAL WRITING TOPICS

1. Ask students to further investigate the topic of citizens' privacy. Based on their research, they could write an argument essay that responds to Mieszkowski's.

2. Students could also investigate the privacy and rights of inmates. How common are Arpaio's tactics? Should webcams be allowed in prisons?

Should inmates be allowed to vote? Should they be allowed to have conjugal visits? Students could write a persuasive essay about any of these topics.

3. To help students prepare for the above prompts, ask them to write a brief essay that explores the topic that interests them most from items 1 or 2.

CONNECTIONS WITH OTHER TEXTS

1. The Kenneth Cole ad that students examined before this reading also dealt with the issue of privacy. Ask students whether they find Cole's ad or Mieszkowski's essay more effective. Which is more convincing? Which is more memorable?

2. Mieszkowski does not state her view on this issue in the beginning of her essay, although it can

certainly be inferred from her tone and word choice. Readers do not get a sense of her opinion until near the end of her essay. Charles Young's "Losing: An American Tradition" (p. 423) works in a somewhat similar fashion. Although there are clues early on regarding Young's view, we do not know what it is for certain until the last few pages. Ask students to discuss this strategy in an essay that analyzes the essays by Young and Mieszkowski. Students are used to presenting a view early on with a thesis statement. Is it better to present one's view early on or to let readers discover it as the essay progresses? What are the advantages and disadvantages of each strategy?

SUGGESTIONS FOR FURTHER READING, THINKING, AND WRITING

print

Lessig, Lawrence. *The Future of Ideas: The Fate of the Commons in a Connected World*. New York: Random House, 2001.

Sykes, Charles J. *The End of Privacy*. New York: St. Martin's Press, 2000.

[www.] *web*

www.howstuffworks.com   This interesting web site explains how various things work. Students might find the articles on computer security and facial recognition systems to be helpful.

www.privacy.org   This web site features news and information about privacy issues, and it suggests actions to be taken to ensure privacy.

Links for the selections in this chapter can be found at www.seeingandwriting.com.

[www.] Re: Searching the Web

For an alternate assignment, students could examine the language of computer security. Ask them to research the meaning and history behind such words as *virus, Trojan horse, cookie, hacker, web bug, spyware, firewall,* and the like. How well do these words describe the meanings attached to them in the computing community? How much do they rely upon their roots outside of computing? Alter natively, you could have students examine the software that offers security and privacy—the names, the icons, the packaging (i.e., art and text). How do the details present the issue and sell the software?

Students can complete the Re: Searching the Web exercises online at www.seeingandwriting.com. Additional tips and links for each exercise are also included.

Karal Ann Marling, *They Want Their Mean TV*

GENERATING CLASS DISCUSSION AND IN-CLASS WRITING

Marling is troubled by the television shows—such as *Jackass* and *Fear Factor*—that appeal to younger crowds with "an unbridled meanness that represents the flip side of the entertainment of optimism purveyed to those who follow E.R." (para. 5). Marling does observe that the concept of humiliating people on television is not new: The "golden age" television show *Beat the Clock* made people "do stupid pet tricks for prizes" (para. 6). However, she finds recent "reality" shows to be "symptomatic of a broader trend toward cultural nastiness that crept up on us with the advent of Jerry, Maury, Ricki, Montel" (para. 8). As Marling notes, "These so-called 'reality' shows are about watching ordinary—albeit cute-in-a-swimsuit—people sweat, fret, scream, scheme, eat bugs and diss one another in nastily amazing ways" (para. 7).

In her attempt to figure out why people watch such shows, Marling notes that viewers take pleasure in ridiculing the less-than-glamorous "stars": "it's easier to wish ill to an un-pretty, un-famous face with missing teeth and acne scars" (para. 9). She also observes that viewers can feel superior to their television guests: "There's a class bias at work, too. Clearly, these shrieking, incest-ridden families are not our kind of people" (para. 9).

As she considers the effects of such television, Marling makes a common claim: "The medium might be the real message here: nasty television produces nasty audiences" (para. 11). When she observes the "boorish" behavior of her undergraduates, she is reminded of *Big Brother* residents. Marling does not pursue this simple cause-and-effect idea for very long, though. For her, watching these "nasty" shows does not directly cause "nasty" behavior—it's "unconsidered spectatorship" that leads to such behavior (para. 12). She believes her undergraduates watch without a sense of responsibility or empathy: "they have no responsibility for the yelling and the bloodshed—no stake in the mayhem, which makes it all too easy to enjoy wickedness from a distance. Merely watching things happen absolves the viewer of any responsibility for them" (para. 12).

Marling does not offer any suggestions as to how society can go about creating a thoughtful, empathetic audience. She does imply, however, that television shows might be able to draw audiences away from "Mean TV" if they were to become more edgy and unpredictable: "But old-fashioned hourlong drama can, perhaps, be indicted for being so predictable, so formulaic, so comfortable that young viewers go looking for a little edge—and wind up in the clutches of Mean TV" (para. 14).

You might begin discussion by asking students to list five shows they watch regularly. Do the "mean" shows listed by Marling show up on the lists? Ask students who watch such shows to describe the appeal. What about these shows turns off the students who do not watch? Or you could tape an episode of *Jackass, Fear Factor, Big Brother,* or *Jerry Springer* and watch a few minutes of it before addressing the essay.

As you analyze the essay with students, ask them to comment on Marling's use of humor. For instance, early on she sets a humorous tone when she describes herself: "I'm in that pathetic demographic nobody pays any attention to—the 'early geezers' that advertisers write off or consign to bleak celebration of incontinence products and denture cleaners beginning with the nightly news" (para. 1). Does she lose credibility by using such humor? Or does her humor seem fitting given the light subject matter?

ADDITIONAL WRITING TOPICS

1. Put students into groups and ask each group to remove the humorous aspects from Marling's essay. Have them locate humorous phrases and re-write them in a serious tone. Ask each group to read some of its best revisions. As a class, discuss how these changes influence the overall effect of the essay.

2. Assign an essay in which students explore the relationship between television and society. How do they influence each other?

3. Ask students to write an essay that considers how values and personality influence which television shows a person chooses to watch. Students can interview parents, teachers, siblings, and fellow students. They should also attempt to explain their own viewing habits.

CONNECTIONS WITH OTHER TEXTS

1. In "Creating the 'Real' in Bright Yellow and Blue" (p. 391), Robert Pinsky praises *The Simpsons* for its ingenuity and its humanity. Based on Marling's criticisms of the shows discussed in this essay, how do your students think she would react to an episode of *The Simpsons*? How would she respond to Pinsky's essay?

2. Divide students into groups and ask each group to choose a "mean" television show listed by Marling (or one similar to those listed). Each group should tape an episode and present 5 to 10 minutes of the show to the class, assessing the show, explaining why people are drawn to it, and leading the class in a discussion about the show.

SUGGESTIONS FOR FURTHER READING, THINKING, AND WRITING

print

Marling, Karal. *As Seen on TV: The Visual Culture of Everyday Life in the 1950s.* Cambridge: Harvard University Press, 1994.

web

Links for the selections in this chapter can be found at www.seeingandwriting.com.

VISUALIZING COMPOSITION: **Point of View**

GENERATING CLASS DISCUSSION AND IN-CLASS WRITING

Students will probably not have much difficulty discussing the perspective and bias evident in the Wolfschmidt vodka ad. The vodka bottle is clearly expressing a male perspective. The bottle sees it necessary to persuade the tomato (a woman) that he's not like other men, those who lie to women and use them. When he speaks to the orange (another woman), he feels the need to woo her with compliments: "You sweet doll. I appreciate you." The orange, though, questions him, suggesting that she might be suspicious of all men: "Who was that tomato I saw you with last week?"

Students might have a harder time understanding the issue of bias. There are a few ways to approach this issue. You could engage students in a discussion about biased language, using sexist language as the most obvious example. You might generate a few sentences that include only one sex in reference to a group (e.g., "A *nurse* needs to be careful around *her* patients"; "A *student* should always turn in *his* work on time"). Most students will probably know to avoid sexist language, but they will usually use the awkward *his/her* phrase to fix the problem. Instead, show them how to correct sexist language through use of the plural form: "*Nurses* need to be careful around *their* patients." Sexist language is, of course, not the only form of biased language. An extended discussion of biased language can be found in most handbooks.

Handbooks, however, do not discuss as extensively other ways in which bias can be present. You could start a general discussion of how bias can be tended to by developing better audience awareness as well as self-awareness. Students should not only be aware of their audience's experiences and beliefs but notice their own as well. They will have difficulty discussing and writing about their own prejudices at first. You might ask them to generate a list of words that classify them. For instance, one list might begin "Female, young adult, American, middle-class, daughter, sister, painter, math major, long-distance runner . . ." You might then direct students to consider how the classifications could include certain perspectives and prejudices.

The best way to tend to bias is by responding to it in student writing. When students are made aware of how bias can weaken their credibility, they will learn to look for similar instances of bias in their other writings.

ADDITIONAL WRITING TOPICS

1. For more in-class writing, ask students to generate lists about the prejudices built into certain points of view. For instance, students could think about the prejudices that might be expressed by a student writing an argument paper about whether college students should live in dorms or at home with their parents. Then, ask them to think about the prejudices that might be expressed by a parent writing about the same issue. For more practice, ask students to come up with lists for the prejudices that men and women might bring to essays about gender issues.

2. Invite students to bring to class an essay that they wrote earlier in the semester. Ask students to exchange essays and write a new one that analyzes the point of view and bias apparent in another student's essay.

3. Have students choose an essay from the text to analyze for bias. They should read the headnote, classify the author, and generate a list of possible prejudices. Then they should write an essay that analyzes bias within the essay.

CONNECTIONS WITH OTHER TEXTS

1. James Twitchell's essay "In Praise of Consumerism" (p. 411) is a good illustration of how careless reading can result in a misunderstanding of the author's point of view. In the essay's tenth paragraph, Twitchell explains how cultural studies teachers view the media. For example, he seems to state, "The masters of the media collude, striving to infantilize us so that we are docile, anxious, and filled with 'reified desire'" (para. 10). However, he separates the teachers' point of view from his own at the beginning of the paragraph. If readers overlook the first three words, "To these critics," they are likely to read the following statements as coming from Twitchell's point of view.

2. David Guterson's essay "No Place Like Home" (p. 157) presents a bias against planned communities. Divide students into groups and ask them to examine Guterson's essay for instances of bias, particularly in his use of word choice and comparison.

3. In her essay "They Want Their Mean TV," Karal Ann Marling discusses "Mean TV" and how the youth respond to it. She raises the issue of her age and her position as a college professor. You should discuss with students how these characteristics might lend to certain biases. Ask students to read the essay again, looking for instances of bias from Marling.

www. Links for the selections in this chapter can be found at to www.seeingandwriting.com.

Gerard Jones, *Killing Monsters*

GENERATING CLASS DISCUSSION AND IN-CLASS WRITING

In this essay, Jones argues that violent media can be used in healthy ways. His essay was written in response to parents, teachers, and "pop psychologists" decrying violent entertainment and blaming violent behavior upon it (para. 7). You might note that students do not need to explicitly state the motivations behind their writing in the way Jones does; however, their writing will be more interesting if they can find a purpose that goes beyond "because it was assigned." Since a major impetus behind the essay was the spate of shootings at high schools, you might discuss some of those cases as you read Jones's essay. You could begin discussion by asking students not only about what they thought were the reasons behind the shootings, but also about the many reasons they heard from various pundits in the media. Students are bound to recall fingers being pointed at the music of groups such as Marilyn Manson and at the violence in videogames.

Jones begins the essay by recalling how the Incredible Hulk, a comic book character, helped him overcome a passive, lonely, and repressed childhood: "I had a fantasy self who *was* a self: unafraid of his desires and the world's disapproval, unhesitating and effective in action" (para. 4). This fantasy self helped Jones make friends—"other sensitive geeks chasing their own inner brutes"—and become a writer (para. 5). Jones does not rely only upon his own experience. Fans of his work have told him how violent entertainment has helped them develop: "Across generations, genders, and ethnicities I kept seeing the same story: people pulling themselves out of emotional traps by immersing themselves in violent stories" (para. 5). He also notes that his son (para. 6) and two girls (paras. 13–15) have had similar experiences, using violent stories to face fears and develop self-control.

Other evidence behind Jones's claim comes from discussions he's had with psychologists over four years as he's developed his "Art and Story Workshops, in-class programs to help young people improve their self-knowledge and sense of potency through storytelling" (para. 10). Through these discussions, he's learned "about the ways in which children use stories, including violent ones, to meet their emotional and developmental needs—and the ways in which adults can help them use those stories healthily" (para. 10). One of these healthy ways involves using the imagination to overcome a sense of weakness: "Pretending to have superhuman powers helps children conquer the feelings of powerlessness that inevitably come with being so young and small" (para. 11).

Jones also notes that kids can learn from how comic book heroes struggle with dual identities, public and private selves. Learning this concept "helps kids negotiate the conflicts between the inner self and the public self as they work through the early stages of socialization" (para. 11). If students do not understand the dual-identity concept, you might give Spider-Man or Batman as examples. Students might recall how some of the high school shooters were reported to have different public and private selves. At school, they were quiet and meek. In private, they fantasized—through writing and drawing—about the violence they would later commit. Are the people who acted on their enraged fantasies examples of the influence of violent media? Or are they examples of people who might have been helped had they been taught to handle their rage?

Jones believes that violent media can be used to help children handle rage, an emotion that, he observes, they are taught to fear and suppress. He notes that rage is an unavoidable emotion for children and that creative violence can help them to channel rage in a useful direction: "Through immersion in imaginary combat and identification with a violent protagonist, children engage the rage they've stifled, come to fear it less, and become more capable of utilizing it against life's challenges" (para. 12).

Jones is not claiming that violent entertainment is completely harmless; indeed, he believes that "it has helped inspire some people to real-life violence" (para. 16). He states that fears about youth violence have been overblown and that hiding children from violent entertainment will do more harm than good: "We act as though our highest priority is to prevent our children from growing up into murderous thugs—but modern kids are far more likely to grow up too passive, too distrustful of themselves, too easily manipulated" (para. 16). He claims that rage is a "natural aggression" that youngsters should be taught to understand: "When we try to protect our children from their own feelings and fantasies, we shelter them not against violence, but against power and selfhood" (para. 17).

ADDITIONAL WRITING TOPICS

1. Brainstorm lists about possible influences on children's violent behavior.

2. Ask students to freewrite about their childhood and/or adolescence. What helped them get through difficult times? Some students might respond that television, movies, or music—each as heavily criticized as comic books—helped them. If this is the case, ask them to write an essay that defends the medium that they found invaluable.

3. Invite students to read several comic books and write an essay that analyzes how violence is depicted in them. You might suggest that students look into several comics that offer varying degrees of violence (e.g., Superman, Batman, and Spawn, or Wonder Woman, The X-Men, and The Punisher).

CONNECTIONS WITH OTHER TEXTS

1. Students might recall that in his essay "Inside Every Superhero Lurks a Nerd" (p. 439) Neal Gabler claimed that the *Spider-Man* film succeeded at the box office largely because it spoke to teens' feelings of powerlessness and their desire for power: "[Spider-Man] is transformed from an outcast into the toughest kid in the school. No wonder teenagers respond" (para. 4). Ask students to consider recent superheroes in television and film that have fulfilled the needs of certain audiences.

2. Ask students to research the role of the media, finding arguments for and against Jones's claim. Based on this research, they can write a paper that puts forth their own position.

SUGGESTIONS FOR FURTHER READING, THINKING, AND WRITING

print

Jones, Gerard. *Honey, I'm Home! Sitcoms: Selling the American Dream*. New York: St. Martin's Press, 1993.

———. *Killing Monsters: Why Children Need Fantasy, Superheroes, and Make Believe Violence*. New York: Basic Books, 2002.

(www) *web*

www.pbs.org/wgbh/pages/frontline/shows/kinkel/   PBS page offers in-depth study of a school shooter, including material about the influence of violent media.

www.pbs.org/wgbh/pages/frontline/teach/tvkillguide.html   PBS teaching guide for its video *Does TV Kill?*

Links for the selections in this chapter can be found at www.seeingandwriting.com.

audio/visual

Does TV Kill? 90 min. 1995. Videocassette. Distributed by PBS. A *Frontline* study on how television violence affects people.

Talking Pictures

Before you give the assignment, you might bring a television show or film to class that demonstrates product placement. To give students some direction, you could brainstorm with the class certain television shows and films that would be best to watch.

A slight variation on this assignment might be to have students watch television shows or films that have different audiences. Then ask the students to write an essay that compares and contrasts the products and how they are presented to each audience. Again, you would probably want to brainstorm a list of shows and films.

James Rosenquist, *Professional Courtesy*

GENERATING CLASS DISCUSSION AND IN-CLASS WRITING

This painting presents two hands, each holding a gun pointed directly at the other against a red background. Before students read Rosenquist's quote, you might ask them to freewrite about their reaction to the painting. Then ask them to share their writing with the class. Do they see the painting as a "stark look and confrontation of a handgun"? Do they sense Rosenquist's intention to make viewers "question the idea of who really is the target"? How does the title affect their reading of the painting? (For further discussion of the title, you could direct students to the text's second Writing question.)

How do your students read the red background? Does it suggest urgency? blood? Ask them to consider why Rosenquist only shows the hands of the figures holding the guns. Would faces distract us from the guns? Would we attempt to attach a motive to a face? Some students might note that they feel as though they are a part of the painting since the gun in the foreground seems to extend from the viewer's position. If some students have difficulty understanding the positioning of the guns, you might ask how the painting would be different if the guns were presented horizontally, extending directly from the sides of the painting.

 For an interactive visual exercise for this selection, go to www.seeingandwriting.com.

ADDITIONAL WRITING TOPICS

1. Using Rosenquist's painting as one example, ask students to write an argument essay about whether images can inspire change in society.

2. Ask each student to create a different title for the painting and to write a brief essay that explains how that title would affect the painting's meaning.

3. Some students might take issue with Rosenquist's statement regarding how "[y]oung people are confused by the way guns are depicted in the movies and on television." Have students write an essay that explains why they agree or disagree with Rosenquist.

CONNECTIONS WITH OTHER TEXTS

1. Whether or not you assign the first Additional Writing Topic above, you might wish to discuss it in class. For other examples, you could discuss other images in the chapter—Goya's anti-war etchings, the anti-drug ads, and Kenneth Cole's privacy ad.

2. Rosenquist is concerned with the pervasiveness of guns in our society. You might ask students to discuss the gun as an American icon. To help start the discussion, you could ask students to imagine a handgun alongside Betty Boop, James Dean, and the Statue of Liberty in the storefront window captured in David Butow's photograph (p. 521). Is such an image outrageous? Do some students see it as plausible?

SUGGESTIONS FOR FURTHER READING, THINKING, AND WRITING

print

Goldman, Judith. *James Rosenquist*. New York: Viking, 1985.

web

www.artcyclopedia.com/artists/rosenquist _james.html   Artcyclopedia's web page on Rosenquist.

Links for the selections in this chapter can be found at www.seeingandwriting.com.

Office of National Drug Control Policy, *Parents, the Anti-Drug (Tommy)*

GENERATING CLASS DISCUSSION AND IN-CLASS WRITING

This anti-drug ad features a boy holding a skateboard, walking down a deserted street. The ad's text advises parents to watch their children, even though they may feel as though they are violating their children's freedom: "Keeping an eye on your kids is not taking away their freedom. It's actually the best way to keep them away from drugs." Before students turn to the ad, you might ask them to comment on how their own parents balanced matters of privacy with protection. How did their parents limit their freedom to protect them from drugs?

You might ask students to consider the attributes that make Tommy the poster boy for kids who need to be watched. Students might observe that he is alone on a deserted street. They might read his demeanor as being smug or suspicious. His skateboard and clothing might indicate that he's willing to fit into a particular group's style. You could also ask students to consider how the background adds to Tommy's situation. Once students imagine the background as a suburban street or a high school, they can see how the barred windows and endless bricks do not allow any soft, safe imagery. The gray street clashes with the boy's bright clothing, suggesting that he is not supposed to be there.

ADDITIONAL WRITING TOPICS

1. Ask students to consider the short phrases that urge parents to "Talk/Know/Ask/Keep an eye on them." In a freewriting exercise, have students associate specific activities with these phrases. How would these activities be carried out?

2. Direct students to write a narrative essay about what helped them stay away from drugs or what influenced them to try drugs. In the essay's conclusion, they should write about what others can learn from their example.

SUGGESTIONS FOR FURTHER READING, THINKING, AND WRITING

 web

www.theantidrug.com   Web site that features a number of anti-drug ads, including this one.

www.whitehousedrugpolicy.gov/   The White House's official page on the government's drug policy.

Links for the selections in this chapter can be found at www.seeingandwriting.com.

VISUALIZING CONTEXT: **History Repeats Itself**

GENERATING CLASS DISCUSSION AND IN-CLASS WRITING

This Visualizing Context section asks students to examine how similar messages—in this case, an anti-drug message—are conveyed by different techniques and strategies over time. Students are first asked to consider the classic 1987 anti-drug ad that featured an egg frying in a pan and included the line: "This is your brain on drugs." The simplicity of the ad and the boldness of the metaphor made it unforgettable. The 2001 ad about heroin addiction used similar imagery but in a different way: Instead of focusing on the damage done to the user's brain, the ad showed an actress demolishing a kitchen with a frying pan to show heroin's effects on the user's brain, dignity, friends, and family. You might ask students to consider why the 1987 ad could not just be rehashed for contemporary audiences. Students might infer that an increase in heroin use might have prompted the need for a specific and daring ad. Others might note that the original tagline "This is your brain on drugs" lost its effectiveness by being too familiar. Is the 2001 ad successful because it references the earlier ad? Or does this allusion weaken its effectiveness?

You might also discuss how other popular ads have changed. Early commercials about the dangers of drinking and driving featured the line "Friends don't let friends drink and drive" and sometimes included sound effects of cars crashing. Recent commercials have carried this theme a bit further, including pictures and video footage of people killed by drunk drivers.

ADDITIONAL WRITING TOPICS

1. Ask students to research how cigarette or alcohol ads have changed over time. Based on these ads, students can write a paper that analyzes how tobacco or alcohol companies have changed their messages and methods over time.

2. Direct students to study a variety of anti-drug ads. Which ones do they find most effective? least effective? Ask them to write a paper that explains why certain strategies are more effective than others.

3. Have students imagine that they have been assigned the task of directing the country's anti-drug campaign. Students can either design an anti-drug ad or write a memo that identifies and explains the strategies and messages the campaign will utilize.

1. In your discussion, the anti-smoking ads by www.thetruth.com might have been mentioned. The methods used by the ads are often clever and sometimes shocking. You might ask students to compare and contrast one of these ads with the "Tommy" ad (p. 590).

SUGGESTIONS FOR FURTHER READING, THINKING, AND WRITING

 web

www.thetruth.com   This web site promotes awareness of the dangers of smoking and exposes the advertising methods of tobacco companies. Includes an archive of the group's anti-smoking ads.

Links for the selections in this chapter can be found at www.seeingandwriting.com.

PORTFOLIO: **Sebastião Salgado**

GENERATING CLASS DISCUSSION AND IN-CLASS WRITING

You might ask students to explain how these photographs fit the series title *Migrations: Humanity in Transition,* and you could direct them to the text's Seeing questions after they've examined the pictures on their own. It might be worthwhile to have students react to the pictures without first reading the captions. The first photograph shows a rooftop filled with dozens of babies in various states—sleeping, crawling, rising, playing—against a background of towering buildings. The skyline features peaks and dips as the buildings vary in height; the babies in the foreground create a similar effect. The shot is brilliant in its contrasts: Flesh-and-blood babies—still in the beginning phases of their development—are set against metal, concrete constructions that represent fully developed ideas of engineering and human achievement. Before reading the caption, one can see transition in the babies and the buildings representing different points of development: The babies are beginning to rise and crawl, and eventually they will enter that world behind them or help create more of it. A lack of progress could also be seen here in stunning display: Why are these babies crowding this rooftop and not residing in the homes in the background? The caption reveals that they are on the rooftop of the Foundation for Child Welfare, an institution that takes care of abandoned babies.

The second photograph also shows the disintegration of families. In a dark building, children stand by a window. Light and dark are here, but they only contrast each other in the photograph's composition. The light blazing through the window seems hopeful at first, but the lack of anything beyond the window makes the light equal to the darkness, especially when it seems as though most of the people in the picture are in the dark room to take shelter. The caption explains how these young boys are avoiding being pulled into the civil war in southern Sudan.

The third photograph features a pipeline running through the middle of a town that consists of ramshackle houses. As the caption notes, the pipeline is carrying drinking water to wealthier parts of Bombay. The pipeline, like the buildings in the first photograph, is an invention, an achievement of humanity. However, progress is called into question by the pipeline's callous placement: Since it carries drinking water, the inference can be made that the people who live by and walk on this pipeline do not share in the life-sustaining element it carries. The water within the pipe is moving toward wealth; the people who walk along it will not make the same transition.

Two men stand by a replica of the Statue of Liberty in the fourth photograph. The statue raises a dove in one hand and holds flowers in the other. You might ask students why it is holding a dove instead of a torch. According to the caption, the statue was made by a refugee and stands at the entrance to a detention camp. The statue and the dove represent freedom, America.

The fifth photograph is a sweeping shot of the State of Roraima, which has become eroded due to deforestation by settlers and cattle ranchers. The previous pictures have depicted how humanity has been impacted by the migration and transition of humanity. This photograph shows the ruin brought upon the earth itself by the action and movement of humans.

ADDITIONAL WRITING TOPICS

1. Ask students to freewrite about each image before they read its caption. Have them share their freewriting with the class.

2. Invite students to write a brief expository essay about the photo that affects them the most. For a longer essay, students can compare and contrast the photo with the others.

3. Ask students to research one of the subjects raised by Salgado's photographs and to write a paper that explains the causes of the problems and offers possible solutions.

1. Students might find a better way to define Salgado's style by comparing his photographs to Raghubir Singh's vivid, colorful portraits of India (pp. 198–99).

2. When students discovered that Joel Sternfeld's *Taylor Hall Parking Lot* (p. 186) was taken at the site of a shooting, they probably imagined the incident in the context of the photograph. Salgado's last picture is similar in that it is devoid of people and presents the area after that damage has been done. Ask students to freewrite about the activities that must have occurred on this land.

SUGGESTIONS FOR FURTHER READING, THINKING, AND WRITING

print

Salgado, Sebastião. *The Children: Refugees and Migrants.* New York: Aperture, 2000.

———. *Migrations: Humanity in Transition.* New York: Aperture, 2000.

 web

www.pdnonline.com/legends/ This Photo District News site features a gallery of Salgado's work.

Links for the selections in this chapter can be found at www.seeingandwriting.com.

Michael Kimmelman, *150th Anniversary: 1851–2001; The Assignment Is to Get the Story, but the Image Can Rise to Art*

GENERATING CLASS DISCUSSION AND IN-CLASS WRITING

To begin discussion you might put students into groups and ask each group to find a different photograph from the text to analyze for its artistic merit. Each group should try to arrive at an agreement as to how it defines *art*. As you discuss Kimmelman's essay, ask each group to discuss its photograph in terms of how Kimmelman defines artistic photographs.

In the opening paragraphs, Kimmelman describes memorable photographs taken on September 11. Although they have become unforgettable and even symbolic, they are not, Kimmelman says, art. He states that it is difficult for photojournalists to achieve art in their work: "All photojournalists hope their best pictures are good enough to be considered art, but most of the time they don't succeed" (para. 4). To become a work of art, a picture must convey "more than information" (para. 4). Even if a photograph achieves this task by presenting beauty or conveying an event, it does not necessarily become art. A photograph becomes art when it transcends the event it captures. For an example of a photograph that has "shape[d] history" but does not transcend the event, Kimmelman refers to "Eddie Adams's unforgettable photograph of the South Vietnamese police commander shooting a Vietcong prisoner" (para. 5).

A transcendent picture is one that is not limited to the event it captures. It causes us to recall other images and represents something universal. As Kimmelman states, it is an "echo of some previous images we have seen . . . , which are stored in our memories as archetypes and symbols, so that the photograph, by conscious or unconscious association and special variation, is elevated from the specific to the universal" (para. 6).

Kimmelman describes two photographs that have transcended their events and become art. He mentions each photograph in relation to a picture that is more important, more newsworthy. However, each time the less newsworthy picture rises to art. The first photograph "shows a boy, arms out, face heavenward, standing before a wall of electric fans that belong to an artwork at the P.S. 1 Contemporary Art Center in Queens" (para. 10). The more newsworthy photograph is "a fairly straightforward spot-news shot of Radislav Krstic, a Bosnian Serb general, on crutches, in The Hague, where he was found guilty of genocide" (para. 10). The photograph of the boy reminds Kimmelman of "the famous Cartier-Bresson image, a surreal masterpiece of a Spanish boy, eyes skyward, arms out, as if in ecstasy" (para. 11). Note how Kimmelman's sentence about the artistic photograph is more elegant and vivid than his sentence about the "fairly straightforward" picture. Naturally, his prose is more striking for the photograph that excites him, but his prose also affects how the reader "sees" each photograph.

A similar effect can be seen in his discussion of the other artistic photograph, which is contrasted with the more newsworthy image of Governor Bush during his presidential campaign. Note the lackluster description: "Gov. George W. Bush is shown behind the lunch counter in a drugstore in Grinnell, Iowa, pretending to wait on customers for the benefit of news cameras, which you see beyond the counter" (para. 16). The second photograph "shows mourners around the dead body of Ali Paqarizi, a 19-year-old Albanian killed by a Serb booby trap" (para. 17). The picture is not of his military funeral; it is of "his family's living room, where his mother, surrounded by grieving women, cried over her son's corpse" (para. 17). Again, Kimmelman's prose becomes vivid as he describes the picture: "The formal geometry of this image, with the semicircle of mourners, is locked in place by the horizontal body of the dead man in his striped shroud and by the vertical axis of his mother's foreshortened arm, his impassive mask set against her explicit grief" (para. 18). This photograph rises above its event because "it articulates the larger meaning of the conflict in the Balkans and, most important, of suffering generally" (para. 18).

ADDITIONAL WRITING TOPICS

1. Before students read the essay, you could ask them to write a brief paragraph that explains what they think would constitute an artistic photograph. You could open discussion by asking students to discuss their views in comparison to Kimmelman's.

2. Ask students to keep a journal that records the news photographs they see online, on television, and in magazines and newspapers over one week's time. Which photographs catch their eye? Which photographs stick in their memory? Which are more newsworthy? Do they see any patterns in the pictures that stand out or linger in the mind? They should consider these questions in their journals. This could be assigned before students read the essay and used as discussion material, or it could be used afterward as essay material.

3. If students write a paper that responds to Kimmelman's essay, you could suggest that they interview photography majors or local photographers about their views on artistic photographs.

CONNECTIONS WITH OTHER TEXTS

1. Ask students to examine the September 11 photographs in Chapter 3. Would any of these match Kimmelman's criteria of an artistic photograph? What about the popular photograph of the firemen raising the American flag?

2. Invite students to bring a photograph to class and write a brief paragraph that explains how it fits the artistic criteria set forth by Kimmelman.

SUGGESTIONS FOR FURTHER READING, THINKING, AND WRITING

print

Kimmelman, Michael. *Portraits: Talking with Artists at the Met, Modern, Louvre, and Elsewhere.* New York: Random House, 1998.

www. *web*

Links for the selections in this chapter can be found at www.seeingandwriting.com.

Looking Closer:
The Ethics of Representation

In this section the textbook moves from a consideration of reading words, whether in print or on screen, to an emphasis on reading photographs. Readers are asked to consider to what extent they can rely on the photographic image to represent "reality" in contemporary media, particularly the news media.

Mitchell Stephens, *Expanding the Language of Photographs*

Stevens mentions three examples of digitally altered news photos: Tonya Harding skating with Nancy Kerrigan in *New York Newsday*; the pyramids in an issue of *National Geographic*; and Governor Ann Richards in *Texas Monthly*. Instead of assuming that altering news photos is like lying, Stephens suggests that altering photographs, even news photographs, is necessary for the evolution of photojournalism. He argues that because photos are already altered in many ways through choice of angles, filters, contrast, and depth of field, the act of digitally altering does not render them any more subjective than they already are. He also points out that language itself routinely refers to what is not there. (He does make the point that digitally altered photos should be labeled as such, though.)

Stephens asserts that altered photos "will allow us to peek, however hazily, into the future: showing not just how Harding and Kerrigan might look together on the ice but how that new building might change the neighborhood" (para. 9). He thinks the assumption that photographs represent reality has always been "something of a misperception." Further, "if we are to take advantage of the great promise of digital technology, we'll have to wise up" (para. 14).

George Hunt, *Doctoring Reality to Document What's True*

This black and white photo demonstrates some of the ways in which supposedly "real" photographs have always been manipulated, even before it was possible to alter them digitally. Here we see the fiction that is used to create the "truth" of a Kwakiutl woman and her weaving. The backdrop is being held up in order to create a better picture of the "authentic" woman at her task. Is the photograph therefore less true? Is it a less authentic representation than an unstaged photo would be?

John Long, *Ethics in the Age of Digital Photography*

In this essay, Long discusses how unethical changes to photographs have damaged journalism's credibility. He refers to some of the same examples mentioned by Stephens, but he takes the opposite view: "In the context of news, if a photo looks real, it better be real" (para. 22). Regarding the altered photo of Governor Ann Richards, Long notes that the labeling of digital alterations does not make the alterations permissible (para. 22). He seems to believe that changes "that make the photo more readable" are "neither ethical nor unethical—they are merely technical" (para. 24). Long notes two different kinds of changes made to the content of photographs: "Essential changes change the meaning of the photograph and Accidental changes change useless details but do not change the real meaning" (para. 25). However, he feels that any change to content is wrong. Changes diminish the power of the photograph to capture a moment as it happened. He notes how certain photographs have changed "the hearts and minds of the people," and they achieved this power by being real: "They are powerful and they get their power from the fact that they are real Moments captured for all time on film" (para. 37).

Shark Photo Hoax

The first still image shows Charles Maxwell's shark jumping out of the water and Lance Cheung's *Members of the 129th Rescue Squadron*. The two images below it were spliced together and edited to make the version that was spread via e-mail as *National Geographic*'s "Photo of the Year." In the essays by Long and Stephens, students read about the possible consequences of professional journalists altering photographs. What does it mean that such alterations can now be done by almost anyone with a computer and an average photographic program? How does the availability of such technology complicate the truthfulness of images?

Newsweek, *Bobbi and Kenny McCaughey*

In this photograph, Mrs. McCaughey's teeth have been digitally altered to look exceptionally white and healthy. Ask students to consider why this touch-up was made. How would viewers' reaction to and assumptions about the McCaugheys differ if the teeth had not been altered? What does this reveal about our cultural assumptions?

U.S. Postal Service, William Hopson

This example of a digitally altered photograph is exactly what Mitchell Stephens is arguing against in "Expanding the Language of Photographs." He maintains that when a photograph is altered, it should be clearly labeled as such and should not be used to deceive.

ADDITIONAL WRITING TOPICS

1. Ask students to write a journal entry addressing the issue of truth in photojournalism. Direct them to examine their own assumptions about the reality of news photos.

2. Instruct students to draft an essay analyzing the photographs they find in one edition of their local newspaper. Which ones are coded for truth, and which ones are not? Have students write down their observations about the criteria in the photos that signal "real." Have them also write about the specific elements of the non-news photos that signal "not real."

3. Ask students to watch a documentary on television. Then, have them list and explain in an essay the elements of the show that were staged and those that were not. For example, what is the role of people? Are there actors in the show? If not, how is the story presented visually—with animals? with old war footage? Are the cameras visible? Is there a voice-over narration that informs the viewer about the images being presented, or do the images speak for themselves?

CONNECTIONS WITH OTHER TEXTS

1. Ask students to consult the *Oxford English Dictionary* for definitions of the word *ethics*. Discuss with them the original meaning of the word, and apply it to the texts in this section. To what extent are these representations ethical or not?

2. Bring in copies of a magazine such as *National Geographic,* and ask students to examine the photography and evaluate their sense of its authenticity. How do the qualities of these photos differ from the many advertising photos found in the textbook?

SUGGESTIONS FOR FURTHER READING, THINKING, AND WRITING

print

Anonymous. "Magic (Airbrush Art)." *The New Yorker*, 3 February 1992: 24ff.

Edwards, Elizabeth. *Anthropology and Photography, 1860–1920.* New Haven: Yale University Press, 1992. Includes an essay on George Hunt and his work.

Stephens, Mitchell. *The Rise of the Image, the Fall of the Word.* New York: Oxford University Press, 1998.

Zane, J. Peder. "Sanitizing History on a Postage Stamp." *New York Times,* 27 October 1996: E3 (N). This brief article includes pictures of Franklin Delano Roosevelt without his cigarette, Winston Churchill without his cigar, and Andre Malraux without his cigarette.

web

www.theatlantic.com/issues/98may/photo.htm An excellent three-part article on photo doctoring that focuses on nature and ecological issues.

www.uta.fi/ethicnet   This is the "EthicNet" databank for European codes of journalistic ethics. It has the listing of the official codes for over twenty countries, providing an opportunity to see what different societies regard as the most pressing ethical issues.

Links for the selections in this chapter can be found at www.seeingandwriting.com.

audio/visual

A Brief History of Time. Directed by Errol Morris. 84 min. NTSC, 1992. VHS videocassette, rated G. Distributed by Paramount Studios. Errol Morris is a master of riding the thin line between documentary and fiction film. His production values are pure Hollywood, but in this movie his focus is on making Stephen Hawking and his complex scientific theory comprehensible to the audience—a wonderful marriage of science and art.

The Matrix. Directed by Larry Wachowski and Andy Wachowski. 136 min. 1999. DVD, rated R. Distributed by Warner Studios. Performers include Keanu Reeves and Laurence Fishburne. A technological thriller that raises questions about the future of virtual reality and the role of ethics in representation.

Nanook of the North. Directed by Robert J. Flaherty. 69 min. NTSC. VHS videocassette. A black and white documentary about one year in the life of Nanook, an Eskimo (Inuit), and his family; the film explores trading, hunting, fishing, and other aspects of the daily life of people who have barely been touched by technology. It was hailed as "the first full-length, anthropological documentary in cinematographic history." This film incorporates many staged shots and would be a good accompaniment to the discussion of Mitchell Stephens's essay, "Expanding the Language of Photographs," concerning the ethics of altering an image and calling it "truth."

Appendix

The theoretical texts we've chosen for the Appendix address the two areas that *Seeing & Writing* highlights in composition instruction: sharpening your students' abilities to read and write about images (Berger, starting on p. 622), and making connections—and identifying differences—between the verbal and visual dimensions of American culture (McCloud, p. 636).

John Berger, *Ways of Seeing*

GENERATING CLASS DISCUSSION AND IN-CLASS WRITING

Instructors could begin by asking the class to closely analyze the first sentence of this piece: "Seeing comes before words." Berger's essay can be used as a lens through which to re-examine any visual selection in the book. How might students rethink their interpretations of images in the book after reading Berger's piece?

ADDITIONAL WRITING TOPICS

1. Para. 43 (on reproduction) is an especially important—and provocative—passage to teach. You might want to invite students to apply Berger's discussion of image reproduction to *Seeing & Writing*.
2. What does it mean to include/reproduce such a huge variety of images of visual selections (some difficult, some pleasant; some familiar, some new) in a textbook?
3. Have students write an essay in which they explain how this is different from reproducing images on a T-shirt, in a museum, in an ad, or in a poster.

CONNECTIONS WITH OTHER TEXTS

1. Have students compare John Berger's discussion of photography (para. 8) with Susan Sontag's in the Chapter 3 selection from Sontag's *On Photography* that begins on p. 292.

www. Links for the selections in this chapter can be found at www.seeingandwriting.com.

Scott McCloud, *Show and Tell*

GENERATING CLASS DISCUSSION AND IN-CLASS WRITING

If John Berger delves into reading visual images, the selection from Scott McCloud speaks to the changing differences—and significance—of cultural roles. McCloud's piece would serve as an excellent instructional companion to any one of the Pair selections in *Seeing & Writing* that are placed shortly after the beginning of each chapter. This selection from McCloud provides a lens through which to continue any comparison of a verbal and visual representation of a similar theme. In this respect, you might ask students to discuss the differences between "showing" and "telling." How do the selections in *Seeing & Writing* demonstrate such similarities or differences? Compare, for example, Tibor Kalman's Portfolio in Chapter 6 (starting on p. 494) with W. E. B. DuBois's "Double Consciousness" (p. 243) in the Chapter 7. Both selections deal with the cultural construction of race.

ADDITIONAL WRITING TOPIC

1. Have students write an essay in which they argue for—or against—the proposition that images have replaced words in importance in contemporary American culture.

CONNECTIONS WITH OTHER TEXTS

1. If you are interested in comparing and contrasting the selections from Berger and McCloud, you might ask students to explore the notion that "the medium is the message" in both selections.

2. Have students consider what specific compositional strategies Berger and McCloud have employed to convey their points.

www. Links for the selections in this chapter can be found at www.seeingandwriting.com.